Praise for *A Manager's Guide to Project Management*

"Mike Bender has applied his considerable expertise to crafting straightforward and pragmatic guidelines on making project management work for your enterprise. Now it's up to you. This is how you add value to your organization."

—**Kimi Hirotsu Ziemski**, PMP, VP Community Relations, PMI SFBAC; author,
When Opposites Collide: Leadership Beyond Gender;
and contributing author, *PMBOK® Guide*, 4th Edition

"Were I an executive moving my organization to take advantage of new challenges, I'd want this book to ensure I achieve the most out of my project portfolio. Michael Bender distills the essentials of project management into what executives need to know without overwhelming them. He treats projects as capital investments for executives to achieve greater returns in this ever challenging economic environment."

—**Michael F. Malinowski**, PMP, IT Manager, Exelon Corporation;
and author, *IT Maintenance: Applied Project Management*

"*A Manager's Guide to Project Management* by Michael Bender is without doubt the most accessible book I've read on the topic for the past five years. Michael manages to step back from the more mundane technical aspects of program management and instead enable one to see how program management fits into the organization as a whole and how it brings value.

"He reinforces the need to think holistically about every system and process in the company and, in doing so, certainly elevated my thinking on the need for clarity of goal alignment right from strategic executive level down to 'boots on the ground' individual project contributor levels.

"In essence, the book is a recipe for how to achieve alignment in an organization striving to achieve maximum efficient delivery of common goals through execution of the projects the company chooses to pursue.

"Finally, program management in any company cannot thrive in isolation. Executive management must sponsor, sanction, and enable its existence. This book details the mechanisms by which this sanction can be pragmatically implemented. In short, well worth the read—I recommend it wholeheartedly."

—**Shay Conway**, Senior Director of Program Management, SiRF Technology

"Michael's *A Manager's Guide to Project Management* is a wonderful read. Clear, concise, and full of examples, checklists, and tools to help managers and executives alike. Michael has done an exceptional job of covering a wide range of topics from strategic planning to scorecards, as well as project management, but does so in a systematic and integrated fashion, deserving of virtually anyone in an organization and something very worthwhile to MBA students. Fantastic—I plan to use it as a quick guide staple that will sit close at hand."

—**Robert Van Zant**, PMP, Sr. Business Consultant, BT Global Services

"This book is an advocate for the science of project management and helps senior management understand what their project managers are or should be doing to maximize their projects' profitability. Mike does an excellent job of showing how clever project management techniques can align an organization's goals and strengths in order to maximize the organization's portfolio potential."

—**Andrew Courier**, PMP, Assistant Group Director,
QinetiQ North America | Foster-Miller Inc.

"Finally someone has tackled the difficulties that executives in most organizations have with projects. Methodically, the book takes the reader through the issues that confront executives and gives solutions that can be implemented and communicated. In addition, this book is incredibly useful to the project manager who needs to understand the issues at the executive level so that the project manager can ask the right questions to bring about best practices. The discussions on using a goal breakdown structure for strategic alignment and on project resource conflicts in a matrix organization are especially enlightening for both executives and project management professionals."

—**Norma Sutcliffe**, Ph.D., Associate Professor, DePaul University

A Manager's Guide to Project Management

Learn How to Apply Best Practices

MICHAEL B. BENDER

FT Press offers excellent discounts on this book when ordered in quantity for bulk purchases or special sales. For more information, please contact U.S. Corporate and Government Sales, 1-800-382-3419, corpsales@pearsontechgroup.com. For sales outside the U.S., please contact International Sales at international@pearson.com.

Pearson Education LTD.

Pearson Education Australia PTY, Limited.

Pearson Education Singapore, Pte. Ltd.

Pearson Education North Asia, Ltd.

Pearson Education Canada, Ltd.

Pearson Educación de Mexico, S.A. de C.V.

Pearson Education—Japan

Pearson Education Malaysia, Pte. Ltd.

Library of Congress Cataloging-in-Publication Data

Bender, Michael B.
  A manager's guide to project management : learn how to apply best practices / Michael B. Bender.
    p. cm.
  ISBN 978-0-13-713690-2 (hardback : alk. paper) 1. Project management. I. Title.
  HD69.P75B446 2010
  658.4'04—dc22

                    2009021922

Vice President, Publisher
Tim Moore

Associate Publisher and Director of Marketing
Amy Neidlinger

Acquisitions Editor
Jennifer Simon

Editorial Assistant
Pamela Boland

Development Editor
Russ Hall

Operations Manager
Gina Kanouse

Senior Marketing Manager
Julie Phifer

Publicity Manager
Laura Czaja

Assistant Marketing Manager
Megan Colvin

Cover Designer
Alan Clements

Managing Editor
Kristy Hart

Project Editor
Anne Goebel

Copy Editor
Krista Hansing Editorial Services, Inc.

Proofreader
Leslie Joseph

Senior Indexer
Cheryl Lenser

Compositor
Nonie Ratcliff

Manufacturing Buyer
Dan Uhrig

To my father, who crawled out of the coal mines of Pennsylvania and climbed the corporate ladder, but never sacrificed his time with his family. You taught me more about business than both of us ever knew.

Contents

Part I   Understanding Projects and Project Management

Part II   Aligning Project Management with the Organization

Part III   Project Management Oversight

Part IV   Projects as Capital Investments

Part V   Globalization and Resource Optimization

*NOTE: Chapter 15 is available for free online at www.ftpress.com/title/9780137136902.

Acknowledgments

I wish to offer special thanks to these people:

Mr. Stephen Gershenson, my very good friend and colleague, for all the help, insight, and time you invested in helping me create this book.

Mr. Richard T. Balog, my very good friend and colleague, for your support, financial wisdom, and time you invested in helping me create this book.

Mr. Jack Adams, without your many years of program management experience, this book would have never been written.

Mr. Russ Hall, author and editor, who helped me find my voice smoothly and graciously.

About the Author

Michael B. Bender, PMP, began his career working in high-technology computer-based projects. With more than 30 years of practical experience, Mr. Bender has worked on such projects as the Hubbell Space Telescope; air traffic control systems for Taiwan, the United Kingdom, and the United States; and the U.S. Doppler weather radar system. He has also helped put communication satellites into orbit and developed cable television automation and switching systems, advanced imaging for aircraft simulators, and many other systems.

Mr. Bender began Ally Business Developers in 1996 to help clients successfully implement projects and project management in both nonprofit and for-profit organizations. Since then, he has consulted and led seminars for literally thousands of individuals across hundreds of organizations, including Fortune 500 companies, nonprofit organizations, city and state governments, museums, and religious organizations.

Mr. Bender is a speaker for the American Management Association, International; Global Knowledge; the National Center for Continuing Education; and DePaul University's MBA program. He has been an elected public official and served both school boards and township committees.

Preface

Project Management Is a Value Strategy

Value. That term has taken on new importance in the last few months. As I sit here writing this preface, the Dow Jones Industrial Average has been down for the previous eight days, down some 2,000 points since the United States Congress passed the $700 billion economic recovery bill, and some 35 percent from its peak only about a year ago.

This "economic event" was caused partly by derivatives, instruments that derive their value from some other instrument that has value. Derivatives appear to serve two purposes: 1) to offer alternative methods for exchanging an instrument with intrinsic value (futures and options, for example) and 2) to disguise the true value of the instrument, to sell it for more than it's worth (in this case, mortgage securities). According to reports, companies have hired mathematicians and physicists to develop derivatives of such instruments. Now the United States Treasury is considering buying these instruments (called "toxic mortgage securities" by some newspeople) because no one knows what they're worth. The Federal Reserve Bank (the "Fed") is planning to take equity interest on some banks, to help finance banks holding such instruments.

Value. Perhaps it's coincidental—or perhaps it's fate—that this book was published shortly after these events. The reason: the core theme for this book is that projects and project management add value to an organization.

> **Adding value to an organization is the only reason
> to engage in a project or in project management.**

My quest in this book is not just to present project management—enough books cover that. My quest involves the next steps in project management evolution: to offer you, the executive, ideas, tools, and concepts to improve project management to increase the value of your organization.

The Project Manager's Secret Society

Project management is an extremely well-defined discipline. Inside the discipline is a suite of tools designed to conquer any challenge. Enough books have been written about project management to fill a small library. Sadly, however, the pundits have failed in one very important area—to communicate our wisdom and needs to the rest of the world. To outsiders, project management is still a secret. These pundits have focused only on the discipline itself, finding yet another way to describe the ubiquitous work breakdown structure

(WBS) or embellish even more on scope definition or risk management. We have enough books that teach project managers how to run projects.

As we browse the library of project management books, we find a small and dreary section: the section that looks outward from project management to embrace those not directly involved in the discipline—what project managers call stakeholders. This book's theme is based on the value of projects and project management. This theme is certainly not new— the book's target audience, however, is.

This book is designed for executive managers, the group that has the most influence on and control over projects and project managers. This group defines which projects should be done, which should be cancelled, and how project management should be implemented. Yet for all its influence, this group has been neglected in literature for too long.

This book is designed for you, the executive manager. I tear down the walls that hide the secret society. You will see how project managers put plans together to achieve your goals. I present your role in projects and project management, and I give you tools to handle those roles. I help you to successfully implement project management in your organization, whether you're a for-profit or not-for-profit organization.

Because the only purpose for a project is to add value, I also show you how to add real value to your organization.

How to Use This Book

This book is designed both as a straight read-through and as a reference book. It builds on concepts continuously throughout the text. If you're reading Chapter 4, I assume that you're familiar with the material in Chapters 1–3. I attempt to cite where you can find previously presented material, where reasonable.

The book is a high-level "how-to" book. It presents concepts and tools, and then suggests how to implement such concepts and tools. It is not a detailed "how-to" book; it does not contain all the details you need for implementation. For that, I would need several volumes. Besides, you have subject matter experts that work for you. If they have been well trained, if you give them clear direction, and if you work with them, you cannot fail.

Consider this book a consultant, an advisor. As a consultant or advisor, I can offer only ideas, tools, and concepts.

> **I can lead a horse to a watering trough. I can show the horse the water.**
> **I can point the horse's head toward the desert we're both about to enter,**
> **but I can't make that horse drink that water.**

You, the executive, must decide what to do with these ideas and tools. You can take a glib approach (not recommended) and half-apply the ideas, with little understanding. Just don't blame me or project management when it fails. You can take this book at face value (also not recommended), implement it exactly as written, and then later discover that different people do things differently. You can challenge every concept in this book (highly recommended), knowing that the additional thought processes will foster your understanding and enable you to implement the concepts and tools your way. Or you can delegate this book to someone else within your organization. (Okay, as long as you delegate it to the right person—and, of course, that you buy another copy.) The choice is yours.

Read this book. Study it. Bounce its ideas off your own experience, your own management style, your own perspective, and your subject experts. If you do that, whatever your decisions are, your organization will be better—and we will have done our job.

The Book's Layout and Roadmap

This book is divided into parts, each containing two or more chapters. Each part has a core theme, with the underlying chapters providing supporting details. We provide the outline here.

Part I: "Understanding Projects and Project Management"

This part provides a foundation on project and project management that's necessary to develop advanced concepts.

> Theme: Project management, when supported, already defines sufficient tools and techniques to achieve project success.

This part includes three chapters:

> Chapter 1: "The Goals of Project Management"
> Chapter 2: "Project Management Framework and Structure"
> Chapter 3: "Project Definition and Planning"

Part II: "Aligning Project Management with the Organization"

Part II examines the role of project management in the organization and presents tools and concepts to successfully integrate it with other organizational activities. Integration is achieved through alignment, thus gaining buy-in and improving organizational efficiency.

> Theme: Projects are not ancillary activities to our real jobs; they are an integral part of all organizations.

This section includes four chapters. The first two focus on strategic alignment, making sure that your project's goals align with the organization's goals. The third takes an organizational focus: defining organizational structures designed to align communication and decision making. The fourth focuses on project activities themselves, concentrating on integrating and aligning project processes with other organizational processes.

Chapter 4: "Strategic Alignment"
Chapter 5: "A Framework for Strategic Alignment"
Chapter 6: "Organizational Alignment"
Chapter 7: "Process Alignment"

Part III: "Project Management Oversight"

Part III develops concepts and tools to help you make sure your projects are running correctly.

> Theme: As with all organizational disciplines, project management must be managed.

This part contains three chapters, each building on the previous to develop a complete system for oversight.

Chapter 8: "Project Cost Management"
Chapter 9: "Project Oversight"
Chapter 10: "Project Management Oversight"

Part IV: "Projects as Capital Investments"

Part IV expands on the concept that projects add value and are capital investments.

> Theme: Projects are capital investments.

This part contains three chapters. The first focuses on financial benefits and presents the basic building blocks for a balanced portfolio. The second chapter builds on these concepts, recognizing that not all benefits are financial and develops a balanced portfolio. The third chapter demonstrates how you might apply the different techniques in different situations.

Chapter 11: "Projects as Capital Investments"
Chapter 12: "Developing a Balanced Portfolio"
Chapter 13: "Balanced Portfolio Techniques in Action"

Part V: "Globalization and Resource Optimization"

Part V builds on the concepts in all earlier sections to develop advanced concepts for dealing with globalization, strategic outsourcing, and multiproject resource optimization.

> Theme: Globalization and advanced techniques enable us to optimize resources.

This part contains two chapters:

Chapter 14: "Globalization and Strategic Outsourcing"
Chapter 15: "Optimizing Resources in a Multiproject Environment" at
www.ftpress.com/title/9780137136902

1

The Goals of Project Management

Every organization, whether for-profit or not-for-profit, embraces a strategy to move into the future. Sound strategies involve a synergy of goals working together to move the organization toward its vision. Organizations engage in projects, processes, operations, and research to achieve these strategic goals.

In this book, we explore one of those key actions: projects. I present projects not from the classical project manager's perspective (enough books have been written about that), but from yours: the executive. We examine your influence over projects, whether intentional or unintentional. You will see how the decisions you make, the culture you generate, and the direction you present determine the successes and failures of projects and programs. I present a sound, comprehensive, yet simple architecture that generates a successful project management business environment—optimizing resources, eliminating waste, achieving all organizational and strategic objectives, and ensuring growth and increased value.

I begin with a brief story.

A Day in the Life of Alex

Alex woke at the usual time, but this routine bothered him now. He used to love his job, but now it just seemed like a tedious sequence of uncoordinated events strung together, serving no purpose. Alex was an electrical engineer, specializing in radio transmitter modules for integrated circuits—a job he loved—or, at least, used to. It seemed like he just didn't get to do a lot of engineering anymore.

Alex was working on a project to upgrade an existing chip design. His design was due Friday, and it was already Tuesday. He wouldn't be able to finish the design by Friday, let alone go through a proper design review in time. He had dropped subtle hints to Diane, his project manager, but he hasn't formally informed her of the delay. He needed to do that today—they had a status meeting scheduled for 3:00 p.m.

Alex arrived at work at the usual time. "The unbroken pattern is continuing," he thought to himself as he got his coffee and sat down at his desk. He used to arrive at work at 8:30, but time pressures led him to start earlier in hopes of getting a few hours of real work done before the interruptions began. Now 7:00 a.m. was the norm. The earlier arrival hadn't helped. By the time he plowed his way through the array of e-mails and cleared his desk from the previous day's chaos, most of that extra time had vanished.

"Today will be different," he thought to himself. "Today I get on top of this design. At a minimum, I need to put a plan together so that I can tell Diane when I'll be done."

He gathered the papers strewn across his desk into one large pile and placed them on the floor behind his chair. He turned off his e-mail server, knowing that even looking at the list of unread e-mails would distract him too much today. Today he would focus on only one thing—the new design. He knew tomorrow he'd pay for this—tomorrow he'd need to confront that stack of papers and those e-mails, but not today. Today he was determined to break the pattern. He rummaged through his desk, gathering the papers he needed for his design. He fired up his computer and arranged the windows in the usual way. His energy level was rising, his motivation returning.

It took Alex almost 20 minutes just to get organized and figure out where he'd left off. "That's okay," he thought, "at least now I can get to work." He had left off in the middle of improving the thermal stability of the first-stage amplifiers. Initially, the work went slowly, but he gathered speed. Finally he was doing what he loved and what his project manager wanted him to do. "I'll stabilize this stage," he thought, "and then work on a plan to finish the design for the 3:00 meeting."

However, Alex's productivity was short-lived. Not a half-hour later, Jim, the head of production, came to visit. Jim usually arrived at 9:00, but he was in early today. "Didn't you get my e-mail this morning?" he asked as he poked his head into Alex's cube.

"I'm trying to get this design finished for Diane by Friday," Alex replied.

"They're having problems making a working prototype of the XR–120 chip. Call them immediately—we need to get that chip out to production in three weeks!" Jim commanded as he turned and left.

By "them," Jim was referring to the company's prototype and manufacturing partner in China. As an engineer, Alex was often required to handle prototyping and production problems. He had actually been to the facility once but had never gotten to see the country—they had worked him 18-hour days while he was there.

Alex knew this wouldn't be an easy problem. They had rushed the design and shortened the review cycles of that chip. The original project plan was sound, but last-minute requirement changes put the schedule into a tailspin. "I'll bet the chip's getting too hot," Alex thought to himself. He turned back to his desk. He looked at his computer screen, with his windows in perfect placement for designing, his papers organized precisely the way he liked them, and his tools staged to carry out his commands. He sighed, "I guess today isn't the day after all," he said out loud.

He gathered his papers into a stack and placed them behind his chair next to the previous one. "Phone conversations with China are difficult—I'd better do my homework," he thought as he closed the design diagrams for his current chip. He learned that reading their e-mails worked better than phone conversations—his contacts in China could write English better than they could speak it. He suspected that it was because they could review and rework the e-mail before sending it.

He fired up his e-mail server to discover nearly 25 e-mails, almost half of them marked "URGENT!" They hadn't been there the night before, but that's one of the problems working with China. The time difference caused e-mails to stack up from one side of the planet while the other side slept. "It's just after 6:00 p.m. over there," Alex thought. "I'd better get moving on this while someone is still at the plant."

The rest of Alex's day was similar to all the rest—dealing with the prototype problem, appeasing the vice president of marketing's concerns regarding the ease-of-use issues their clients would have integrating the chip with their products, and helping out the younger engineers struggling through their issues. He even got a change on the thermal requirements for his current chip design. "Well," he thought, "I guess I'm glad I didn't finish the thermal stability design—it wouldn't have worked for this new requirement anyway."

Alex could have been a biochemist for a pharmaceutical company, a plant designer for a soft-drink manufacturer, a researcher for a polymer manufacturer, an infrastructure architect in an advertising firm's IT department, the exhibit designer for a museum, or a product manager for an insurance company. Alex's problems are not technical—they're based on the way his organization runs projects.

Project management has mushroomed as a serious, recognized management discipline only within the last two decades. Twenty years ago, project management was an esoteric discipline, restricted to large systems integrators (such as RCA, Martin-Marietta, Raytheon, and Sperry-Univac), the construction industry, and a few savvy midsize organizations. Today you can get an MBA in it.

However, only this recognition is new. Project management is as old as mankind. The project managers who built the Egyptian pyramids used the same techniques in place today. Labor relations might have differed, and they might have used different terminology, but Gantt charts (perhaps called Prometheus charts back then), precedence diagrams, and resource leveling were critical to successful pyramid building.

The Problems You Face

Alex's problems aren't tactical—they're based in the organization's culture, environment, and lack of strategic planning. The problem in China was caused not by bad project management practices, but by a reactionary corporate environment. Although project management offers excellent tools for managing scope change, political, cultural, and environmental factors frequently derail these efforts, plunging the project team into a series of emergencies. Simple concepts and techniques employed at the senior-management level create the right environment to manage project scope change. You can trace most emergencies to either poor project management or, more frequently, their surrounding environment. Alex's emergency will now cause another: the delay of the current project, which will cause that project to be rushed, which will then cause another emergency, which will cause the next project to be rushed, which will....

As an executive manager, you help establish the personality of the organization. You set the culture, processes, morals, and ethics (both personal and work ethics) for the organization. You do this intentionally or unintentionally, architected or happenchance, planned or evolved—but you do it.

The discipline of project management is well defined. The Project Management Institute (PMI) has written a standard for project management practices (ANSI/PMI 99-001 2008), also known as the *Guide to the Project Management Body of Knowledge*,[1] in its 4th edition at the time of this writing (*PMBOK* Guide[2]). It codifies 42 processes with well-defined inputs, tools and techniques, and outputs. Whether your organization conforms to this standard, another standard, or your own methodology, project management is quite well defined as a discipline.

If your organization struggles with projects, it's not the discipline's fault. For now, we will blame it on evolution. The practice has evolved from the middle out. Project management in its current format was developed primarily in the 1940s–1950s (Prometheus charts notwithstanding). It concentrated on its own internal processes. With those processes now well developed, it must look outward—or, in our case, upward.

As a seminar leader and management consultant, I frequently find that clients have skilled project managers, yet the organizations still struggle to get projects done on time and on budget. Their problems do not lie within the discipline of project management. Their problems might be the organizational culture, the way project management is viewed within the organization, political strife, structural flaws, departmental silos—a variety of issues can plague even the best project managers. In this book, we pursue these issues and attempt to address them from the executive manager's perspective.

Starting with the assumption that our project management is sound, let's examine the influences senior management can have on project success.

Wasted Resources

All MBA programs address resource utilization. As an executive manager, one of your primary objectives is to get more things done (in our case, projects) with fewer resources. You look around your organization and see people working hard, staying late at night; you see a beehive of activity, yet you can't seem to get projects done on time and on budget. How can such a high level of activity surround the company, yet its projects are constantly delayed or never finished?

Let's look at some of the results of the cultures we create.

The Project du Jour

Overly dynamic project priorities cause resources to quickly switch among projects and among activities, without finishing the original project or activity. Then suddenly priorities switch again. The result is a string of half-completed projects, exhausted staff, demoralized teams, and little accomplishment.

The Warm-Body Syndrome

When I started training in project management, one common problem facing project managers was a lack of human resources. Today the complaint is not the lack of resources, but the fact that the resources have the wrong skills. Attendees continue to complain that the teams they're given have little experience in the disciplines they need. Perhaps the most notable example: I often find administrative assistants taking advanced multiproject management seminars with no basic project management training. Their bosses have asked them to manage a major project in addition to their regular responsibilities. Opportunities, situations, and emergencies pop up seemingly without warning. In an attempt to capture the opportunities, handle the situations, or manage the emergencies, we grab the next warm body and throw them at the problem, whether or not that person is qualified.

Staff Doing Project Work and Their Real Jobs

The phrase "my real job" grew out of one of the greatest problems facing project management today: the concept that projects are ancillary activities, falling into the "other jobs as assigned" category of formal job descriptions. They're viewed as distractions, annoyances, and things that make us work late.

The truth is quite the opposite. Projects are an integral part of business activities. They are as much a part of the organization as process, operations, and research. One of my key objectives in this book is to present tools and concepts to help you successfully integrate these activities, ensuring success on all organizational fronts.

The Need to Multitask

Whether the perceived need to have all employees multitask derives from lack of planning, a truly dynamic environment, or some other cause, multitasking seems to be a requirement of every individual. Yet individuals are just that—individual. Some are good multitaskers, some are specialists. Some people quickly skim across the top of subjects; others delve deeply into them. Demanding that every employee multitask is as ridiculous as demanding that every employee specialize. Organizations need both, and projects need both. Your objective as an executive manager is to build a culture that balances these skills and employees across organizational activities—in this case, across projects.

Projects Not Achieving Their Goals

Good project managers know how to develop project plans that achieve goals. The assumption, of course, is that the goals are defined, clear, and (to some degree) static. Consider some common problems related to achieving goals:

We Didn't Think of That!

As the project evolves, key stakeholders realize that they forgot something. They rush to the project manager to implement their new requirements—but by doing so, they re-create the same problem. In their haste to get something into the project, they don't think it through. So it happens again and again. It's a prime cause of scope creep. The scope of the project creeps upward and onward. This is simply the result of poor planning.

Politics Interferes with Sound Business Decisions

All organizations have their politics. As clever managers, we understand that politics can be beneficial to the organization. Yet as the political power and influence change among the key stakeholders, so do their underlying projects. In such organizations, the project managers keep revising their plans as the political landscape changes, rarely achieving the projects' goals.

Things Just Change

We live in a dynamic universe—things just change. Project management has well-developed tools and techniques for handling legitimate change and for staving off illegitimate change—all for the mutual benefit of the client, performing organization, and other key stakeholders. The question remaining for the executive is whether your organization supports these techniques or whether political influences, culture, and environmental factors thwart sound change-management practices.

We Get Smarter

As the project evolves, so does our knowledge of it. Clients, the key stakeholders, and senior management all get smarter. Does your culture constantly throw these new ideas at the project manager without regard to schedule or cost, or does your culture evaluate enhancements and judge their value?

Project Overruns and Delays

A variety of issues can cause project overruns and delays. Many of these issues are legitimate, expected, or even planned. Project managers, for example, will recognize new, innovative technologies or dealing with new vendors as project risks and develop contingency plans, time, and money. These examples are not the topic of this discussion. Here we examine those delays and overruns that you can overcome by improving the culture and organizational management. Specifically, we examine the following potential problems.

Forced Deadlines

As humans, we started experiencing forced deadlines the day we were born: nap at 2:00, bottle at 6:30. We continue to see the same effect as we get a bit older: "The book report is due Thursday and you'll have an outline for me by Monday's class." So we grow up developing schedules based on deadlines set by superiors (not necessarily in the skills or intelligence sense, only in the authoritative sense). The results: We learn to back into those deadlines. It doesn't matter whether the tasks are doable, it doesn't matter that we have a dozen other items on our lists or what our availability is, and we don't care whether we throw quality out the window. We're taught to meet the deadline. It's a habit, the way we're brought up. Our estimates are not based on the work and the resources doing the work; they're based on dates chosen for political reasons by dictatorial personalities. In such cultures, overruns and delays are inevitable.

Poor Project Finance Management

The discipline of project management contains tools and techniques for managing project finances. Interestingly, in our profit-driven culture, these techniques are rarely enforced and frequently poorly implemented. Whether you're a for-profit company or a not-for-profit organization, sound financial project management is critical to fiscal stability and growth.

The Definition of Done

Did you ever stop working on a task that was almost complete (or one you thought was complete) and later discovered that it wasn't? Do you remember the time and energy it took you to pick that task back up again and really finish it?

Interestingly, this is one area in which project management has been historically lacking. Although technologies improve, our culture tends to rush us to the next hot task, forcing us to abandon our current task prematurely. You'll hear statements such as "It's good enough for government work," "Ship it—we'll fix it in the field," and "It's good enough for now—we have this other problem….” These decisions are usually time driven, foregoing quality and, interestingly, cost considerations; the more time we wait to finish the task, the more money and waste we incur.

The Goals of Projects and Project Management

Ultimately, both projects and project management have only one goal: to add value to your organization. You, as an executive manager, establish the values important to the organization. You then communicate these values and establish a strategic plan to foster and improve the organization along these values.

**Projects are the actions an organization
performs to increase its value.**

Projects cost time and money. The value the projects add must be greater than the expense incurred. In addition, the projects undertaken must be the best choice in furthering these values.

Project management, as with all activities an organization undertakes, must also add value; again, the value it adds must be greater than its cost. Perhaps a bit oversimplified, the goal of project management is to reduce the cost and time for completing projects.

To manage projects, you hire project managers and pay them a salary. They then add more activities to the project for planning, management, and oversight, which all add to the cost and time of the project. However, these costs and activities must reduce both the cost and time for the project by increasing efficiency and reducing rework. For both time and cost:

$$Project\ Planning + Efficient\ Execution$$
$$<$$
$$Inefficient\ Execution + Rework$$

Specific Goals for Project Management

Let's examine some more specific goals for project management.

Your Clients Are Happy

You and your project managers share this goal. Of course, this is one of the key goals of project management. However, you will see that client satisfaction in projects is much more complicated than it might initially appear. Clients rarely know what they really want. Many of those that do know have difficulty articulating it in terms the project team can understand. The client's goals frequently conflict with other key stakeholders' goals, including yours. Political strife, conflicting objectives, and organizational silos all combine as barriers that inhibit project managers from achieving this goal.

You're Making Money or Being Fiscally Responsible

If you are a for-profit company, this is one of the critical success factors for most projects. Yet many management structures fail to either enforce profitability during project definition or measure it after project completion. Many organizations that do attempt it fail to capture important information, which produces false results.

If you are a not-for-profit organization (I cover both in this book), then, at a minimum, you must maintain sound fiscal strategies. Although your primary objective might be preserving and presenting history; spreading a religious belief; running a city, state, or federal government (or department); or looking for a cure for cancer; fiscal responsibility is a core competency for any not-for-profit organization.

You're Achieving Your Strategic Objectives

Organizational success relies on goals synergy, a collection of strategic objectives that work in unison for organizational betterment. Of all the activities that an organization embraces, projects are activities specifically undertaken to achieve these goals. In this book, I use simple techniques to ensure that your collection of projects works with the same synergy—reducing waste, reducing rework, and achieving your strategic goals efficiently and effectively.

You Optimize Your Resource Usage

Your resources are your most valuable (or, at least, most expensive) asset. Wasting resources is almost criminal. Yet organizations incorporate and cleave to practices that generate incredible waste. Constant resource shuffling, dynamic project reprioritization, and ever-changing goals all cause staff to abandon, postpone, or half-complete activities, in an attempt to meet a deadline.

These practices are not the only resource-wasters. Projects that don't align with organizational objectives employ precious resources that actually hinder organizational growth. Abandoned projects, or projects that don't achieve all their goals, absorb resources that could have been applied more productively elsewhere.

I address all these issues, making sure your resources run efficiently and focus on the organization's vision.

Things Are Getting Better

My last objective, perhaps, is our simplest. No matter where you are, no matter what condition your projects might be in, and no matter how well your organization manages its projects, you want things to get better. Fortunately, improving project management is as simple as improving any business process. Also fortunately, the techniques are the same. I seek to present project management in the correct light to enable you, the executive, to promote improvement throughout your organization.

How We Achieve These Goals

I've arranged the book based on several overriding themes. Although these themes weave throughout the text, I've divided the book into sections that focus on each theme:

- **Part I, "Understanding Projects and Project Management"**—When properly supported, project management already defines sufficient tools and techniques to achieve project success.

  Your role as an executive is to identify those aspects of project management that are critical to your organizational success and then to promote and improve those aspects. Chapter 2, "Project Management Framework and Structure," and Chapter 3, "Project Definition and Planning," cover project management to help you better understand the discipline for this purpose. These chapters also present key concepts needed for executive management and strategic planners for improving overall management, planning, and communication at the senior staff level. Even if you're knowledgeable in basic project management, these chapters offer insight into those areas of project management needed for the overall architecture of the organization.

- **Part II, "Aligning Project Management with the Organization"**—Projects are not ancillary activities to our real jobs; they are an integral part of all organizations. Successfully aligning project management within the organization involves three aspects: strategic, organizational, and process.

  - **Strategic alignment** ensures that project goals align with and support organizational goals. When properly structured, this alignment reduces scope creep, overly dynamic priorities, resource shuffling, and activity waste. Fortunately, project management itself offers tools for such alignment.

  - **Organizational alignment** integrates project resources and activities with the rest of the organization. We examine committees, teams, and other structures to help facilitate project success and resource utilization, and improve communication and decision making throughout the organization.

  - **Process alignment** examines project management as a formal business process. By examining the interfaces among project management processes and other business processes, senior management can improve product hand-off, resource hand-off, and communication among all organizational activities.

- **Part III, "Project Management Oversight"**—As with all organizational disciplines, project management must be managed.

  As an executive, you are responsible for managing all disciplines employed within your area. Project management is no different. Each organization must employ sufficient oversight to make sure that work activities are being done correctly, that phase reviews occur at the right times and for the right reasons, that resources move smoothly between project work and other organizational work, that project managers correctly manage their budgets and finances, and that clients are satisfied.

- **Part IV, "Projects as Capital Investments"**—Projects are capital investments. Projects invest resources and capital to achieve goals. The project's primary objective might be profit, more efficient processes (process improvement projects) that will save money over the long run, or increased market share to create more sales. The organization's strategic plan incorporates multiple objectives, all designed to move the organization forward. Projects are the means by which you invest your capital and resources to obtain these objectives.

- **Part V, "Globalization and Resource Optimization"**—Globalization and advanced techniques enable us to optimize resources. Globalization has created a true need for strategic outsourcing for both manufacturing and project management. I present techniques to add flexibility and improve the organization's capability to outsource both projects and activities within projects.

I also present advance resource optimization techniques, including Dr. Goldratt's Theory of Constraints, queuing theory applied to a dynamic project environment, centralized resourcing, and others.

Project Management Maturity

Project managers need to create a unique product that satisfies multiple, conflicting stakeholders using resources that don't report to them under tight budgets and time constraints—simple, right? As we will see, project management is a vast topic. It can't be learned in a day. Project management takes years of experience to master the art and the science.

Organizations are no different. As individuals within the organization mature in their ability to manage projects, so does the organization.

As the software industry began to grow, the U.S. government contracted with the Software Engineering Institute (SEI) to develop a model that ranks an organization's capability to perform projects. That model is called the Capability Maturity Model (CMM). Later the SEI generalized and further developed the model to include all projects. The later model is called the Capability Maturity Model Integration (CMMI).

Figure 1.1 shows five maturity levels: initial, managed, defined, qualitatively managed, and optimized. To be rated at each level, the organization must demonstrate that it can achieve all the defined goals for that level. You can use this model as a roadmap to help you mature your project management capabilities in a controlled and predictable manner. SEI's Web site is www.sei.cmu.edu. SEI is tied to Carnegie Mellon University.

Figure 1.1   CMMI maturity levels

Summary

Project management is an evolving discipline. Historically, the discipline concentrated on itself—focusing on the tools, processes, and techniques for successfully executing projects. Now that these are well developed, the discipline must look outward, focusing on its environment. Executive management shoulders the responsibility to conceive, design, implement, and manage the organization's overall objectives, culture, environment, and processes for all disciplines, including project management.

Focusing on these key areas will help you drive your organization's success in projects and programs:

- **Foundations**—Establishing an understanding for sound project management practices

- **Alignment**—Ensuring that projects align with all the organization's activities

- **Management**—Tracking, measuring, and improving project management as an organizational discipline

- **Investment**—Ensuring that the capital and resources invested in project activities yield valuable results

- **Resource optimization**—Using outsourcing and advanced technologies to improve resource optimization

2

Project Management Framework and Structure

This chapter describes the overall framework and core concepts employed in managing projects. Most of the framework derives from the Project Management Institute (PMI) standard. In some cases, I alter the presentation slightly to improve understanding to those outside the discipline. I also incorporate other standards or perspectives where appropriate.

Core Concepts

I begin this chapter with a discussion regarding the basic concepts rooted in all projects: that they involve work. Understanding work and its relationship to projects helps us develop a comprehensive framework for project management.

The Purpose of Work

If you have children in grade school, try this exercise (this frequently works in junior high and high school as well). Ask your children if they have homework. If they do, ask them what the homework is. Finally, ask them the purpose of the homework. If you have children, you already know how they will respond to these questions. Consider this typical conversation:

"Hi Jimmy, how was school today?"

"Fine," responds your child in a dull, monotone voice.

"Do you have any homework?"

"Yes," he replies sadly.

"What homework do you have?"

"I have a book report due on Friday."

"That's interesting," you respond in a vain attempt to generate some enthusiasm. "Why are you doing the book report?"

You'll get the obvious answer to this question: "Because my teacher told me to."

Now take the next step. Let's see if Jimmy really understands what knowledge or skill he's supposed to gain out of this homework exercise.

"Well, there must be some learning objective for the book report. What does your teacher want you to learn?"

The answer: "I don't know."

This pattern started before kindergarten. Someone in authority tells us to do something, so we do it. We frequently don't know why we do it. We don't know the purpose of the task we're asked to do, but we do it anyway. Why? Because that's the way we've been raised. So Jimmy does the book report, gets a decent grade, and learns nothing except how to please people in authority.

Now Jimmy's 30 years old and the situation hasn't changed. Here's the allegorical version in business, what I call *rock fetching*:

The vice president says, "Jimmy, go fetch me a rock."

Jimmy nods affirmatively, goes out into the parking lot, and finds a rock. He finds the vice president and hands it to him. "Here's your rock, boss." He smiles.

"This is a really bad rock Jimmy. Get it out of here and go get me a good rock."

"What's a good rock?" Jimmy asks hopefully.

"You're the expert—that's why we hired you! Now go get me a good rock!"

Now disgruntled, Jimmy wanders back into the parking lot to find another rock. He finds one but has no idea whether it will please his boss, but he gives it a try.

"You're really bad at this rock fetching, Jimmy," replies the vice president. "Now this is your last chance. Go get me a good rock!"

The problem older Jimmy is experiencing is the identical problem he had in grade school. Jimmy doesn't know why he's doing the task. In grade school, he knows that if he does what his teacher tells him to do, he will receive a decent grade, which will make his parents happy. However, this all has nothing to do with the true purpose of the activity—imparting some knowledge or skill to Jimmy.

Older Jimmy has the same problem. He knows that if he does what his boss tells him to do, he might please his boss and possibly get a raise (satisfying at least one of Jimmy's goals). However, this might not help his career or the organization.

Because the problems are the same, so are their solutions. Jimmy must learn how to ask "Why?" "What's the learning objective for me doing the book report?" "What will the rock be used for?" Jimmy needs to learn that...

...the purpose of work is to achieve a goal.

If work has no purpose, then don't do the work. As a seminar leader, I tell almost every group this: If you're invited to attend a meeting, ask for its goal. If the meeting doesn't have a clear goal, don't go. You have more important things to do than spend your time in meetings that have no purpose.

Jimmy would be much better off if he knew the learning objectives for the book report. Perhaps his teacher wants him to study character development or perhaps plot development, or maybe he's supposed to analyze literary style. Whatever it is, Jimmy has a much better chance of learning if he knows what he's supposed to learn.

Let's return to Jimmy at age 30:

> "Boss," continues Jimmy, "it might help if I knew what you will use the rock for."

> "Well, Jimmy, you know that my office is on the 15th floor. I like fresh air, so I open my windows frequently. It's quite windy on the 15th floor, so my papers blow off my desk."

> "Oh! You want a paperweight!" Jimmy replies gleefully.

> "Yes, that's what I've been saying. Now fetch me a rock!"

Jimmy now has an excellent chance of finding a rock that will please his boss, because he knows the goal his boss is trying to achieve.

For completeness, we need to add an interim step:

Work produces a product or service that achieves a goal.

Figure 2.1 shows how this process looks.

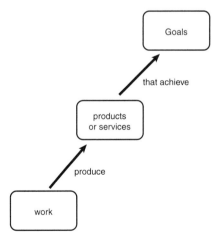

Figure 2.1   The purpose of work

This simple concept becomes the core structure for developing successful projects.

Young Jimmy first performs the work: He conducts an analysis (of plot, character building, or literary style) and writes a book report. The product is the book report itself. The goals are that Jimmy learned something and he gets a good grade.

Older Jimmy also performs a task: searching for, and ultimately finding, an appropriate rock. The product is the rock. Jimmy's boss's goal is achieved: His papers don't blow off his desk. Jimmy's goal is achieved: His boss likes him and feels more confident about giving Jimmy bigger assignments.

Notice that of the three components, work is the least important. It's the product that achieves the goal, not the work. Also notice that the goal is the primary driver. The products and services must be designed to achieve the goal. The work must be designed to build the correct products or perform the right services.

The Project Manager's Triangle of Balance

As with any form of work, projects must have a goal. To achieve the goal, we conduct work to produce products or deliverables. The work expends resources, both human and non-human. Work takes time. Work, resources, and goals interact to form the triangle shown in Figure 2.2.

Figure 2.2 The project manager's triangle of balance

From a high-level perspective, the project management team's job is to strike a balance among time, resources, and goals. Additionally, as one side changes, the others must change accordingly. If you increase the goals, you must also increase time and resources. Similarly, if you don't have sufficient resources to achieve the goals, you won't achieve them.

Also notice the contrary situation: If a project manager has too many resources or time, goals will automatically expand to use the overage. Just like Goldilocks, projects are successful when the three porridges (time, cost, and goals) are "just right."

You can hold one side of the triangle constant while shifting the opposite point slightly from side to side. For example, you can sometimes shorten the time to attain a goal by throwing more money at the project, but these trade-offs wane quickly. The shape must approximate an equilateral triangle.

Progressive Elaboration, Decomposition, and Breakdown Structures

Projects are successful when they are planned from beginning to end. In the early stages, this is done at a very high level. As planning progresses, the project management team continues to plan the project from beginning to end, but each iteration develops more detail and more accuracy. The PMI calls this concept **progressive elaboration.** This theme is similar to the "top-down" concepts familiar to systems developers since the mid-1980s. The concept is to define something at a very high level and then progressively make it more detailed and more accurate.

One of the primary tools to aid progressive elaboration is the concept of the **breakdown structure.** A breakdown structure successively breaks down a large item (a goal, a unit of work, an organization, and so on) into smaller components. A list of ingredients used to make a meal is a breakdown structure. A bill of materials is also a breakdown structure.

To illustrate, let's make a house breakdown structure. The house is at the top of the hierarchy. A house consists of rooms, so rooms is the next level down. Each room consists of walls (we'll leave floors and ceilings out, for simplicity); walls is the next level down. Figure 2.3 shows this graphically. For simplicity, I restrict our house to only three rooms.

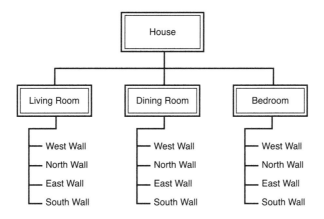

Figure 2.3   A house breakdown structure

Breakdown structures are shown in one of two ways: using the hierarchical chart in Figure 2.3 or using outline format. This is the outline format for the house breakdown structure:

1. House

    A. Living room (LR)

        1. LR west wall

        2. LR north wall

        3. LR east wall

        4. LR south wall

    B. Dining room (DR)

        1. DR west wall

        2. DR north wall

        3. DR east wall

        4. DR south wall

    C. Bedroom (BR)

        1. BR west wall

        2. BR north wall

        3. BR east wall

        4. BR south wall

Several breakdown structures are used in project management. The most common are the work breakdown structure (WBS), the resource breakdown structure (RBS), and the organizational breakdown structure (OBS). The lesser-known goals breakdown structure (GBS)[1] offers executive managers benefits for developing and managing projects within their organization.

Establishing a Common Language

I still frequently find companies struggling with definitions. Improperly used terminology yields waste, rework, and inefficiency. In seminars, one of the goals attendees frequently bring with them is to help develop a common language within their organization. As an executive manager, you have the power to improve your organization's efficiency by helping establish that common language.

The definitions I present are commonly recognized in most circles. Whether you choose these definitions or define your own is not relevant. Simply be aware that if you use the terms differently, you might need to translate them when communicating with the outside world.

Project and Program

The definition for **project** comes directly from the PMI standard:

> **Project**—A temporary endeavor undertaken to create a unique product, service, or result

This definition describes three characteristics for an activity to be considered a project:

1. **Temporary** means that a defined timeframe exists: a beginning and an end.

2. **Unique** means that this project is different than previous activities.

3. The **product, service, or result** is defined.

The formal definition of the term project precludes a size distinction. A project can be an activity that takes half an hour or ten years, as long as it's unique, temporary (has a beginning and an end), and creates a unique, well-defined product. This might be why administrative assistants show up in advanced project management training seminars. However, it would be ridiculous to project-manage a half-hour activity, which is why most of those administrative assistants return to the office feeling unfulfilled.

Although the concepts we apply to project management are appropriate regardless of size, the classical tool sets presented in both this book and most seminars assume that you're managing a project that's typically several months long or longer and involves at least a small handful of people. Small projects can be handled with less rigor than a larger project. Complex, high-risk, or high-visibility projects also require more rigor. The tools I present in this book assume a medium-size project. You can upscale or downscale these tools as needed for your project mix.

> **Program**—A group of projects managed together as a unit

The distinction between a project and a program is sometimes merely semantic; other times the distinction is clear. Let's consider two types of programs. The first is a new product launch program. Here the organization engages in several eclectic projects to effect the new product launch. The technical team must develop the product, the marketing team must develop advertising and marketing materials, the sales team must be trained, a production line development project is required, and logistics must be handled. These are all very different projects, but they must be managed in a coordinated way to successfully launch the new product.

The second example is an air traffic control system. This system involves developing several computer-based systems: one for the airport control areas, one for the en route controllers, a separate system for the towers, another for communications management, and finally one for radar management. The project plans to develop all these systems will be similar because they are all real-time computer-based systems. You can manage this program as a single, large project, blurring the distinction between *project* and *program*.

Programs consist of two or more projects that require coordination. The projects might relate in two key areas. In the previous examples, the projects require coordination because they share a common high-level goal. Projects can also relate because they share a common resource pool. When that occurs, the project managers must coordinate the use of the resources to provide efficiency across the program.

Whether your organization calls this a project or a program is irrelevant. What is relevant is that everyone in your organization uses the terminology consistently, preventing administrative assistants from showing up in advanced project management training programs.

Portfolio

> **Portfolio**—The entire collection of projects and programs an enterprise, organization, division, or department of an organization undertakes to achieve its overall objectives

The term portfolio is well chosen because a portfolio of projects and programs should be managed similar to any other portfolio: an investment portfolio, a photo portfolio for a model, a drawing portfolio for an artist, and so on.

Scope, Requirements, Objectives, and Goals

The discipline of project management offers less clarity for these terms than it should. The definitions I chose align with the standard, but I've tried to provide more clarity based on older doctrine or personal perspective:

> **Scope**—What's included and not included in the project

This might be the most confusing term in the discipline. Although most people can correctly describe the dictionary definition of the term, scope can (and does) refer to several distinct and dissimilar items in project management. We have goals scope (the complete list of objectives included in the project), work scope (all the work included in the project), cost scope (the total project budget, including human resources, capital expenditure, expenses, and so on), resource scope (the complete list of all resources involved in the project), and schedule scope (the total amount of time it will take to do the project). Not long ago, a senior manager would ask a project manager (PM) for the scope of a project and the PM would respond, "It's about a million-dollar project" or "It's about a two-year project." Both answers were correct, depending on who was asking the question.

Today even the PMI standard defines three versions of the term scope: scope (unqualified), product scope, and project scope. The first version refers to all the products, services, and results included in the project; the second version refers to the functional and performance characteristics of the products that the project will create; and the third version refers to the work needed to create those products.

When I use the otherwise unqualified term scope, I refer to goals. These might be business-level goals or product requirements (PMI's **product scope**). When I refer to the entire collection of work included in a project, I use the term **work scope,** making the term more easily understood by nonproject professionals.

Let's continue.

> **Goals**—I use this term to refer to any generic goal, objective, requirement, specification, or target.

> **Objectives**—I use this term to refer to business-level or organizational-level goals. These are the primary reasons to undertake a project, including such items as market share, return on investment (ROI), sales objectives, and membership drive objectives.

> **Requirements**—This term refers to a measurable characteristic of a product or service.

I take slight liberty with the term requirements and employ an older model. My basis for the use of this definition derives from the old military standard MIL–STD–2167A (now I'm showing my age) and other U.S. government project standards of the period. This term clearly aligns with the PMI standard, but I take a more rigorous approach to the concept. Requirements are also frequently referred to as **exit criteria:** characteristics that must be proven to the client or other stakeholders to deem the project complete.

Roles and Responsibilities

The roles and responsibilities presented here follow the classical models. Later in this book, I define additional roles to improve project management in the organization. Here we explore the project manager, project sponsor, and senior management. As with the terminology section, it's less important that you match this model within your organization; it's more important that the roles be clearly defined. Every seasoned project manager is aware of the need for clearly defined roles and responsibilities to get the team to work together toward the project's end goals.

Project Manager

We examine the role of the project manager (PM) from two perspectives. First we look at the PM's relationship with the team, and then we look at the PM's relationship with other key stakeholders.

The Project Manager and the Team

Executive managers commonly misunderstand the project manager's role. The PM's primary job is to manage the team, not to actually do the work of the project. For example, the project manager does not create the work breakdown structure (WBS); the project manager leads the team that creates the WBS.

Three reasons drive this structure. First, the project manager cannot be a subject matter expert (SME) in all the disciplines involved in the project. In areas where PMs possess expertise, they must learn to delegate both the planning and execution to others so that they can manage the other disciplines. Second, when project managers act as both manager and doer, they must manage themselves in addition to the rest of the team. This is similar to self-medication—it yields both bad management and bad task performance. Third, when PMs are performing project activities, they are not managing the rest of the team, which then flounders.

The role of project manager is very different and distinct from the role of task performer. The former is a jack-of-all-trades, a multitasker. The PM must maintain a high-level view of the entire project to make the right decisions. The PM must be able to sense when a project is in trouble and correct it quickly to ensure that it stays on track. The task performer is a specialist, a single-tasker who must concentrate on one item to make sure it meets its quality specifications. Distracting the task performer causes waste and increases the probability that the product will not meet its quality standards.

The project manager is a manager and coordinator. Project managers don't create the project plan; they muster the appropriate experts to create the project plan. The project manager's job is to make sure the experts create a plan that meets the project's requirements and keeps the stakeholders happy. When project execution begins, the project manager makes sure that the right resources are placed on the right tasks and that the team members have everything they need at their disposal to do the job correctly, quickly, and efficiently. PMs also monitor the project to detect when it starts to go astray so that they can correct it quickly.

Project Manager and the Stakeholders

In addition to managing the team, the project manager must "manage" the stakeholders. Formally, project stakeholders include anyone affected by the project or its deliverables. These include the client, functional managers whose people are on the team, senior management, vendors and consultants, and any other departments or individuals involved with the project. Many stakeholders are several layers higher in the organization than the PM, placing the PM in a very difficult political situation. All these different stakeholders have different needs and wants, and many of them will conflict with other stakeholders' objectives and the project's objectives.

Stakeholder management is one of the most challenging, time-consuming, and risky aspects of project management. It requires both political and business savvy, and it distracts the project manager from the [more productive] task of getting the project done.

Executive management plays a significant role in aiding or hindering the project manager's ability to manage stakeholders. Well-defined processes and a positive corporate culture enable your project managers to spend their time managing the project instead of handling conflicting stakeholders.

Sponsor

The project sponsor is an executive-level individual who represents the project to the executive team. The sponsor serves three key roles.

First, in formal project management, the sponsor controls and has complete authority over the project budget.

Second, you might have noticed that the most recent projects seem to get the most attention. The projects that get the most attention also seem to get the highest priority. Those with the highest priority seem to get the most resources. As a result, the older the project is, the more difficulty the project manager has securing resources. Therefore, the sponsor must champion the project at the executive level. The project manager has enough to do making sure that the project stays on track. The project manager is also not at the right level to hobnob with the rest of the executives. One of the sponsor's roles is to help the project manager maintain the project's priority and visibility over time, to prevent other executives from stealing needed resources.

Finally, as executive representative for the project, the sponsor should have enough authority to overcome political issues, allocate resources, and make executive-level decisions on behalf of the project. For example, when the project is internal (the client and project team work for the same organization), the sponsor acts as the mediator between the project manager (who wants the project to absorb a minimum of resources) and the client (who wants every possible feature for free).

Senior Management

Senior management has two roles for the project. First, management determines the project's viability and defines its organizational objectives. This is accomplished through a business case that ultimately results in a project charter (we discuss this later). After the project is approved and sanctioned, senior management must maintain support for the project throughout its life by ensuring that it has adequate resources.

Project Framework

The framework presented in Figure 2.4 is modeled after the 2nd edition (2000 edition) of the *PMBOK Guide.* This framework model is designed to offer more clarity in presenting project flow to executives. I also take the liberty of renaming some of the stages, to improve understanding for those outside the discipline and for those using other models.

The model incorporates five stages. These stages have very clear functions in the overall project plan and create clear deliverables. Table 2.1 offers a brief description of these stages.

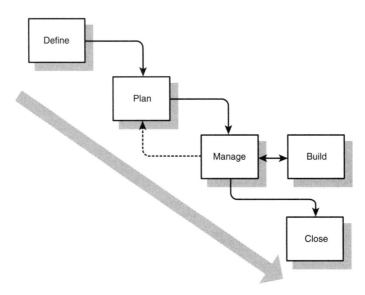

Figure 2.4 Project framework

Table 2.1 Project Structure Stages

Define	Formally authorize the project and define the organization-level success criteria
Plan	Develop the detailed project requirements and plan
Manage	Manage and coordinate the team performing the project activities
Build	Build the products or perform the services defined in the project
Close	Perform activities needed to formally bring the project to closure

Define

All projects start with some stimulus, event, or spark in someone's mind. A competitor announces a new product, some new technology is discovered that could save you money, or the price of fuel oil increases and you need to find an alternative energy source. Someone must determine whether this idea makes sense for the organization. This is the business case.

Formally, this is not part of the project. This stage includes those activities needed to evaluate the project's viability, determine its organization-level objectives, and formally sanction the project. Although the project manager should be included in this stage, the primary responsibility should fall on a business analyst, product marketing manager, strategic planner, or similar role.

The project charter is an executive summary of the business case. When executed by appropriate stakeholders, this charter formally sanctions the project. This means that the project manager is enabled to expend organizational assets (cash, human resources, and so on) on behalf of the project.

Plan

This stage involves the project manager and key subject matter experts developing the detailed project goals, work plan, resource plan, risk management, and other plans needed for successful project execution. The primary deliverable for this stage is the completed project plan.

Manage

The project manager and project management team manage project execution in this stage. The primary outputs or deliverables are status reports and forecasts. Note the dotted line returning to planning. When the plans change, the project management team must revise the plan to keep it up-to-date.

Build

This stage represents the project team developing the products or performing the services defined in the project. The primary outputs for this stage are the project's deliverables.

Close

At first glance, the closing stage appears purely administrative. However, this stage is critical to the future of the organization. Activities in this stage include conducting the final lessons learned, to prevent mistakes from reoccurring; updating the organization's processes to incorporate the new project and its lessons learned; reassigning the team members to their new assignments; reporting on team members' performance, to aid their professional growth; archiving the actual time each activity took, along with the results, so they can be used to improve future estimates; and obtaining both administrative and emotional closure on the project.

Summary

This chapter presents core concepts, roles and responsibilities, and a framework for successful project management. To aid you in your quest for improved organizational efficiency, I offer the checklist in Table 2.2 as both a summary and a guide to successfully implementing project management in your organization.

Table 2.2 Chapter 2 Organizational Performance Rating Sheet

Performance Item	My Organization's Performance				
	High ⟵				Low
My organization uses a common language for project management to prevent mistakes, rework, and other inefficiencies.					
My organization clearly defines and communicates organization-level objectives for each project, enabling the project team to successfully achieve those objectives.					
Someone in my organization defines the products and services to ensure that they will achieve the organization's objectives.					
My organization clearly defines the roles of sponsor, project manager, executive management, and project teams for all projects.					
My organization incorporates an executive sponsor to aid the project manager with executive-level decisions, politics, and the project budget.					
My organization encourages project managers to identify and delegate project planning to appropriate subject matter experts.					
My organization balances time, cost, and goals on a continuous basis to ensure project success.					

3

Project Definition and Planning

his chapter offers an overview of project management, specifically highlighting those areas that help you understand and better support it in your organization.

The purpose of project definition is to make sure the project builds the right things. The purpose of planning is to make sure the project team builds them efficiently. Therefore, this chapter highlights how project definition and planning affect management and execution. I also briefly discuss change management, which is critical to project success.

Project Definition

Project definition is not formally part of the project. Perhaps for this reason, it is the least understood and most poorly implemented part of the project environment.

All projects begin with some stimulus, such as a competitor announcing a new product, the cost of some raw material suddenly increasing, or the strategic planning committee wanting to increase market share by 20 percent. The stimulus initiates an analysis to determine whether it warrants becoming a project. This analysis creates a business case for the project. The business case is summarized in the form of a project charter. The charter is an executive-level summary of the business case that contains, at a minimum, the essential items executive management needs to make a decision on whether to proceed with the project.

The key purpose of project definition is to do the following:

1. Identify the benefits the organization expects out of the project

2. Define the project sufficiently for a qualified project manager to begin developing a project plan

3. Determine the organizational viability of the project

4. Identify and communicate risks, assumptions, and issues currently known about the project to both executive management and the project management team for planning purposes

5. Formally sanction the project and assign the project manager

At this stage, three concepts are key to successful project definition.

- Formally, the project charter is the one project document that cannot change.

  The charter establishes a line in the sand that prevents stakeholders (some of whom might be very powerful and savvy) from growing the project beyond its usefulness and trying to absorb inappropriate resources. In Congress they're called riders, and in projects it's called scope creep. Some director wants to put just a few extra pages on the Web site, or wants to add just one more report to the computer system you're building—the scope of the project keeps creeping higher. One of the key purposes of the charter is to prevent such scope creep.

- The charter is a contract between executive management and the project manager.

  The project manager promises to deliver the products and services itemized in the charter using the estimated time and resources. Senior management promises to provide the resources offered in the charter. Both acknowledge the risks, issues, and assumptions contained in the charter.

  Because the charter is a contract, estimates must be sufficient for the project manager to succeed, yielding our third key concept.

- Appropriate project management and subject matter expertise must be employed in developing the business case, to ensure a balance of scope, time, and cost.

The elements contained in the charter and their level of detail will vary among organizations and types of projects. Executive management is responsible for determining the elements and detail needed. Table 3.1 offers typical charter elements, followed by a sample charter. You can download a soft copy of a charter from my Web site at www. AllyBusiness.com/PMTools.html.

Table 3.1 Elements of a Project Charter

Project mission or goal statement	Describes the key objective for the project. Similar to a company mission statement, the project mission statement should be concise, focused, and wordsmithed. It must also be durable—capable of surviving the entire project without changing.
Business objectives	Lists key goals the organization wants from the project. These might include such elements as market share, return on investment, and technology development.
Deliverables	Briefly describes the key deliverables and any characteristics important to senior management and to project success.
Scope: inclusions and exclusions	Lists the activities or goals both included and excluded in the project. The purpose of the exclusions is to prevent clients and other stakeholders from assuming that they're getting something they're not.
Project manager and level of authority	Identifies the project manager and what he/she is allowed to do. This may include hiring staff, consultants, or vendors; conducting training; or authorizing capital expenditures.
Organizational resources	Provides high-level estimates of resources needed by the various departments.
Approach	Takes an organization-level approach to accomplishing the project. If you have standard procedures, methodologies, or templates, you can itemize them here.
Risks, assumptions, and other issues	Lists key project-level risks and assumptions associated with the project. Using the simple risk/reward business model, you can compare these elements to the business objectives to determine whether to undertake the project.
Initial estimates	Uses appropriate subject matter experts and the help of a qualified project manager to provide initial estimates for both time and cost. Early estimates might include a wide range of values (such as $1 million ±30%).

Sample Project Charter

Project Title: Additional soft-drink manufacturing plant

Key Stakeholders:	**PROJECT PRIORITY:** ☒ 1 ☐ 2 ☐ 3 ☐ 4 ☐ 5
Executive Sponsor	John Smith, President
Project Manager	Michael B. Bender, PMP
Client Point of Contact	Kiran Jonas, VP Operations

Primary Project Mission:

Acquire and make operational a new plant to increase production of the XYZ soft drink line by 35% in an economically distressed area within the United States.

Business Objectives and Justification:

1) Increase production by 35%.

2) Retain current gross margin for all products created in the new plant.

3) Ensure a 7-year payback on the cost of the plant.

4) Products shall meet all existing product quality standards.

5) Plant must be operational in 18 months

6) Project shall not interfere with ongoing operations.

7) Project team shall include outside architectural and engineering consultants to bring fresh ideas into the plant and production design.

Deliverables:

1) Fully operational plant

2) Staff trained to run two shifts

3) Warehouse space for 3 months of inventory

4) 6,000 sq. ft. laboratory space for new product development

5) Tax incentives from community

6) Product distribution plan

Scope:

Inclusions:

Fully operational 200,000 sq. ft. plant with all new equipment. Trained staff to run the plant for two full shifts. 6,000 sq. ft. space for lab equipment for new product development. 5,000 sq. ft. offices for plant managers and administration support. 5,000 sq. ft. offices for executive management. Warehouse space for 3 full months of inventory. Direct access to railroads for distribution. Distribution plan and contracts. Tax agreement with the local township. Offices shall be furnished.

Exclusions:

Lab equipment is not part of this project. Also, no raw materials shall be purchased for this project except for production prototyping and quality control testing.

Departments Involved:

Engineering (5,000 hours), Executive Management (consulting and reviews), Facilities Management (1,200 hours), Finance (800 hours), Purchasing (1,200 hours), Human Resources (1,200 hours), Training Department (1,400 hours)

Constraints:

Budget:	$24 million including equipment
Schedule:	Fully operational in 18 month; buy/build decision in 5 months
Quality:	Production lines shall meet all existing quality standards
Other:	All OSHA, FDA, federal, state, and local ordinances shall be followed

Suggested Approach:

Locate economically challenged areas to take advantage of tax incentives and available labor. Find any existing plants in those areas that are abandoned or for sale that might meet the project's objectives. Evaluate the cost of environmental cleanup necessary for existing plants. Pre-negotiate with local townships to determine willingness to engage in tax incentives. Produce a short list of five plants for executive review. Evaluate the cost of building a new plant for executive review. Executive committee will make the final determination. Acquire/build the plant. Design the production lines. Purchase and install appropriate equipment. Hire and train staff.

Risks, Assumptions, and Issues:

1) Economic conditions may worsen, alleviating the need for the new plant.

2) Commodity prices for raw materials may affect gross margins.

3) No existing plants may exist, and cost to build a new plant may be prohibitive.

4) Ecological cleanup may extend project duration and cost.

5) Changes in township politics may affect the deal during plant development.

6) Build/buy decision may affect cost and schedule. At this point, these costs are viewed as essentially equal as we'll have to refurbish an abandoned plant or build a new one.

7) Financial analysis assumes a 35-year amortization schedule.

8) Dynamic economic environment may affect the cost-of-capital which will affect financial analysis and margins.

Initial Estimates:		
Cost:	Plant: 12 million Furniture and equipment: 6 million Cleanup: 1 million (average of typical cleanups over last 4 years) Misc: 2 million (travel, training, legal and financial services)	
Schedule:	Plant short list: 5 months Plant acquition (if we can purchase one): 9 months Fully operational: 16 months	

Approvals

Title	Signature	Date
President		
Project Manager		
VP Operations		
VP Finance		
VP HR		
VP Engineering		
Facilities Manager		

Project Scope Definition

Project planning begins when all required stakeholders execute the project charter. The project team now develops a detailed scope definition. Recalling that project scope includes both goals and work, this includes both requirements definition and work definition.

Requirements Definition

The first challenge the project management team faces is identifying *all* the requirements and deliverables needed for the project to succeed from both a technical and business perspective. Because the charter is an executive-level document, it does not identify these more detailed aspects of the project. These include how the project manager will report on the project's progress, which technical standards will be used, how project quality will be managed, and how project risks will be identified and tracked, just to name a few.

This stage of the project is usually the most difficult for the project team. In addition to addressing the previous items, the team must address the needs of all the key stakeholders.

Every functional manager who needs to provide personnel to the project is a key stakeholder, even if that functional department receives no benefit from the project. Purchasing, human resources, finance, functional managers, and operations are key stakeholders in most projects.

> **The project management team must attempt to satisfy**
> **all key stakeholders while satisfying the goals identified**
> **in the charter on a limited budget and schedule.**

The Goals Breakdown Structure

Aiding the project team is the first of the formal breakdown structures: the goals breakdown structure (GBS). The GBS breaks down high-level goals into smaller goals. For example, let's say we want to get on the Dean's list in college (get all A's and B's) this semester. We know we're good at mathematics and general test taking, but we're bad at writing papers. For this example, our curriculum consists of Calculus (an easy A because we're good in math), English Composition, and Ancient History. The latter two will be more difficult because they involve writing papers. After the professors provide us with the course syllabus and grading schedule, we can create the following GBS for getting on the Dean's list:

1. Get on the Dean's list
   A. Get an A in Calculus
   B. Get a B in English Composition
      1. Get an A on all tests
      2. Get a minimum of a C on papers
      3. Get a B on at least 2 papers
   C. Get a B in Ancient History
      1. Get an A on all tests
      2. Get a minimum of a C on all papers
      3. Get a B on at least 3 papers

As with all breakdown structures, it's convenient to label the different layers. For projects, the structure shown in Figure 3.1 was devised by Messers Gershenson, Bender, and Syme,[1] and has proven to work well with most projects.

The project charter provides the project team with the business objectives. The team must now create the detailed requirements. After the project scope documents are approved, the technical team will conduct a detailed design to create the design specifications.

The benefits of the GBS are the same as for any of the breakdown structures: The GBS provides us with the complete set of goals, with no extra or unnecessary goals, at all layers of the organization.

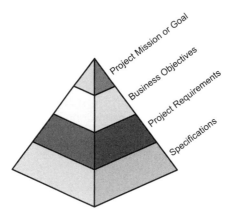

Figure 3.1 Goals breakdown structure hierarchy

A note about project requirements: A large number of organizations use requirements as project **exit criteria.** In other words, the project is deemed complete when the project management team proves to the client that every project requirement has been successfully completed. This is accomplished through a series of tests called the final acceptance test or customer acceptance test. Although it might seem excessive for internal projects, instilling this discipline offers additional benefits and advantages beyond improving project quality. I address these additional benefits later.

Stakeholder Management

The team now must work with the stakeholders to hone and refine the requirements, in an attempt to keep everyone happy. This might involve interviews, meetings, more detailed analysis, prototyping, piloting, or benchmarking. The ultimate goal is to define a complete set of project requirements that will satisfy the project charter and all stakeholders—or, at least, set realistic expectations.

This is one key area where executive management can support the project manager. The project manager must work with all stakeholders, regardless of rank, skill, or agendas (hidden or visible).

> **The project sponsor, in addition to providing funding for the project, must provide political and authoritative support to the project manager when handling difficult stakeholders.**

Work Definition

Once we understand the goals and deliverables for the project, the team can develop the work plan. In this section, I present the work breakdown structure (WBS), project phases and phase gates, and the work package concept. Finally, the team establishes the order in which they should execute the work. They accomplish this using the precedence diagram.

Work Breakdown Structure

The work breakdown structure (WBS) is arguably the best-known construct in project management. As its name implies, the WBS decomposes, or breaks down, a large unit of work into smaller units of work.

The WBS becomes the core of the project plan. The charter, requirements, and product descriptions ultimately contribute to the project's WBS. After it's constructed, the WBS becomes the primary driver for the rest of the project. Risk management, resource planning, estimates, procurement, tracking, and monitoring are all based on the WBS.

You can use several strategies for breaking down the work. You can break down work by department, component, region, cost center, or any method by which the project management team and subject matter experts see fit. Many larger-scaled projects decompose work along multiple strategies. A classic WBS structure employs **phases** at the highest level of the project, followed by **deliverables,** and then **work packages,** as illustrated in this outline. This model is what the Project Management Institute (PMI) refers to as a **deliverables-based WBS** as shown in outline format below**.**

Project Title

1. Phase 1
   A. Deliverable 1
      1. Work package a
      2. Work package b
      3. Work package c
   B. Deliverable 2
      1. Work package d
      2. Work package e
      3. Work package f
      4. Work package g
   C. Deliverable 3
      1. Work package h
2. Phase 2
   A. Deliverable 4
      1. Work package i
      2. Work package j
      3. Work package k

With this structure, work packages build well-defined components of the deliverables. Phases consist of multiple deliverables. As you will see later, this structure offers both project managers and executives many control and monitoring advantages. You can also exploit this strategy to enhance your organization's flexibility in performing projects. Figure 3.2 illustrates this structure graphically.

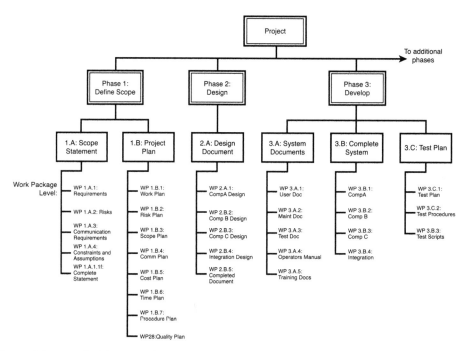

Figure 3.2   Sample deliverables-based WBS

Let's briefly describe the layers.

Project Phases and Phase Gates

Phases are not technically a WBS construct. They are not a decomposition of a high-level of work; they arrange the work to enhance executive and project management oversight.

The purpose of a phase is for executive management to review the progress of the project, re-evaluate the benefit based on current circumstances (which might have changed since the charter was executed), and determine whether the project should continue into the next phase. These reviews are sometimes called **gate reviews** or **kill-points**. The project must pass through the gate to proceed to the next phase.

Each phase consists of the creation of a set of deliverables or subdeliverables (well-defined components of deliverables that might span several phases). Including a deliverables level helps project managers justify the work and ensure they don't forget items.

Work Package

The work package concept is key to developing sound project strategies, both at the tactical level and at the strategic level. I elaborate on this later. For now, I present their use in classical project management.

The definition of a **work package** can be a bit awkward. The work package represents the work needed to create a well-defined component of a deliverable. By "well-defined," I mean that an outside organization (such as the quality control group) can inspect and evaluate the component. Therefore, the component must have clear, measurable, and verifiable specifications. This condition also implies that you can outsource the work for a fixed price. These specifications are presented as the fourth tier of the GBS, illustrated earlier.

To illustrate the work package concept, let's construct a table for a flea market. The table must meet these requirements:

- The table's top must be 6 feet by 3 feet in size.

- The table must hold up to 200 pounds.

- The table's legs must be removable or collapsible for transportation to the flea market.

- The table must not weigh more than 30 pounds.

The table has five primary components: the top and four legs. Our project must include a design. Our small project might consist of eight work packages:

1. Design table

2. Buy materials

3. Create top

4. Create first leg

5. Create second leg

6. Create third leg

7. Create fourth leg

8. Assemble table

Note that each work package creates a deliverable or piece of a deliverable. The first work package creates a design document. The second produces all the materials needed for construction. The third creates the top of the table, and so on.

Also note that you can outsource each of the work packages. Theoretically, we can hire someone to design the table. We can then hire someone to buy the materials. We can hire someone to create the top. As each of these work packages is finished, we can inspect the product for quality and completeness.

Beyond the Work Package

Executive management must ensure that the project's WBS is complete and accurate to the work package level. However, the project management team usually requires the work package to be broken down at least one more level. Therefore, each work package is broken down into a collection of what PMI refers to as **schedule activities.** This layer is designed to improve the accuracy and efficiency of the project plan. If needed, the work package owners or managers can further break down these schedule activities.

Precedence Diagram

The purpose of the WBS is to create the complete list of project activities. Although complete, this list is not necessarily in any sequence. Precedence diagramming involves evaluating the activities to determine their logical sequence and to determine whether you can do any in parallel. Figure 3.3 shows a simple precedence diagram for the first phase of a deck construction project for the fictitious Acme Deck Construction, Ltd., company. At this point in time, the duration, effort, and total cost of the activities might be unknown. We are interested in only their sequence and the degree to which tasks can run parallel. This helps us establish the shortest time to do the project and helps determine when resources will be needed.

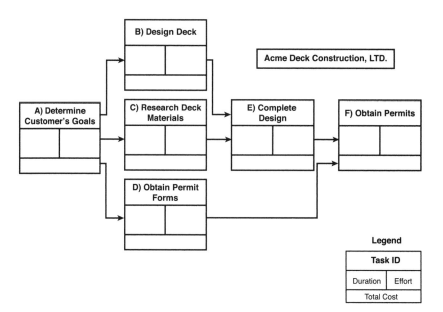

Figure 3.3   Sample precedence diagram

Estimates

When the WBS is in place, the project management team can begin estimating the work. A project manager needs two kinds of estimates: effort and duration. Effort is the actual amount of dedicated work time a person applies to an activity. Duration is the amount of time the task takes on a calendar.

As an executive, you need to know these key concepts about estimating:

- The earlier in the project the estimate is given, the less accurate it is.

- Project archives help in estimating by providing the team with actual results of earlier projects.

- Those responsible and accountable for the tasks should estimate them.

- If tasks are well defined and small enough, most task performers can estimate the effort to complete the task relatively accurately.

- The difference between effort and duration is rarely under the control of either the task performer or the project management team.

Let's briefly discuss each point.

Early Estimates

The earlier a team is in the project, the less knowledge it has about the project. Early estimates must be qualified. Typically, a project manager offers a range of estimates or a core estimate plus or minus some percentage. Estimate ranges of ±30% are typical early in the project. Some high-risk or very unique projects might exhibit an even greater range.

A political game can exist between executive managers and project managers regarding estimates. An executive who forces the project manager to give a firm cost or schedule estimate too early without sufficient planning forces the project manager to pad the estimate, to cover unknowns. Cutting the estimate to compensate for the pad simply forces the project manager to pad more the next time.

Project managers must learn to offer truthful estimates, and senior management must learn to trust those estimates.

Project Archives

Estimates are predictions of the future. The only tool we have in predicting the future is the past. Therefore, accurate estimates depend on two factors:

1. How similar the activity we're estimating is to some past activity

2. The quality of our memory regarding the results of that past activity

The project team has some control over the first factor. Executive management can control the second factor by supporting and enforcing the maintenance of project archives. As an executive manager, you can significantly improve project estimates by creating, supporting, and enforcing accurate archival of project activity information for future estimating.

Accountability for Providing the Estimates

Those responsible and accountable for the tasks should provide the estimates for two reasons:

1. The task performer knows (or should know) the work better than a manager.

2. This generates buy-in and ownership from the task performer.

This concept frequently is difficult for many project managers and executives to accept, or perhaps they don't want to give up control. The difficulty is that you need to rely on and trust your staff to give accurate, unpadded estimates for activities. It's easy to believe that your staff is padding their estimates; therefore, it's easy for you to cut those estimates—especially under pressure from above. When your staff knows you're cutting their estimates, they just start padding more (see the "Early Estimates" section).

As an executive manager, you establish the culture that dictates how your organization handles estimates. Therefore, this topic receives significant attention later in this book. For now, I simply ask you to encourage your staff to offer truthful estimates, to trust your staff, and to enable the task owners and performers to provide the estimates.

Task Definition and Size

Simply stated, the smaller the task is, the more accurate the estimate is. Certainly, a point of diminishing returns emerges. Project managers are (or, at least, should be) well trained on how detailed to make the WBS for estimating and other purposes.

Task definition also plays a significant role in the accuracy of the estimates. The better defined the task is, the more accurate the estimate is. However, project managers are not subject matter experts. They must rely on the subject matter experts to define the tasks accurately enough for the task performer to estimate them.

The biggest complaint I hear in my seminars regarding this issue is that executive management doesn't give attendees enough time for project and task definition. This forces project managers to either pad to cover unknowns or cut corners, resulting in significant rework.

Effort Versus Duration

Effort is the amount of dedicated work time applied to a task; **duration** is the amount of calendar time applied to the task.

Project managers first ask for effort estimates for tasks. This tells the project manager the amount of work required to do the task. The PM then asks the percentage of time the worker can apply to the activity. If the effort estimate is one week but the worker can dedicate only 50 percent of his time to the task, then the task will take two calendar weeks to complete.

In Chapter 1, "The Goals of Project Management," I introduced the Warm Body Syndrome, in which managers grab the first available warm body to do some task, regardless of importance, skill, or the person's current workload. If executive or middle managers grab this worker whenever they need something done, the duration of the task they are on will increase and the project will be late. This issue causes many projects to slip their schedules. It's the manifestation of Alex's problem in Chapter 1.

It is very difficult for either project managers or task performers to tell a vice president "no" when he asks them to do something unrelated to the project they're on. Because most project team members report to a functional manager in a matrix environment, it's even more difficult for a task performer to say "no" to their own boss.

As an executive, you define the culture that promotes or prevents arbitrarily reassigning resources on the fly. You will see later in this book that the fewer distractions a task performer is forced to handle, the more efficiently that person can work.

Critical Path

Few will challenge that we live in a very dynamic business environment. Plans change and emergencies occur. Critical path is probably the most useful tools project management offers for managing resources in a dynamic environment.

Core Concepts

Many people outside project management misunderstand the term critical path. The critical path defines tasks that exhibit the highest risk for schedule delay. They are time critical, not mission critical, as many initially think.

Critical path is a mathematical phenomenon of scheduling. It exists in the physical universe. Through each project precedence diagram, at least one series of activities defines the length of the project. If any task along that path is delayed, an equal delay appears at the end of the project. Not all activities exhibit this characteristic. Some activities can accept a certain delay without affecting the project schedule.

In Figure 3.4, I added effort, duration, and cost estimates to the precedence diagram shown in Figure 3.3.

Note that the sequence of tasks A–B–E–F formulates the longest series in the phase—a total of ten days. Task C takes only one day, but its deliverables aren't needed until two days after it can start. It has one day of **float** (the amount of time a task can float on a calendar without impacting the end date). Task D is a two-day task, but its deliverable isn't needed until four days after it can start. It has two days of float.

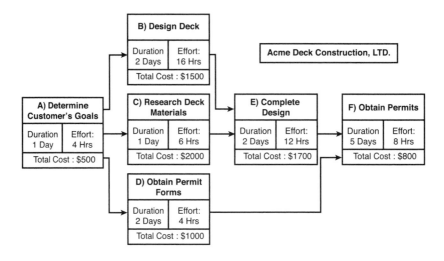

Total Time: 10 Days
Total Cost: $7500

Figure 3.4   Sample critical path

This means that the project manager can reassign the person currently assigned to task C to handle some emergency, client request, or some other nonproject activity for a full day without impacting the end date. Similarly, the project manager can reassign the person currently assigned to task D to a nonproject activity for two days without impacting the end date. However, if any of the people assigned to tasks A, B, E, or F are reassigned for any reason, the phase will be late.

> **The critical path tells project managers where to put their best resources—which resources they can afford to loan out, how long they can afford it, and which resources they can't afford to lose.**

Critical Path and Resource Leveling

Initial critical path analysis assumes that you have enough resources to parallelize and that your resource pool is relatively stable—a difficult assumption in today's business environment. Note that tasks B, C, and D can run in parallel. We would need three people on our team to do that. If we had only two, then one of the tasks (probably C) would need to run after B and D, extending the phase's duration.

The project management team typically determines the critical path assuming an unlimited resource pool. This determines two key planning elements:

- The shortest possible time to do the project
- The makeup of the perfect project team

The project manager then attempts to acquire the perfect team. After negotiations for resources conclude, the project manager must adjust the project plan to account for resource limitations—extending the project's duration. This is called **resource leveling.**

As an executive manager, you recognize that resources are tight and that many other organizational activities also need resources. Therefore, …

> **…executive management determines which projects get the resources and which projects will be delayed.**

The issue is whether executive management does this with forethought, based on the strategic plan, or whether this is done ad-hoc. The former method produces stable priorities that provide clear direction to project managers and functional managers alike. The latter produces what project managers frequently call **priority du jour:** daily readjusting of priorities that causes frequent staff reassignment and chaos. Chapter 4, "Strategic Alignment," addresses this issue.

Supporting Elements

At this point, we have addressed most of the information an executive needs to understand about project management. Most certainly, the previous discussion is highly condensed. The project manager and project management team have many other activities, tools, and responsibilities.

The purpose of this section is to present some additional tools to make the project plan more resilient to interference and risks, and to present typical communication tools that an executive might expect to see in a complete project management plan. If your curiosity gets the best of you, many (perhaps too many) books are available regarding the intricacies of project planning. I provide only a brief description of each.

Risk Management

Projects, by their definition, are unique entities. Therefore, they exhibit risk. Project risk management is a critical part of project planning. The purpose of risk management is to make the project more resilient to external or internal events that might or might not occur. The net result of risk management is a catalog of identified risks, their response plans, and contingency time and money to affect those responses. After consulting with the project sponsor or senior management, the project manager usually adjusts the WBS to incorporate certain tasks, to reduce either the impact or the probability based on management's risk tolerance. Let's look at two key graphs you might see regarding risk management.

Monte Carlo Analysis

Monte Carlo analysis is a computer simulation technique used to determine probabilities of achieving project goals—specifically, cost and schedule goals. For example, one of the classical high-risk activities in any project is getting customer information. Although customers want projects done perfectly, they don't want to (or don't understand the need to) invest time with the project team to describe exactly what they want. The actual act of getting the information is easy and predictable. The risk is scheduling the customer to actually sit down with the team to discuss the project. The resulting Monte Carlo graph of the "gather customer requirements" task for a project might look like Figure 3.5.

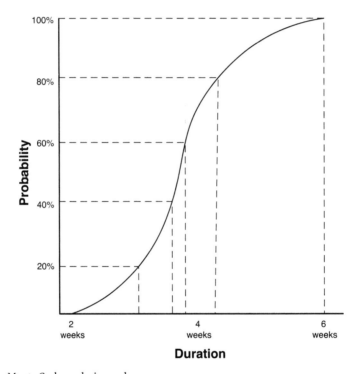

Figure 3.5   Monte Carlo analysis graph

Sensitivity Analysis

Projects exhibit multiple risks, often overlapping and impacting each other. As a result, many project managers run a sensitivity analysis. A sensitivity analysis is also a computer simulation technique and is frequently run with the Monte Carlo analysis. The purpose of this exercise is to determine which risks have the greatest effect on project cost, schedule, or quality. The resulting graph is called a tornado diagram because of its distinctive shape. The tornado diagram ranks the risks, from highest to lowest, based on their effect on the project. Figure 3.6 shows a typical tornado diagram.

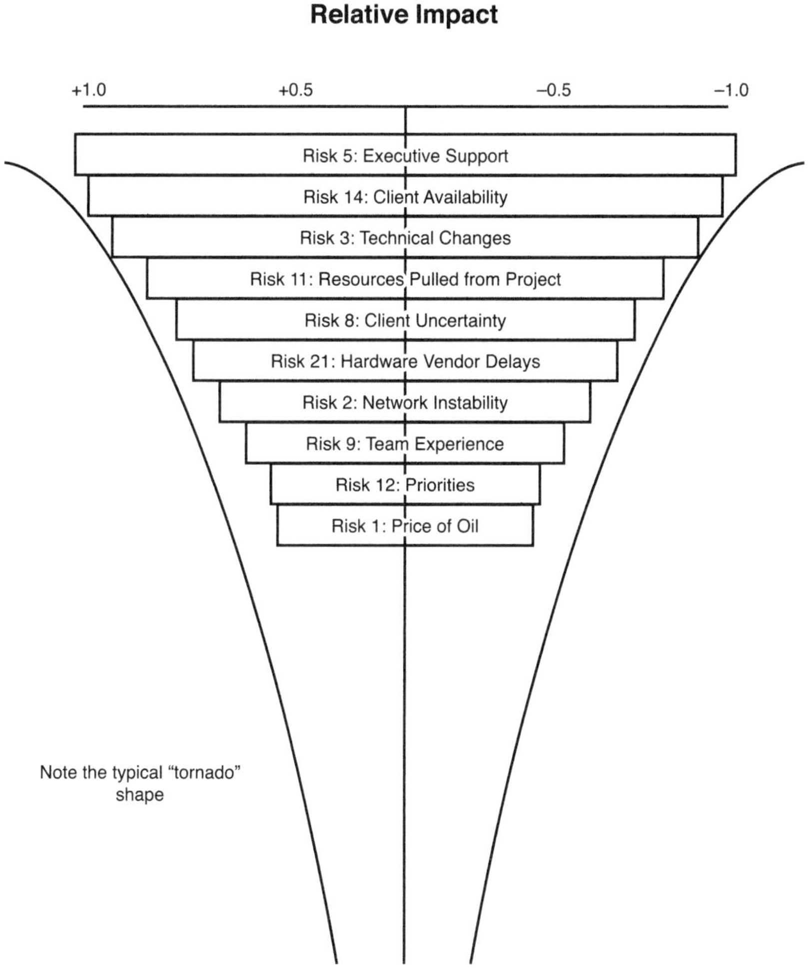

Relative Impact

| +1.0 | +0.5 | −0.5 | −1.0 |

- Risk 5: Executive Support
- Risk 14: Client Availability
- Risk 3: Technical Changes
- Risk 11: Resources Pulled from Project
- Risk 8: Client Uncertainty
- Risk 21: Hardware Vendor Delays
- Risk 2: Network Instability
- Risk 9: Team Experience
- Risk 12: Priorities
- Risk 1: Price of Oil

Note the typical "tornado" shape

Figure 3.6   Tornado diagram

Organizational and Resource Charts

In Chapter 2, "Project Management Framework and Structure," I highlighted the importance of clearly defining roles and responsibilities. Table 3.2 is called a resource assignment matrix (RAM). It identifies which resources are doing which tasks. Note that this version of the chart includes a column for the task owner, an important concept that I explore later in the book. Many versions of this chart exist, including the PMI RACI chart that identifies the "responsible, accountable, consulted, and informed" parties.

Table 3.2 Project Resource Assignment Matrix

Task/Resource	Owner	Louis	Marion	Ed	Reginald	Zel
Create skills competency	Louis	P	A		S	BU
Research competitive jobs	Zel	BU			S	P
Create benefits package per skill level	Zel			S		P
Define training needs	Marion	S	P	S	BU	
Select and hire training company	Ed	S, BU	S	P		
Conduct training	Ed	S, BU	S	P		
Review and promote	Zel	S	A			P

P = Principal contributor   A = (must) Approve

S = Secondary support   BU = Backup

Project Communication Plan

The communication plan describes how the project manager and project management team will communicate and report to the key stakeholders, including the sponsor, client, functional manager, vendors, team, government officials, and other key stakeholders. The document includes communication requirements; report formats, content, and frequency; meeting agenda, attendees, and frequency; escalation procedures and reporting; and any other communication needs.

The Communication Responsibility Matrix (CRM)

Figure 3.7 is called a communication responsibility matrix (CRM). It quickly shows who is supposed to communicate to whom and at what minimum frequency. Note that this is the only chart known in project management that specifically prevents certain groups from interacting. For example, this chart shows that the vice president shouldn't communicate with a team member regarding the project. The purpose of this is not to eliminate information flow, but to prevent erroneous communication flow. You're an executive. You ask an inexperienced engineer a simple question such as "How's it going?" The response you get is a litany of engineering babble that can only confuse and confound you. You can respond by ignoring it or becoming concerned about it. The former only wastes your time, and the latter will inevitably and adversely affect the project. This chart hopes to prevent the latter.

Report To

	Project Manager	Program Manager	Team Manager	Account Manager	Project Sponsor	Vice President	Customer SPOC
i Project Manager		M	W	M	S	A	M
t Program Manager	A		N	S	S	M	M
i Team Member	W	A		N	A	N	A
a Account Manager	M	M	N		A	A	S
t Project Sponsor	A	M	A	A		M	A
o Vice President	A	A	N	M	A		A
r Customer SPOC	A	A	A	M	A	A	

W = Weekly
S = Semi-Monthly
M = Monthly
A = As Needed
N = Never

Figure 3.7   Communication responsibility matrix

The Resource or Staffing Management Plan

This plan describes where and how the project management team will acquire appropriate staff. This might include the criteria needed for entry to and exit from the project team, under which circumstances the project team will obtain outside resources, resource performance reporting criteria (which might also be reflected in the communication plan), roles and responsibilities, rewards and punishment, and other resource and staffing information.

One significant chart included in the project staffing plan is the resource histogram, shown in Figure 3.8.

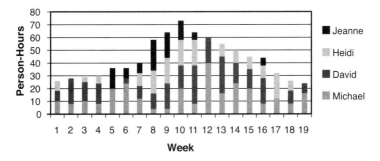

Figure 3.8   Project resource histogram

Procurement Plan

This plan outlines the procedures and criteria for outsourcing project work and resources. The procedures for outsourcing goods and services for project management are no different than that of other disciplines. However, the reasons to outsource can differ, and we address that topic in later chapters.

Milestones and Schedule Charts

More than 100 years ago, Henry Gantt developed one of the most famous project management charts in use today: the Gantt chart. The chart now takes several forms, but essentially it lays out tasks on a calendar. Figure 3.9 shows a typical modern-day Gantt chart. This chart was created by Microsoft® Project.

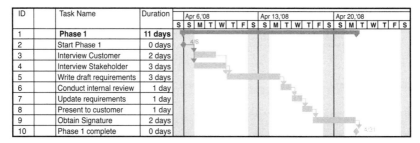

ID	Task Name	Duration
1	**Phase 1**	**11 days**
2	Start Phase 1	0 days
3	Interview Customer	2 days
4	Interview Stakeholder	3 days
5	Write draft requirements	3 days
6	Conduct internal review	1 day
7	Update requirements	1 day
8	Present to customer	1 day
9	Obtain Signature	2 days
10	Phase 1 complete	0 days

Figure 3.9 Sample Gantt chart

A milestone is simply an event that firmly identifies where we are in the project. Completing a deliverable is a milestone, and so is ending a phase. The event doesn't need to be large—it just needs to firmly identify where we are in the project.

Figure 3.10 shows a typical milestone chart.

ID	Task Name	Start	Finish	Duration
1	Requirements Definition	10/8/2007	10/8/2007	0d
2	Systems Design Complete	11/23/2007	11/23/2007	0d
3	System Acceptance	1/23/2008	1/23/2008	0d
4	System Parallel Run Starts	3/31/2008	3/31/2008	0d
5	Full System Cutover	4/30/2008	4/30/2008	0d

Figure 3.10 Sample milestone chart

Change Management

"I wish I had a dime…."

Project change management is probably the simplest and most obvious process in project management. Yet it is the process that continues to confound, confuse, derail, and thwart the greatest and simplest of projects. The process is simple and well known, but often unpracticed—usually for cultural reasons. Let's review the six steps for project change management:

1. Write down the change or change request.

    Any Web site professing project management will have the needed forms, including mine (www.AllyBusiness.com/PMTools.html).

2. Analyze both the positive and negative impact of the change.

3. Review alternatives.

4. Make recommendations.

5. Get approvals (or rejections).

6. If approved, implement the change. If not approved, don't implement the change.

Performing work requires both time and resources. If the scope changes, so do the cost and schedule. One plus one is still two—it's that simple.

Things change—minds change, environments change, competitors change, situations change. Project management has a strategy for handling these changes. Project managers don't mind change as long as there's an appropriate adjustment for schedule and cost. When it comes to change, …

> **…the smart project manager never says "no."**
> **The smart project manager says "when" and "how much."**

Remember these three keys to successful change management:

1. The project must be defined well enough to evaluate the effect of the change.

2. The culture must support serious change management.

3. Whoever is paying for the change must accept the cost.

If the party requesting the change won't pay for it, they really don't need it.

The project manager doesn't (or, at least, shouldn't) care who's paying for the change, as long as the budget and schedule are adjusted appropriately. If an outside client requests an enhancement and marketing wants to give it to the client for free in hopes of future business, the project manager shouldn't be concerned as long as marketing provides the budget increase. However, someone does need to pay. In my opinion, if a project manager accepts a change request without appropriate approvals, she's stealing from her own management.

Summary

The discipline of project management is well defined. The tools are ample. If project management is not successful in your organization, look for the following possible faults:

- Untrained project managers
- Unreceptive culture
- Lack of processes and procedures
- Lack of support from nonproject suborganizations
- Lack of support from executive management

Use Table 3.3 to help you rate your organization's ability to manage projects.

Table 3.3 Chapter 3 Organizational Performance Rating Sheet

Performance Item	My Organization's Performance				
	High ←——————— Low				
My organization's project charters are complete and sufficient for project teams to develop a solid plan.					
My organization offers project managers executive-level support to handle difficult stakeholders.					
My organization incorporates a goals breakdown structure to ensure that projects achieve their goals.					
My project managers build solid work breakdown structures to define the work needed to do the project.					
My project managers incorporate risk management to protect the project against unwanted change or external events that could derail it.					
My project managers use critical path to determine where to put their best resources and which resources they can afford to loan in an emergency.					

Performance Item	My Organization's Performance				
	High ←				→ Low
My project managers clearly define roles and responsibilities in their projects and codify those roles (typically in a resource assignment matrix).					
My project managers accurately estimate the level of work, duration, and cost of project activities and convey those estimates to key stakeholders.					
My organization's culture promotes honesty in estimating.					
My organization's culture discourages arbitrary resource reassignments.					
My organization employs and supports a serious project change management process.					

4

Strategic Alignment

The benefits derived from aligning projects with organizational objectives seem intuitive, yet few organizations either enforce or encourage such alignment. The issue might be a misunderstanding of the true effects of misalignment, a lack of skills or know-how to enforce alignment, or simply an assumption that the staff will automatically align projects themselves. Misaligned projects waste valuable resources at best and can rip organizations apart at worst.

Consider what happens when an automobile's tires are misaligned: Fuel economy plummets, the driver must constantly compensate by steering to either the left or the right, rides get bumpy, passenger safety might be compromised, and tires become lopsided. Many of us know how to prevent, detect, and recover from misaligned tires because the system is essentially mechanical, few variables exist and interventional strategies produce predictable results.

Your organization is not quite so simple. Your organization is a complex suite of systems, structures, people, and processes operating at multiple levels. Many variables exist with numerous moving parts. Cultural, political, regulatory, financial, technical, and social considerations must be coordinated to keep your organization focused and headed in a straight line.

In a utopian organization, all activities, projects, processes, research, and operations support organizational objectives. Any activity that does not support organizational objectives is a waste of your resources and time. Any activities that move the organization away from its strategic path are worse.

Alignment can be challenging in the project world when middle-level and senior-level managers create or advocate pet projects for political or personal gain. Nebulous or conflicting organizational objectives exacerbate the problem. Sales might not agree with manufacturing's goals, or accounting might disagree with both. Even if your managers are loyal to the organization, they are constantly distracted by daily or weekly activities instead of higher-level organizational activities. Infighting, political positioning, and the continuous struggle for resources interfere with even the most loyal and capable middle managers.

Integrating project management into the organization requires you to align it three ways:

- **Strategic alignment**—Project objectives align with organizational objectives.
- **Organizational alignment**—Project resources integrate seamlessly with resources engaged in other business processes, research, and operations.
- **Process alignment**—Project activities interface seamlessly with other business processes.

This chapter and the next focus on strategic alignment: ensuring that the projects themselves align with and support organizational objectives.

Although the strategic plan is an integral part of project alignment, I do not intend to present strategic planning. I leave that for other texts. However, I present the key elements of the strategic plan needed for project and portfolio alignment. Our ultimate objectives are these:

1. Maximize organizational growth by
    A. Aligning all resources to organizational objectives
    B. Enabling an organization to quickly achieve more of its strategic objectives
2. Reduce waste by
    A. Ensuring activity alignment
    B. Reducing political infighting to focus resources on organizational activities
    C. Reducing chaotic resource reassignments caused by dynamic, politically driven, and misguided reprioritization
3. Enhance senior management's control of the organization by
    A. Enhancing communication
    B. Structuring monitoring and oversight
    C. Defining a hierarchically based objective framework

Conflict and Strategic Alignment

Recall that, as a senior manager, you define the characteristics of your organization (whether intentionally or unintentionally). You choose whether you encourage internal conflict and competition for the purposes of creativity, for developing political strength, or for other results you might seek; whether you prefer a more focused and structured approach to improve productivity; or whether you take a more open approach. Although strategic alignment demands a more structured approach, this does not reduce creativity, competition, or even productive conflict. On the contrary, if you structure the organization properly, you can successfully encourage both creativity and competition while still achieving alignment. You must simply determine when and where you want creativity, competition, or conflict, and when and where you want pure production. For example, the strategic plan might demand a specific increase in market share in one market segment, but the products and features needed to achieve that growth might be established through competition or conflict.

The term **conflict** generally denotes negative events, despite its appropriate use in generating new ideas, challenging existing ideas, or finding root causes of problems and issues. Conflict has a place in every organization. However, mismanagement can cause conflict, with devastating effects. For the rest of this chapter, I use the terms **disruptive conflict** and **positive conflict** to avoid confusion.

Conditions for Successful Alignment

Whether you encourage some level of competition to generate new ideas or strive for a more cohesive planning structure, successful project alignment relies on six factors:

1. Balanced and comprehensive objectives
2. Specific and durable objectives
3. Hierarchical framework
4. Measurable objectives
5. Stakeholder agreement
6. Environmental and organizational assumptions

Let's examine each factor.

Balanced and Comprehensive Objectives

Incomplete or unbalanced objectives are one key source of disruptive conflict. Strategic plans, project plans, and project portfolios that omit key goals are sure to generate resource-draining emergencies, political strife, and organizational disruption.

> **Successful and stable portfolios require a balanced, cooperative environment, in which projects and personnel work together for the organization's benefit.**

The portfolio of projects must balance both project objectives and resources based on an agreed-upon strategy—the strategic plan. Such a portfolio does the following:

1. Covers all organizational objectives outlined in the strategic plan
2. Strives to prevent disruptive conflict, even if only at the tactical level
3. Covers all desired levels of risk/reward

Achieving a balanced and comprehensive suite of objectives is neither simple nor easy. This is one area in which you can encourage positive conflict, to ensure that no major holes exist and that all organizational issues are covered. However, you should restrict such conflict to the strategic level and not allow it to filter down to the project or portfolio level. Senior executives might debate whether they should concentrate resources on a new product introduction or upgrade existing products, and marketing and quality control executives might argue whether to focus on product quality or rush out new features. But after they've made the decision, they should provide the project and portfolio designers clear direction.

> **When senior management fails to either make appropriate**
> **decisions or communicate them, the battle lines**
> **fall to the lower levels of the organization.**

Disruptive conflict at these lower levels indicates that the strategic plan is incomplete, unbalanced, or not communicated properly.

Specific and Durable Objectives

Organizational objectives must be stable over time, despite a dynamic external environment. Project managers attempting to hit an ever-moving target will certainly fail. The project manager and project team plan the project to find the most efficient way to do their jobs. Then a senior executive, client, or other stakeholder changes their mind or remembers something they forgot. The project team now must reshuffle plans and steal resources from other projects to try to meet the deadline. Not only did the project take a hit, but so did the projects from which they took their additional resources—a domino effect. That causes another change to occur and the reshuffling continues. Clearly, dynamic objectives breed inefficiency.

To help ensure stability, you must clearly communicate and strictly enforce objectives. Unstable, uncommunicated, or unenforced objectives result in frequent and wasteful resource realignment and redirection.

> **The efficient organization focuses resources on durable objectives**
> **designed to move the organization toward its vision**

Making objectives durable is relatively easy: Simply remove specificity. However, this prevents us from providing the clear direction we need for the organization. The challenge to the strategic planner or executive manager is to strike a balance between specificity and durability.

At the turn of the previous century, the railroad industry was too specific: They considered themselves in the railroad industry. If the leaders of the railroad industry had considered themselves in the transportation industry, they would have been better equipped to survive the advent of the automobile.

In contrast, I once asked a group of seminar attendees for their corporate mission statements. One gentleman raised his hand and said, "Our mission statement is: *We'll do anything for money.*" When I challenged him, he reached into his wallet and pulled out a laminated card with his company's mission statement and showed it to me. It exhibited all the mistakes of a bad mission statement. Although the statement was obviously (and beautifully) wordsmithed, it essentially said that the company would do whatever its clients wanted as long as they paid the company enough. Yes, it was client focused. Yes, it had the financial aspect. Yes, it was beautifully worded. Yet it provided little direction and was considered a joke by at least one employee and one seminar leader.

A hierarchical structure for objectives is useful for resolving this problem. This structure enables the objectives writer to adjust specificity to the appropriate audience. The higher the objective, the more durable it must be. The lower the level, the more specific it must be. A more detailed discussion follows.

Hierarchical Framework

A well-developed hierarchical framework—essentially, a clearly established and understood objectives pecking order—translates high-level objectives to the appropriate level for the task performers, project managers, program managers, and other management and technical functions. The highest levels include the organization's mission, vision, value, and quality statements. These must be the most durable.

Marketing, production, IT, and other senior department managers then can define more detailed objectives for their department. These might include market penetration goals for a group of products, production targets for manufacturing, or network reliability goals for IT. These lower-level objectives roll up to and support higher-level organizational objectives.

Each group within a department then can define more detailed objectives for their group. These might include market penetration objectives for specific products, yield and waste-reduction objectives for a particular production line, or database server size for IT departments. Such a framework prevents activities from steering the organization away from its strategic direction and reduces waste.

Hierarchical frameworks add many other benefits to an organization. They enhance communication by presenting objectives at appropriate organizational layers; improve management by establishing goals at all tiers of the organization; develop a sense of ownership by enabling employees to see where they fit within the organization; and finally promote and enhance continuous improvement at all organizational layers. These frameworks also enhance your ability as an executive manager to develop objectives that are both specific and durable.

Project management itself provides us with the perfect tool for building such a framework. This tool deserves its own chapter, and we cover it in Chapter 5, "A Framework for Strategic Alignment."

Measurable Objectives

One common cause for resource conflict lies in understanding *how much is enough*. Staff members might become overachievers in an attempt to please their boss or to satisfy their own pride. An electrical engineer might try to make an amplifier more sensitive, or an IT specialist might keep working to get a few more messages per second out of a message processor, while the lazy and glib employees expend enormous effort to achieve the absolute minimum. The project manager must know when to push for more performance and when to stop and move on to the next activity.

Measurements and metrics offer business analysts, project managers, product marketing managers, and other project stakeholders clear guidelines for balancing project objectives. When you offer structured metrics, you enhance the project designer's ability to develop a project plan that supports the organization.

One such framework uses three achievement levels for organizational or project objectives. These include minimum, target, and stretch metrics:

- **Minimum**—Minimum acceptable metrics tell the project designers the lowest acceptable value for an objective. Project designers might drop to this measurement under pressure to achieve balance in other areas. By definition, if the project or product cannot meet this minimum criterion, the project should be rejected or abandoned.

- **Target**—The target metric represents the strategic plan's goals for the area. After this target is achieved, the project designers can focus on other areas. The target metric is the normal, steady-state metric that the portfolio and project designers should try to achieve.

- **Stretch**—Stretch metrics are objectives the organization strives to achieve, to capture innovative ideas or unplanned opportunities. Frequently, these represent upper limits that the project designer should not exceed, to keep from overloading the resource pool. Achieving stretch metrics should not be the norm. If every project designer attempted to achieve stretch metrics, resource shortages would impair the chances of strategic success in other areas. These metrics are reserved for special situations or to capture unexpected opportunities.

You can use this model for all types of objectives: schedule, cost, resource, technical, and quality. Let's look at a couple examples.

Imagine that we run an automobile plant. One of our target metrics is to ensure that the average number of defects per car coming off the production line does not exceed 9, with a stretch metric of 6 and the minimum metric set to 13. Under normal circumstances, the plant would tool up and establish quality processes to achieve the 9 average defects-per-car target.

Now consider that gasoline prices just shot up quickly, forcing the company to change to more fuel-efficient designs ("green" cars). Senior management decided that it wants to capture this new market quickly. To shorten the line modification project timeline, the plant manager and project designer might decide that the 13 defects-per-car metric would be allowed to get the new cars to market quickly. When the new cars were in the market, they could quickly retool the plant to return to the 9 average defects-per-car target.

Let's look at another simple, yet common example.

Diane's Dilemma: Balancing Goals for a Product Upgrade

Diane is a product marketing manager working on features for the next release of her product. She has been doing well with her product, meeting sales and profit margin targets for years, but globalization has caused increased competition in the most recent year. The product has been losing market share because overseas competitive products have more features than her product, and they are now selling for a similar price. Diane's company makes 40 percent of its yearly sales during the holiday season. Therefore, new product releases must be available for the holiday rush. Furthermore, marketing, production, and distribution must be ready to meet this real business deadline. Diane faces a classical set of three conflicting objectives: adding features to meet or beat competition; meeting a real, tangible business deadline; and lowering price.

In a company with a clear goals framework, Diane's approach becomes clear. She needs to push the envelope on features and cost without sacrificing the holiday season. She goes for the stretch limits on features and minimums on gross profit and schedule.

First, she works with her marketing team, production, and distribution to determine the latest dates for critical milestones. These dates would reflect the minimum acceptable metrics for scheduling. She then works with the product development manager and key subject matter experts to determine the optimum set of features that can make those milestone dates.

These actions will help keep her from losing more market share, but Diane needs more than that. Diane needs to recapture the market share she's lost. She decides to drop the gross profit margin from the corporate target level to the corporate minimum level, reducing the selling price to recapture market share.

Diane's dilemma is quite common. In a company without an established metrics structure, Diane competes with other product marketing managers, project managers, and functional managers in a virtual free-for-all environment in which the best negotiators and politicians win. Although this Darwinist survival approach might seem appealing for building future senior managers, product marketing requires a different set of skills. The politicians will absorb resources needed for other projects without regard to strategic direction, injuring the organization's growth and ability to compete.

Establishing a framework for balanced objectives enables middle management to distribute resources based on strategic direction, keeping the entire organization moving ahead. Fortunately for Diane, her company does employ a structured metrics framework. Other product marketing managers use only those resources needed to hit their targets, giving Diane easier access to resources to help get her through this tough time and rebalancing the organization's market penetration to meet strategic goals.

Don't confuse this approach with complacency. It does not prevent target metrics from being aggressive. It does not profess that organizations should have an overabundance of resources. It simply creates a framework to offer clarity to project and portfolio designers in meeting strategic organizational objectives. Executive committees and boards of directors should make decisions about rate of growth and management style, then communicate these in the form of minimum, target, and stretch metrics.

Stakeholder Agreement

The requirement for stakeholder agreement should be self-evident. If stakeholders disagree with the objectives of the organization (or project), conflict will disrupt progress, even to the point of project sabotage—a situation that exists much more frequently than many realize. Of course, it is impossible to have every stakeholder agree with every objective, strategy, project, or approach. However, agreement on the whole is not impossible and is encouraged.

Go ahead and have the debates, engage in negotiation, and battle at the strategic level behind closed doors. But when all is done and the strategic plan is in place, make sure it's supported—your projects will run much better.

Environmental and Organizational Assumptions

Assumptions are part of every organization's (and project manager's) objectives and plans. Financial managers make guesses at inflation rates, costs of capital, and other financial metrics; product marketing managers estimate market penetration and sales figures; and IT managers speculate on server loads in anticipation of new software packages. Organizational strategies are no different.

In too many organizations (and projects), we make decisions based on assumptions, record the decision, and forget the assumptions. This is an area in which both executive management and strategic planners can take a lesson from seasoned project managers. We know the influence assumptions can make on a project plan. We write them down, confirm them, and store them. We then identify risks in case the assumptions are wrong or change. We monitor and track these risks throughout the life of the project. If the assumptions do change, the decisions based on those assumptions become suspect and must be reconsidered.

Although this level of rigor might seem extreme, it's one of the key tools seasoned project managers use to ensure success. As you lay out your project portfolio, you must identify, codify, communicate, and manage these assumptions—and their associated risks.

The Alignment Architects

Proper strategic integration requires a collaborative effort among senior management, the strategic planning committee, middle managers, project managers, and subject matter experts. To aid in our understanding of the alignment function, consider the description of two roles: the portfolio designer and the project designer.

Portfolio Designer

The portfolio designer is the person, team, or committee that translates the strategic plan into a defined project portfolio. Specifically, the portfolio designer must do the following:

1. Work with executive management to establish project selection criteria and procedures

2. Translate strategic objectives into a comprehensive collection of defined projects or programs

3. Hedge organizational risks across the portfolio

4. Balance the project mix across time and resources

5. Ensure continued balance through portfolio tracking and adjustment

The successful portfolio designer exhibits skills in strategic planning, program management, and business analysis. The function is slightly different from that of the classical portfolio manager. It focuses on portfolio design and on maintaining alignment among the projects' and the organization's objectives, instead of a more tactical focus of just keeping projects on track.

Project Designer

The project designer is the person, team, or committee that takes a project from its initial stimulus and develops a business case based on the stimulus, strategic plan, and existing portfolio. This role is similar to the role of the project initiator defined by the Project Management Institute (PMI). The project initiator takes the project from inception (the stimulus) and develops a business case codified in the form of a project charter. The project designer assumes the same role but adds one new responsibility: balancing the proposed project with the existing portfolio, not just the project's objectives. The project designer must have these specific skills:

1. Developing a business case for a project or program
2. Aligning project requirements with organization's objectives
3. Working with project managers and subject matter experts to establish reasonably accurate early estimates for the project
4. Working with project managers and portfolio designers to successfully integrate the project into the existing project mix

The role of project designer is a combined business analyst and organizational integration function. The role doesn't need to be a full-time or separate position. A properly developed organizational culture combined with appropriate processes and training would enable existing personnel to fulfill this function. For example, product marketing managers would easily fill this role if they are not threatened with competition for resources, are well aware of and loyal to the strategic plan, and can work with an experienced portfolio designer.

The role, however, does require political clout. The IT business analyst, for example, is commonly caught between an IT project team that wants to minimize project resources and a client that wants as many features as it can get. The successful IT business analyst requires not only loyalty to the strategic plan, but also support from a project sponsor, chief information office (CIO), or strong portfolio designer to ensure the proper balance of resource utilization and product features.

The project designer is not the project manager. The project designer defines the project's objectives, and the project manager implements them.

The Balanced Portfolio

Earlier, I claimed that organizational objectives must be both specific and durable. Specificity clarifies and focuses middle management and staff toward the organization's objectives. Durable objectives help prevent resources from working on one project and then being reassigned to another project before finishing the first. Durable objectives are certainly a necessary condition for a stable, balanced portfolio. However, objectives are not the only factor to cause such reassignments. Dynamic prioritization, frequently driven by politics, can be even more devastating.

The Problem with Priorities

Consider an old anecdote ....

> An employee walks up to a senior manager and says, "I have five projects to do and I have time to do only three. Which are the highest priorities?"
>
> The senior manager responds, "All of them."

The manager knows that any other answer will prevent one or more of those projects from being completed. Priorities have only one purpose: to determine what to abandon or postpone when you're out of resources or time. If organizations had sufficient resources to accomplish all their work, priorities would be unnecessary. Therefore, prioritization means that the organization is understaffed—it doesn't have enough resources to do all the desired work.

> **Prioritizing, by its nature, is a method to determine**
> **what project, activity, or group will lose.**

The core issue is the dynamic nature of priorities. Even people loyal to the organization view situations differently; therefore, they prioritize differently. Combine this problem with an ever-changing political, organizational, and environmental landscape, and project priorities can change continuously. Resources are quickly moved to handle emergencies or work on the hot project du jour, and then are reshuffled a short time later as the priorities readjust. The results are half-done projects, overworked employees, and little accomplishment. Attempts to stabilize priorities are classically fruitless. Through prioritization, management incites disruptive conflict, infighting, and political structures.

Building Blocks for the Balanced Portfolio

As with all management tools, prioritization has its place in any organization. Every organization must prioritize its objectives (such as forgoing profit to buy your way into a market, or focusing on one product group instead of another). Every organization must select or reject projects based on their relative contribution, risk, and resource requirements. The organization should prioritize at the top to establish durable objectives and to select projects. However, organizations must attempt to avoid dynamically reprioritizing projects after they have been selected and scheduled.

I make a clear distinction among prioritizing, selecting, and scheduling projects.

- **Prioritizing**—Prioritizing projects means you rate projects to determine where to focus resources.

- **Scheduling**—Scheduling projects means that you spread projects out in a timeline based on some criteria. As I demonstrate in later chapters, these criteria include strategic need combined with resource-balancing techniques.

- **Selecting or rejecting**—Selecting or rejecting projects means that you either commit or do not commit to do a project. Project selection and rejection involves some level of prioritization. However, this activity occurs before the project is active, not afterward.

Dynamically reprioritizing causes inefficiency. Therefore, organizations should do the following:

1. Prioritize their organizational objectives at the top

2. Communicate those objectives in the strategic plan

3. Select or reject projects that support the mix of objectives, based on the projects' contribution, risk, and resource requirements

4. Schedule projects to balance resources

After selecting and scheduling a project, executive management and middle management must fully support it.

Select and schedule projects to balance resources; don't prioritize them.

To complete the discussion, let's review three more terms: **rejection, abandonment,** and **postponement.** Think of them with respect to the waste they can generate.

- **Rejection**—Not selecting a project for execution before it starts

  Rejection is part of the normal strategic planning (or portfolio design) process and part of doing business. Not every idea that spawns in someone's mind has a right to become a project. Although some time is expended to determine the relative merits, costs, and risks associated with the project (the project's business case), alternatives to developing a business case to establish project viability are generally more costly and detrimental to the organization. Therefore, the resources employed to evaluate projects are not considered waste.

- **Abandonment**—Starting the project and prematurely terminating it, either intentionally or unintentionally

  The primary difference between rejection and abandonment is that, at some point, the organization decided to accept the project; it expended resources toward the project but later abandoned it. The expended resources were wasted.

- **Postponement**—Delaying a project for some time period

  Postponement can occur before or after the project starts. If the project is started (or restarted) later, little waste occurs, assuming that the project can restart efficiently. If this condition is not met, the project expends some amount of wasted effort in getting reorganized when it restarts. Therefore, …

…reducing waste requires appropriate project selection, rejection, and scheduling, but avoids dynamic prioritization and abandonment.

Although projects can be postponed after they start, they should be properly scheduled based on an understanding of the organization's goals and resource constraints. If they must be postponed after they start, the project should be cleanly closed so it can restart efficiently later.

An Alternative to Prioritization: The Balanced Portfolio

The alternative to dynamic prioritization is the **balanced portfolio**: a portfolio in which selected projects receive the resources they need when they are needed, and enabling the portfolio to meet *all* the organization's objectives. To accomplish this, the organization defines and communicates its objectives, its portfolio includes the appropriate mix of projects to achieve those objectives, and the projects are scheduled to ensure that they have sufficient resources to succeed. An organization can use these steps to successfully implement a stable portfolio:

1. Define its objectives (starting from vision and mission statements down through the strategic plan)

2. Establish a clear set of acceptable criteria for project selection

3. Reject or select projects based on a clearly defined process, ensuring that all objectives receive sufficient support

4. Schedule projects according to the strategic plan, market conditions, and resource availability

5. Commit to all selected projects at all organizational levels

This balanced portfolio approach removes the constantly changing nature of prioritization while maintaining control over resources. Subsequent chapters offer more details and mechanics of creating and maintaining a balanced portfolio.

This concept does not remove competition or creativity. It simply adds clarity to the project-selection process, establishes clear requirements for project selection, and helps ensure that selected projects will be completed. Additionally, the level of competition, degree of rigor employed, and decisions regarding resource commitments remain where they belong: at the top.

The stable portfolio is not an all-or-nothing proposition. You, as a senior executive, might choose to enable dynamic prioritization in certain areas of the organization while offering a stable portfolio in other areas.

Summary

Strategic alignment is not a passive event. Senior management must actively pursue project and portfolio alignment. Your quest for alignment begins with quality and stable organizational objectives, a strategic plan, and the buy-in of that plan. You must constantly communicate these items and develop processes to enforce alignment with strategic direction. Hierarchical frameworks and durable and specific objectives provide clarity at all levels of the organization. Finally, a stable portfolio keeps resources working efficiently, helping to ensure project success. There's a time and place for conflict, prioritization, and infighting; there's also a time and place for productivity. Use Table 4.1 to help you rate your organization regarding strategic alignment. Then, use it as a guide to help you improve in this area.

Table 4.1   Chapter 4 Organizational Performance Rating Sheet

Performance Item	My Organization's Performance				
	High ◄——————— Low				
My organization has a clear strategic plan that prioritizes the organization's objectives.					
My organization's objectives are both specific and durable.					
The strategic plan is clearly communicated to portfolio, program, and project designers.					
My organization uses a hierarchical framework to define goals at all levels of the organization.					
My organization selects projects based on their contribution to the strategic objectives, risk, and resource requirements.					
Executive management supports selected projects.					
My organization schedules projects based on strategic need and resource requirements.					
My organization avoids dynamically reprioritizing projects after they're started.					
My organization supports multiple levels for objectives, such as minimum, target, and stretch objectives.					
My organization records assumptions and manages the associated risks.					
My organization employs portfolio and project designers to ensure that projects not only align with the organization, but also integrate into a balanced portfolio.					

5

A Framework for Strategic Alignment

T
he previous chapter presented core concepts for aligning projects with the organization's objectives and strategic plan. In this chapter, I present a structure and framework to achieve that alignment. First, I expand on the goals breakdown structure introduced in Chapter 3, "Project Definition and Planning," and apply it to the entire organization. Then I present how to structure elements that already exist in your organization to promote alignment, ranging from your mission statement to your strategic plan. Finally, I offer a model for characterizing projects to improve resource balancing throughout the organization.

For simplicity, I use the term **project(s)** to refer to both projects and programs for the rest of this chapter.

The Goals Breakdown Structure

Chapter 3 presented the concept of the goals breakdown structure (GBS): a process that translates organizational objectives into project and product requirements and, ultimately, component specifications. In this section, I expand the use of this tool beyond projects and exploit it to create a framework for aligning all projects with strategic objectives.

The GBS in project management originates from an advanced concept known as **requirements traceability.** This concept requires the project team members to demonstrate how the products and services they create will support and map to the project's requirements. This concept ensures that the final product will meet the project's requirements. The GBS is a more structured and proactive approach. Use it as a planning tool in addition to an analysis tool.

When we expand the concept to the organization as a whole (let's refer to this as the **organization goals breakdown structure [OGBS]**), we start with the highest goal in the organization: the vision statement. We then determine the characteristics that the organization must portray and the actions it must take to achieve that vision. We present this information in the form of mission statements, value statements, quality statements, and so on. We then use these statements to create the organization's strategic plan. The strategic plan identifies the organization's objectives or goals for the foreseeable future. These goals may include market penetration for product lines, developing patents in new technologies, or expanding into new foreign markets. The goals defined in the strategic plan then become the business objectives for projects.

Let's say a company makes three kinds of light bulbs: incandescent, florescent, and halogen. The strategic planners may want to increase market share of all bulbs by 10 percent in two years. Appropriate experts and portfolio designers might define three projects based on their understanding of both the current and the future marketplace: increasing incandescent penetration by 8 percent, florescent light penetration by 11 percent, and halogen penetration by 12 percent. If each project is successful, the company will achieve its strategic goal.

This decomposition creates a hierarchical linkage between lower-level objectives and higher-level objectives. To avoid confusing this concept with other disciplines, I use the term **value track** to describe this linkage.

> **Value track**—The track that links low-level objectives to high-level objectives.

The OGBS has clear benefits:

- Aligns with popular and successful standards, including the balanced scorecard,[1] strategic planning processes, the GBS and requirements traceability
- Offers metrics for tracking, benchmarking, oversight, and quality assurance
- Offers a holistic approach, covering strategic, cultural, process, and tactical business areas
- Defines and communicates objectives at all levels of the organization

OGBS Rules

Two rules exist for constructing an OGBS. These rules are identical to the ones for the GBS and for conducting a work breakdown structure (WBS) taught in basic project management classes and presented in Chapter 2, "Project Management Framework and Structure," and Chapter 3, "Project Definition and Planning." The rules for constructing a GBS are

- The breakdown of each goal must be complete and sufficient to satisfy that goal (nothing missing).
- The breakdown should include no additional elements (nothing added).

When done correctly, the first rule demands that each layer be complete and self-sufficient, ensuring success at the next-higher level. The organization's mission statement, quality statement, and value statements (or similar statements) must properly define an organization that will achieve the vision. Similarly, the organization's strategic plan must contain sufficient goals and actions to meet the mission, quality, value, and similar statements. The organization's portfolio must contain the right project mix for the strategic plan to succeed.

Finally, to eliminate waste, no layer should contain items that aren't needed to support the layer above. An example is riders in Congress (also known as pork-barrel projects): minor projects appended to important legislation that have nothing to do with that legislation. We have enough of this in government; we don't need to promote this practice in our organizations.

Process for Constructing an OGBS

The process for developing both a GBS and an OGBS is easy:

1. **Start with a high-level objective.** The OGBS starts with the highest-level objective. For a project, this is the project goal or mission statement; for an organization, this is the vision statement. When properly written, these statements clearly communicate the primary objective for the project or organization.

2. **Break it down into smaller objectives.** The next step is to decompose the objective into smaller, more detailed objectives. This next tier must be complete, leaving nothing to chance.

3. **Ensure layer integrity.** Ask the question "Is this tier complete and sufficient to ensure the success of the above layer?" If not, more goals are needed or existing goals require elaboration. The second question is, "Are any objectives not needed to ensure success of the above layer?" If so, remove or adjust the unnecessary goals to prevent waste.

4. **Add measurements.** As you complete each tier or subdivision, establish the targets, metrics, or other measurements needed to balance, monitor, and track success. The measurement might be a single target, or it might incorporate the three-tiered minimum, target, and stretch model presented earlier. Note that this step may be omitted for the highest layers of the OGBS.

5. **Continue the process.** As you complete each tier, continue progressively, decomposing the layers into more detailed and elaborate goals.

The (O)GBS develops a structure for answering the questions "Why?" and "How?" Figure 5.1 illustrates this process. To traverse down the (O)GBS, ask the question "How will we accomplish this objective?" The specific answer to that question should be clearly identified in the next lower tier.

Question: How will you obtain a 10 percent increase in market share in light bulb products?

Answer: By increasing market share of incandescent bulbs by 8 percent, florescent bulbs by 11 percent, and halogens by 12 percent.

Conversely, the answer to "Why are you doing that objective?" is answered in the tier above.

Question: Why are we increasing market share of halogen bulbs by 12 percent?

Answer: So we can achieve a 10 percent increase in the market share of all bulbs.

If the (O)GBS does not sufficiently satisfy these questions, the (O)GBS is insufficient or incomplete.

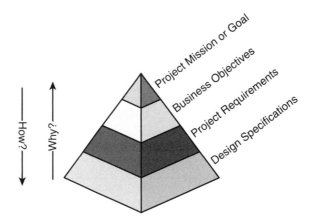

Figure 5.1   Using GBS to answer the questions "Why?" and "How?"

Constructing an OGBS

This section presents strategies for building the OGBS. My aim here isn't to have you restructure your organization (well, not yet, at least). My aim is to help you align your projects with your organization's objectives. Of course, to accomplish this, your organization's objectives must be clearly defined.

Although the process for constructing an OGBS is simple, actual development can be complex. The organization incorporates multiple disciplines, spans substantial periods of time, achieves objectives across multiple value tracks, and undergoes change. Although the same can be said for the project, the OGBS must cover the entire organization, include all business areas, and endure for a longer period of time, despite extensive environmental change. Although different organizations might develop unique structures, we develop the OGBS along four different, coordinated, and synergistic value tracks in this book:

- **Organizational**—Breaking down your organizational objectives by department (human resources, finance, marketing, and so on)

- **Business unit**—Breaking down your organizational objectives by business unit, product line, or revenue track

- **Cultural**—Breaking down your organizational objectives by desired cultural characteristic (responsibility, respect, and so on)
- **Time**—Staging your organizational objectives across time periods

An Organizational Decomposition

Organizational decomposition takes two perspectives. The first divides and allocates organizational objectives to specific departments. This is a **horizontal decomposition**—allocating objectives to the organization's disciplines. After each department is assigned its organizational objectives, it can further decompose those objectives within its own department—allocating objectives within a discipline. This is **vertical decomposition.** Figure 5.2 illustrates horizontal and vertical decomposition.

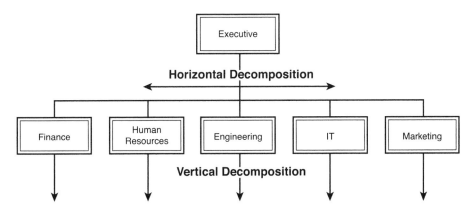

Figure 5.2   Horizontal and vertical decomposition

Horizontal Decomposition

First, you must break down organizational objectives and allocate them across organizational departments. This clearly defines the roles for each department. For example, one of the finance department's objectives might be to establish procedures for capturing accurate and compliant financial information from all organizational activities.

These objectives then help justify projects within the department. If a financial regulation (Sarbanes-Oxley, for example) changes, the finance department is justified in beginning a project to change the financial tracking procedures to accommodate the changes.

Objectives also justify cross-functional projects. Let's say the project management department wants to update its standard processes. It is justified in asking the finance department to update the financial tracking procedures because these clearly fall within its business objectives. These objectives help reduce conflict at the executive and middle-management tiers of the organization. They also help the department managers work more as a team, reducing infighting across departments.

Many objectives span departmental boundaries, such as a requirement that all departments start using activity-based costing (ABC). Other objectives can be handled within a single department, such as expecting marketing to understand the customer base and define products (or services) that satisfy those customers. You might expect a museum's exhibition group to design an exhibit that will increase attendance by 10 percent for a given period, but all groups must support the team in designing, developing, and rolling out the new exhibit. Although you might expect the finance department to establish financial policy and reporting, all departments are expected to support those policies and provide timely and accurate information for those reports. Establishing high-level organizational objectives not only provides clear direction for the department primarily involved in the project, but it also generates buy-in from other involved departments.

The executive management team must ultimately decide which business objectives are allocated to each department.

The department heads and subject matter experts must certainly participate in this allocation, but the final decisions rest with executive management.

Vertical Decomposition

After the objectives have been defined for the departments, the department managers can allocate or break down the objectives as they deem appropriate within each department. Let's use our earlier example, where the department manager for finance is asked to define processes for accurate and compliant financial reporting for all organizational activities. The resulting breakdown may include project activities, sales and marketing activities, operations, and supporting activities. The department manager might assign each of these activities to a different individual, establish teams for each, or create subdepartments for each.

The executive management team assumes a different role when decomposing goals within a department. It's not senior management's job to tell an entry-level engineer what to do, despite the joy many senior managers find in doing just that.

It is senior management's job to provide direction, infrastructure, support, and oversight to enable department managers to achieve their departmental objectives.

Business Unit Decomposition

Executive management must also divide and allocate organizational objectives to business units, segments, or regions. In a for-profit organization, this decomposition creates separate value tracks for financial benefits along each primary business area (such as product sales, maintenance and support, and consulting services). Conglomerates might allocate sales, gross revenue, and profit value tracks to divisions; smaller organizations might allocate profit value tracks to particular products or product groups.

Not-for-profit organizations similarly allocate objectives across different value tracks. Churches might allocate growth objectives for parishioners, children's Sunday school, adult learning classes, and special group participation. Museums might allocate objectives for membership, donations, exhibition attendance or revenue, school tours, and special uses.

Cultural Decomposition

The next decomposition line is cultural. Here the executive management team selects the characteristics of the organization's culture, establishes clear objectives, and breaks down these objectives into tangible actions. Cultural goals include such areas as integrity, communication, respect, intellectual and management growth, work–life balance, family-oriented atmosphere, and other cultural characteristics.

Time Decomposition

Decomposing the organization's objectives across time translates the organization's long-term goals into achievable medium- and short-term objectives. For example, a company might want to become the number one widget maker in the U.S. market within five years. Market research predicts that the company would need to achieve a minimum of a 40 percent market share to meet that goal. Let's assume that the organization currently holds an 18 percent market share. Decomposing the long-term objective into short-term and medium-term objectives might result in the following goal breakdown: Achieve a 20 percent market share by next year, a 25 percent market share by year 3, and a 40 percent market share by year 5. Figure 5.3 shows these goals graphically.

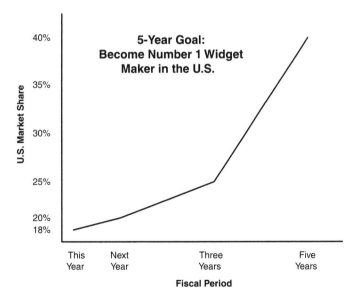

Figure 5.3   Breaking down goals over time

Applying this concept to an internal process–oriented project produces similar results. For example, an organization that decides to become ISO 9000 certified within five quarters might divide the organization into five segments, allocating compliance for specific departments within particular quarters.

A Complete Example

When you combine both the project GBS and the organizational OGBS, you achieve the framework that traces even the smallest decision back to long-term organizational objectives. For an example, let's assume that you manufacture recreational vehicles (RVs).

Your strategic objective is to be the number one seller of RVs in the United States within five years, as measured in sales dollars.

After the marketing department's experts complete an analysis, you determine that you need to achieve at least a 10 percent increase in sales this year, one of your short-term strategic objectives. This objective is transferred to product marketing for a more detailed analysis.

Your research indicates that one of the biggest reasons people select competitors' vehicles is that your vehicles are known to rattle within the first 25,000 miles. Marketing also predicts that the rise in gas prices will continue to affect buying habits. Marketing decides to promote a 100,000-mile rattle-free guarantee and requires that the vehicle designers increase the gas mileage by 15 percent. These objectives are handed to engineering.

Engineering decides that the best approach to handle the mileage objective is to reduce curb weight 10 percent by using stronger but lighter materials. However, engineering is concerned about the rattle-free guarantee because they've noticed that the spot welds that hold the frame to the chassis frequently rust and break, causing squeaks. With the guarantee, the dealers will need to re-weld the chassis and frame to make the repairs, but this will be prohibitively expensive. Engineering decides to fasten the chassis to the frame using the lightest and smallest bolts and nuts they can, employ lock washers, and establish the correct torque. This will increase the number of miles before squeaks to 80,000–100,000. The dealers can easily fix the RVs that do squeak with standard parts, minimizing repair costs. Figure 5.4 shows this combined GBS example graphically.

Note the value track: The bolt selection supports the design specifications, which support the product requirements, which support the marketing objectives, which support the strategic objective. The value of each decision tracks up and down the organizational hierarchy.

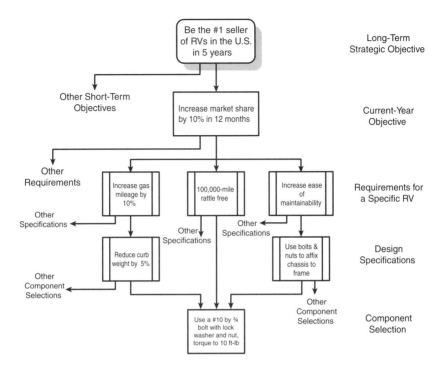

Figure 5.4   Combined GBS example

Specific Tools for Strategic Alignment

Contemporary management frequently communicates its goals and values in the form of mission statements, vision statements, value statements, and quality statements. Frequently, these are written for rhetorical or marketing purposes, placed on Web sites, and promptly ignored. However, when they are well written and supported, these become excellent focal points for project alignment and the highest tier for the OGBS. I collectively refer to them as the **organization definition statements.** When written properly, they provide clarity, direction, and guidance to middle management, staff, and project managers.

Rhetoric and Reality

> **Vision, mission, value, and quality statements designed**
> **as rhetoric will achieve their goal: rhetoric.**

These statements must be useful. They must provide clear direction and have executive management support and commitment. Commitment does not mean more rhetoric. Real commitment means that executive management must be willing and able to provide resources, political clout, infrastructure, and oversight to achieve the objectives stated in the organization definition statements. They are the ultimate answer to the question "Why?" The organization definition statements drive the strategic plan. The strategic plan then drives the project or program portfolio, which, in turn, drives the projects. See Figure 5.5.

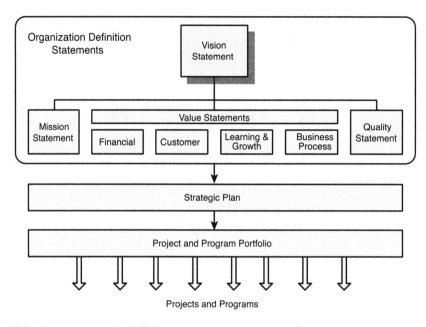

Figure 5.5 Using organization definition statements as strategic tools

Additionally, the organization definition statements need to provide clear, tangible direction to the entire organization. A finance value statement that declares that the organization will employ fiscal responsibility tells the finance department to follow recognized standards, and not employ aggressive or nonstandard fiscal approaches. An organization's commitment to be of the finest quality cannot release a system without quality control's approval, despite looming deadlines.

Executive management's actions must match the speech making.

Otherwise, project managers, portfolio designers, and the technical staff will design to one standard and implement to another.

Finally, the organization definition statements are useful to define and mold the organization's culture. Respect, commitment to quality, employee attitudes, communication, and other cultural issues can be ultimately tracked to the organization definition statements when they are properly written and implemented.

The Organization Definition Statements

The organization definition statements are the highest layer of the OGBS and define the organization. Clear, supported, definition statements become the rallying cry for the organization as a whole.

Vision Statement

The vision statement is the highest level of the OGBS. This statement simply and succinctly states the ultimate long-term objective for the organization. This statement must withstand the test of time and be durable. However, it must also offer management, staff, and other stakeholders clear and concise direction. For example:

The vision of Acme Automotive, Europe, is to be the motor vehicle manufacturer of choice for Europeans.

Mission Statement

To achieve the organization's vision, the organization establishes the current, primary goal. This primary goal is the focal point for decisions and is usually described in the form of a mission statement. Many leadership models describe a group as a collection of people with common interests. A team is a group of people with a common goal. The mission statement states that goal. All other objectives—strategic, organizational, project, process, and operations—must support the organization's mission and vision statements. The mission statement is not rhetoric; it must provide clear direction.

Consider this example of a bad mission statement: Be the best automobile manufacturer in the world.

Now consider this example of a good mission statement: Acme Automotive, Europe, shall provide safe, sound, cost-efficient, and reliable transportation to the average European.

The first statement is unclear. Are we manufacturing the best car, are we the best manufacturer, are we flooding the market with inexpensive cars to ensure volume, or do the cars have the highest quality or most features? The second statement is more specific. Although marketers and visionaries might argue the use of the term *average,* this mission statement offers clear and concise direction for the organization. We're not building the most expensive, highest-featured car, nor are we trying to flood the market with inexpensive, unreliable vehicles. We are trying to appeal to the largest market segment and are trying to address their need for a sound, sensible, safe, and practical means of transportation.

Also note that I selected the word *transportation,* not *automobile.* This enables the company to expand into motorcycles, mopeds, or other means of transportation. This makes the mission statement more durable.

Quality Statement

Similarly, the quality statement dictates the organization's level of support and commitment to quality. The same rules apply: Quality statements must be clearly stated and seriously supported by executive management. Making claims about product quality and then ignoring those claims under financial or schedule pressure sends incongruent messages to middle management, staff, and project managers. The message is that it's okay to skimp on quality if your project is late. In one company I worked for, after telling us to ship a system that wasn't quite ready, a vice president humorously proclaimed, "We might not be good, but we're fast!"

Value Statements

Value statements usually contain four high-level characteristics or values of the organization. You can model these values using a balanced scorecard approach, as I've done in the example, or you can create your own. They complete the categories into which all organizational objectives must fall. Similar to mission statements, value statements are not advertising campaigns. They clearly state, for both public and internal consideration, the *true* and *supported* values of the organization. One important characteristic of value statements is that they cover all aspects of the organization, including employee concerns, business processes, finances, customer concerns, community concerns, and other critical issues.

> **The value statements are the organization's first opportunity to include all key organizational stakeholders in the organization definition statements.**

This approach not only aligns with recognized tools such as the balanced scorecard, but it also supports the stable portfolio concept presented earlier.

Example: Branch-Smith Printing

I use a 2002 National Malcolm Baldrige winner, Branch-Smith Printing, as an example of organization definition statements. Consider the company's vision, mission, and quality statements:

- **Vision**—Market-leading business results through an expert team providing turnkey solutions to customer partners.

- **Mission**—The mission of the Branch-Smith Printing division is to provide expert solutions for publishers.

- **Quality**—Branch-Smith Printing will seek to continuously improve results for all stakeholders through the application of its Innovating Excellence process.

Branch-Smith Printing took a slightly modified balanced scorecard approach to its value statements. The company's leadership was able to include its religious heritage and commitment in its corporate value statements, without expanding past the classical number of four statements. The company's four value statements taken from its 2002 Baldrige application are as follows:

- To honor God in all that we do (reflecting its commitment to business ethics and to faith)

- To pursue excellence with integrity and commitment (balanced scorecard: business process perspective)

- To help people develop as individuals and as a team (balanced scorecard: growth and learning perspective)

- To grow profitably by committing ourselves to our customers' success (combined balanced scorecard: finance and customer perspective)

The organization then uses these statements to define its corporate culture, its ethics, its continuous improvement process, its target market and sales figures, the way to interface with its clients, how it addresses the marketplace, how it manages its employees, and all other aspects of the organization.

Strategic Plan

The strategic plan is the highest level where actions meet objectives. It incorporates the OGBS across value tracks, including: time, business unit, organizational structure, and culture. Although the strategic plan serves many functions, for our purpose, the primary function of the strategic plan is to foster a solid, balanced project portfolio. For clarity, I restrict our treatment of the strategic plan to defining those characteristics needed for project alignment. You can turn to other texts for other characteristics of strategic plans, the method for developing the strategic plan, and other planning issues.

Characteristics of a Successful Balanced Portfolio

The strategic plan should define the organizational objectives for strategic projects. Although qualified portfolio and project designers should perform detailed project definition, the strategic planning committee must define projects in sufficient detail to balance resources, time, and costs across the organization.

The strategic planning committee must involve appropriate subject matter experts, including portfolio and project designers, to develop accurate estimates. An overabundance of time or resources will produce waste; if you give a project team ten months to do a six-month project, the six-month project will take ten months. Conversely, if time and resources are inadequate, it forces the portfolio and project designers to reduce quality to compensate. Additionally, it spawns political infighting as project managers, project designers, portfolio managers, and other managers struggle to meet unrealistic deadlines with inadequate resources. Successful strategic alignment demands that the strategic plan exhibit

- Clear, measurable targets at a sufficient level of detail to enable project definition

- Sufficient resources so that portfolio managers and project designers can create a balanced portfolio

- Stability over time
- Durability during environmental changes

Assumptions and Constraints

All strategic plans include assumptions and constraints, either written or implied. From a portfolio management perspective, constraints place boundaries on the portfolio and project designers. They establish some level of risk on the portfolio and, subsequently, the projects. Assumptions place additional risks on the portfolio and projects. Codifying and communicating assumptions and constraints enables the portfolio manager to identify and track risks, establish contingency and mitigation plans, and hedge the portfolio against those risks.

The Balanced Portfolio

Portfolio management is a complex topic, becoming its own discipline within the project management arena. In this section, I present only those aspects needed to align the portfolio with the organization; I reserve other discussions for later chapters.

Earlier, I indicated that a portfolio is the complete collection of programs and projects an organization undertakes to achieve strategic objectives. Therefore, the portfolio must contain all programs and projects needed for strategic success. It must also contain projects that are not included in the strategic plan but that are still important to the organization. These might include projects to capture unexpected opportunities or handle problems.

**The portfolio is the mechanism that allocates
project resources to all organizational objectives.**

The portfolio includes the complete list of projects and programs. Therefore, the portfolio is the primary link between project resource allocation and all organizational objectives. The four conditions for successful balanced portfolio development follow:

1. The portfolio must be sufficiently robust to support all strategic objectives.

2. The portfolio must contain a balance of projects to isolate the organization from individual project failure.

3. The portfolio must enable a dynamic organizational environment, both internal and external.

4. Each project must support organizational objectives.

For simplicity, let's define five types of projects:

- **Strategic**—Projects that are established by the senior management team and are regarded as critical to organizational success
- **Creative**—Projects not included in the strategic plan, but inspired by it

- **Opportunistic**—Projects that attempt to capture unexpected opportunity

- **Mandatory**—Projects undertaken to remain compliant with regulations

- **Consequential**—Projects undertaken to resolve a problem or issue

The strategic planning committee defines **strategic projects.** These include internal business process projects that span departmental boundaries. They might also include projects that bring the organization into alignment with the organization's definition statements, projects that commit the organization to standards (ISO 9000, for example), organization-wide research projects, or mission-critical strategic projects.

Creative projects are driven by the strategic plan but defined within the organization itself, typically by business analysis, project marketing analysis, process owners, and other appropriate organizational leaders. The strategic planning committee, for example, might establish clear market penetration objectives, and then ask marketing to define the projects to support those objectives. Or, the committee may want to improve some aspect of the corporate culture but solicit project ideas from the rest of the company to develop the plan, using an idea bank or project idea contest. Some organizations have an ongoing process for collecting project ideas from the staff for inclusion in the strategic plan.

Creative projects have a clear link to the strategic plan or organizational definition statements, and they are designed to help the organization move along its strategic path.

Opportunistic projects spawn from unexpected opportunities. These might include technological or scientific discoveries, an unexpected invitation from a new prospect or market segment, an unexpected external event (geopolitical, weather related, and so on), or sudden, unexpected success within the organization. The organization must be careful when considering such projects because, in its euphoria, it might remove resources from other, critical strategic projects. If that occurs, the result might be more detrimental than beneficial.

Mandatory projects are those required by regulation or other legal event. It's important to distinguish between mandatory and optional projects. Any regulation, restriction, or legal mandate has a penalty for noncompliance. However, the cost of compliance might exceed the cost of noncompliance. Therefore, the philosophy exists that no project is mandatory; all projects are optional. To be clear, I do not necessarily advocate some Thoreauistic regulatory disobedience. However, if you are a food producer and a state that comprises only 5 percent of your sales suddenly demands that all sold foods be free of trans fats, it might be less painful for you to stop selling in that state than to convert your entire menu. Also, you don't need to comply with Sarbanes-Oxley, but you might go to jail if you don't. Clearly, only appropriate high-level executives or committees can make such choices.

Consequential projects, by their definition, are waste. These are projects that would not occur if previous processes and projects had been done properly. They include repairing faulty equipment, upgrading a product to fix problems, or appeasing a disgruntled customer. They also include unknown or unexpected events that occur outside the organization. For example, a competitor might announce a new product that you didn't expect, or Congress might pass a tax hike for your industry. You can claim that many of these events are unpredictable, or you can claim that it's the job of marketing and the strategic planner to predict such events. But unless you're perfect, these projects will arise. The better you are at your own internal processes, and the better you monitor and track your environment, the fewer consequential projects you'll face.

The difficulty with mandatory and consequential projects is that they don't add value to the organization; they prevent a reduction in value. Table 5.1 illustrates their less flexible time-cost-scope trade-off.

Table 5.1   Aligning Portfolio Projects

Project Type	Time	Cost	Quality or Scope
Strategic			
Creative	Balanced by the strategic plan		
Opportunistic			
Mandatory	Set by regulation	Minimize	Sufficient to meet regulations and the organization's definition statements
Consequential	Minimize	Minimize	Sufficient to resolve the issue or problem

Aligning Project Types

Let's examine how to align the different project types.

Aligning Strategic Projects

Strategic projects are often the easiest to align. They frequently are designed by the same committee that establishes the strategic plan. The strategic planning committee must be careful not to ignore organization definition statements when defining strategic projects. By supporting these statements, the strategic planning committee demonstrates its support for these statements and encourages other project designers to do the same. Additionally, the committee should enable subject matter experts to actually write the project requirements. Writing project requirements is a defined and honed skill and should be done by experts.

Aligning Creative and Opportunistic Projects

Creative and opportunistic projects are the most difficult to align. These projects are designed by business analysts, product marketing managers, researchers, internal business process owners, and other leaders within the organization. They are inspired frequently by whim. The project designers constantly face political battles and daily distractions, in addition to having their own personal goals. Without clear and active executive leadership, creative and opportunistic projects will absorb unwarranted resources and pull the organization away from its strategic path.

> **The quality of goals, guidelines, and leadership dictates the level of organizational alignment.**

Aligning Mandatory and Consequential Projects

By their nature, these project types prevent the organization from losing value. Therefore, they should absorb minimum resources and be scheduled at the most appropriate time. The most appropriate time is when resource demands are minimal. Many large organizations retain representation in state and local governments to direct or at least predict regulatory changes. (You call them lobbyists.) Smaller organizations cannot afford such representation, yet the regulations still apply. Fortunately, local, state, and federal governments usually attempt to allow organizations sufficient time to adapt to new regulations.

> **A wise executive management team allocates some, albeit small, percentage of resources to handle mandatory and consequential projects.**

You can use historical data to establish a percentage, and then track your progress and adjust the percentage as the strategic plan unfolds. Resources you don't need for these projects become available for opportunistic or creative projects.

Other Issues Concerning Organizational Alignment

In my consulting and training practice, I find three other issues that frequently interfere with organizational alignment. These include project momentum, communication, and project oversight. I address each of these in the following sections.

Project Momentum

Physics students study a concept called the **conservation of momentum.** It is this concept that causes automobile accidents. A car traveling 50 miles per hour through an intersection under a green light suddenly confronts someone on the intersecting road traveling 50 miles an hour through the red light. The drivers slam on their breaks in hope of overcoming the conservation of momentum.

Projects are not automobiles; they don't have mass, but they do have momentum—even before they are formally started or sanctioned. We frequently engage in or continue projects that fail to support the organization for political reasons or simply for their momentum. It's difficult to stop a project after it's started. We select a project based on only one concern: its ability to support the organization relative to its cost. Projects under consideration for inclusion in the portfolio absorb organizational resources. They should live and absorb those resources only if we can track their value to the organization's high-level objectives. In a utopian organization, the project must be the best approach to achieve those benefits. The portfolio designer, with a well-defined strategic plan and a clear understanding of the organizational visions, mission, values, and quality objectives, can make sound project-selection decisions. As with any profession, the quality of the tools and supplies the portfolio designer possesses defines the quality of the portfolio itself. A poorly defined organization will surely have many project *accidents*.

Communication

Exacerbating the problems facing modern executive management is the problem of communication. We live in a society of information overload. Ask your staff how many e-mails they receive each day. Then ask how many required a thoughtful response and how many were FYI[2] or CYA[3]? Finally, ask them how they can discriminate between useful and useless information. The paradox now reveals itself: To determine whether an e-mail is useful, you must at least scan its contents. For the executive management team, this means only one thing: a distracted staff.

**Modern project management demands
a more active executive management role.**

Simply putting your organizational definition statement on your Web site will not keep your staff focused.

> A vice president once complained to me, "I tell my people to do things, and they don't do them!"
>
> I asked, "How many times did you tell them?"
>
> "Once," he replied.
>
> My response: "Assume that you have to tell them a minimum of three times."

Overcoming this barrage of distractions requires a concerted effort from executives. Organizational objectives and the need for alignment must be clearly, consistently, and actively communicated. Project managers face the same issue. Developing a WBS and assigning a resource to an activity is insufficient for project success. Project managers must hold weekly project review meetings, partly to reinforce assignments and deadlines. The project managers must then spot-check progress throughout the week, employing management by wandering around[4] (MBWA) or other mechanisms to ensure that the assigned resources didn't get distracted or pulled from their assigned task. For the same reason, executive management must develop a comprehensive communication plan that establishes and maintains focus on the organization's goals.

Project Oversight

Earlier, I proposed that it is your responsibility as an executive manager to help ensure project alignment. The exact mechanics might vary among organizations, but the responsibility does not. For example, project managers must manage all project stakeholders, regardless of their position within the organization. This means that they, to some degree, try to manage people higher than them in the organization's pecking order. This can derail even the simplest project. Similarly, middle managers can direct technical staff to go off into different directions, altering a project's results. Therefore, project alignment requires the active and coordinated efforts of executive management.

Imagine a major street with a speed limit sign in a small township. When the sign is first installed, most drivers respect the sign and obey it, at least to some degree.

Now consider what would happen if the township never enforces the sign. Although some drivers will continue to obey the sign, many will begin to disregard it and drive at a speed more important to them. As time continues, drivers will observe the violators. Some will object to the violators, and others will disregard the sign and become violators themselves. If those who object are not heard, they will eventually disregard the sign as well. Ultimately, anarchy will take over.

Two mechanisms can prevent total anarchy: 1) Major accidents occur and the township people decide to obey and enforce the speed limit, or 2) The township decides to enforce the limit. Clearly, if you're trying to avoid accidents, the latter approach is better.

The recent economic cataclysm inspired by unregulated derivatives and unenforced regulations clearly demonstrates this concept.

You can prevent these catastrophes in several ways. Executives can actively participate in alignment activities; executives can define and enforce processes that ensure project alignment; or executives can delegate alignment activities to appropriate committees or groups, either inside or outside the organization.

Sufficient oversight requires the project designer to demonstrate how the project aligns with and supports organizational objectives. In project management, this task is frequently called a **scope review.** The project designer presents the top two or three levels of the GBS to the appropriate committee and demonstrates how these project objectives will support the organization. The project designer must also itemize any relevant assumptions, open issues, and risks. If the designer fails to demonstrate sufficient alignment, the project is rejected or terminated.

Clearly, if we require that the project be aligned at its inception, sufficient alignment must also prevail for the life of the project. When facing political obstructions, project managers must have a mechanism to escalate issues to a high enough level to enforce alignment throughout the project's life. A robust and enforced change management process can significantly reduce the problem, especially in a well-defined organizational environment. However, situations still arise that require senior management's intervention. Senior management must provide and support an appropriate process or procedure to enable project managers to escalate alignment issues. Later chapters offer suggested approaches for this process.

Summary

This chapter introduced these core concepts for aligning projects and the organization:

- The organization's character, culture, goals, and values must be clearly stated and communicated.
- The OGBS offers a technique for decomposing and elaborating on the organizational objectives to create a strategic plan and project portfolio.
- The roles of a portfolio designer and a project designer involve defining the portfolio and projects, respectively, which satisfy organizational objectives.

    Such roles can be handled by business analysts, product marketing managers, business process owners, or similar positions.

- Senior management must enforce alignment through oversight.

    Whether senior management itself provides the oversight or it's accomplished through delegation, project and portfolio designers must demonstrate how their projects support the organization.

- Senior management must overcome the constant barrage of distractions through consistent communication.
- Senior management must send a clear message of commitment by aligning action with rhetoric.

Table 5.2 allows you to rate key characteristics in your organization regarding project alignment.

Table 5.2 Organizational Development Checklist

Performance Item	My Organization's Performance				
	High ← → Low				
My organization definition statements provide clear direction for portfolio and project designers.					
Executive management actively supports the organization's definition statements.					
My strategic plan contains sufficient objectives to meet organizational objectives.					
Executive management constantly communicates and reinforces the organizational definition statements and strategic plan to overcome distractions.					
My strategic plan contains sufficient objectives to create the proper organizational culture to meet business objectives.					
Executive management actively supports the strategic plan.					
My portfolio contains sufficient projects and programs to meet all strategic objectives.					
Executive management actively supports the organization's portfolio.					
Portfolio and project designers must demonstrate how projects align with the organization's goals.					
Executive management is able and willing to provide sufficient resources and infrastructure to support the portfolio, strategic plan, and organization definition statements.					

6

Organizational Alignment

his chapter presents tools and concepts to help you review the roles, responsibilities, and structure of your organization to integrate project management successfully. While these tools and concepts are relatively simple, you may discover a significant cultural push-back when you attempt to address this issue. I first examine the origin of this resistance and then suggest mechanisms for successful integration.

Managing Projects in a Process-Oriented Organization

Since Henry Ford developed mass production (and probably well before that time), most organizations' structures have been based on process and operations, not projects. If projects didn't exist, the common matrix management structure would work quite well. A matrix structure (shown in Figure 6.1) exists when the organization is divided by functional departments or disciplines. The departments must transfer decisions, information, products, and personnel among themselves for the organization to work as a whole. The repetitive nature of process and operations enables the mechanics of these transfers to develop over time. Projects do not enjoy that luxury.

Projects don't always have the benefit of repetition; they are unique. Individual work packages might demand skills that aren't available in any department. The transfers among departments are different than normal and might be different for each project. Projects create short-term work overloads followed by periods of light workload. Overstressed project and functional managers frequently grab staff as needed, often with little or no coordination, and sometimes without regard to skills possessed or needed (what I called the "Warm Body Syndrome" in Chapter 1, "The Goals of Project Management").

If you work in a matrix environment, this is your plight. The structure works well for business processes, but projects take a back seat.

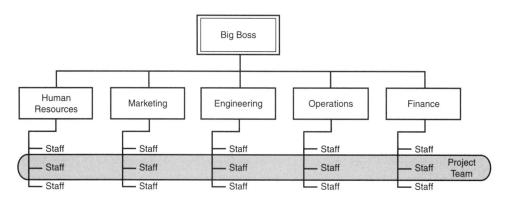

Figure 6.1 The matrix organization

The Plight of the Functional Manager

Functional departments are structured, financed, and managed based on business processes—routine, predictable work. For example, functional managers establish budgets based on the previous year's budget, making adjustments for growth and their own internal initiatives.

However, functional managers need to supply resources to manage their internal business processes as well as for projects. Resource needs for internal business processes are well known and predictable. However, unless they are properly planned in advance and communicated, resource needs for projects are unpredictable.

Denise's Budget Predicament

Denise manages the compliance department for a medium-size insurance company. Her department's primary job is to review regulatory changes in the states where they sell policies; communicate those changes to the other departments and their clients, when appropriate; and adjust policies to comply with the new state regulations. Denise is good at her job and, although individual state legislatures can be unpredictable, the aggregate workflow is generally balanced. Several states sometimes make regulatory changes almost simultaneously, but then she gets a quiet time to recover from the overload.

Denise's communication flow with the other departments is also well established. Her team of people knows what changes need to be communicated, and to which departments. Her people know the other players in those departments, and they know how to get things done. In general, things run pretty smoothly for Denise and her team.

However, things just aren't going well this year. The company is recovering from the financial burden of a few natural disasters. Although Denise's team's workload isn't directly affected by the disasters, senior management has decided to expand the product line and venture into new states, to help balance the overall risk. These new projects have overloaded her department, and she is now falling behind on other compliance issues. Denise knows that the states can come in and audit the company without warning—and if the audits fail, they can be fined and even shut out of that state.

Anticipating the new suite of projects, senior management decided to train some of their people in project management. Although they seem to be doing their job, the results aren't visible. While they were recently trained, they are inexperienced and trying to cope with a process-oriented culture. Projects are very late and cash flow for the entire organization is strained.

Now, it seems like every day, project managers are telling Denise that the people she loaned them will have to stay on the project a bit longer, and other project managers are demanding more people. Denise is trying to support the initiatives, but she can't keep up with all the changes.

Denise's dilemma is typical. She based her budget on routine work and the previous year's experiences. Her budget doesn't include new, unexpected projects, yet she is required to support those projects by supplying resources.

It's easy for both executive management and functional managers to blame the project managers for these types of problems.

However, the problems go deeper than the project managers; the problems are systemic. Executive management tried to use project management to get through this period, but they discovered that a few newly trained PMs didn't solve their problems. Anticipating the increased workload, both executive management and the functional managers should have allocated additional funds for hiring new employees or contractors, based on the project manager's staffing plans—assuming that a few newly trained people would develop accurate plans. They also needed to spend more time working out communication, roles, responsibilities, and authorities for the new and unique project work.

The Projectized Organization

In contrast, consider the projectized organization (see Figure 6.2). Here, the organization is divided across the project base. Project managers hold and maintain their team's personnel folders. Project managers hire, fire, and conduct performance reviews of their team members. Team members have only one boss—their project manager.

The projectized organization is useful for organizations that are project based. Small consulting or custom-work firms (for example, firms that do customer software development or custom engineering) are frequently projectized. Organizations that primarily perform large-scale project work for government or industry also work this way. These larger firms might divide their team by discipline underneath the project manager. So project managers might have an engineering department, IT department, production department, and so on within their projects.

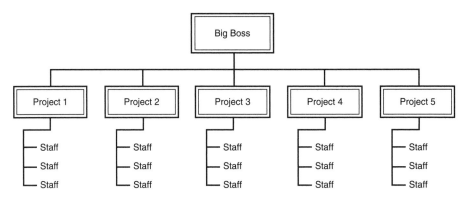

Figure 6.2 The projectized organization

These organizations typically don't exhibit the same difficulties as the matrix management organizations regarding project work, so we limit our focus in this chapter to the matrix organization.

Goals for Organizational Alignment

In the previous two chapters, we achieved alignment for both departments and projects through the organization definition statements, strategic plan, and goals breakdown structure. In this chapter, we improve efficiency by adjusting the organization to enhance the transfers of decisions, information, products, and personnel among departments and projects.

Our goals for organizational integration include the following:

- Coordinate the transfer of resources between project work and functional work
- Ensure that functional managers have sufficient time to develop the needed skill mix through training, contracting, or hiring
- Ensure that each department knows its role in projects and buys into that role
- Improve the communication among executive management, project management, and functional management to enhance the transfer of information and decisions regarding project work

In the next chapter, "Process Alignment," we examine the actual products, information, and decisions that are transferred.

True Organizational Alignment

All organizations include a mixture of process work, project work, research, and other work. The organizational structure you select should be based on the majority of the work categories; therefore, you need to find a way to integrate the other categories of work into the structure. There is no cookbook solution. Multiple answers exist for the question, "What organizational structure is right for me?"

In my experience, both as an employee and as a consultant, I've come to realize that…

> **…well-defined roles and responsibilities**
> **are more important than structure.**

In other words, the wrong structure will still work as long as the roles and responsibilities are well-defined. The right structure will not work if the roles and responsibilities are ill-defined.

If the people within the structure know what's expected of them, know their job, and know how to do it, the structure is less important. Conversely, if a structure is good but people within the structure don't know their roles, their responsibilities, or what's expected of them, the structure is insufficient to achieve organizational effectiveness.

Ownership—A Management Model

The concept of **ownership** aids us in our quest for organizational alignment by solidifying roles and responsibilities. Although the concept is neither new nor misunderstood, I present ownership in a new light to develop a tangible, workable model that can significantly help us integrate and align project work into the organization.

To properly develop our model, we must first agree on the definition of three terms: responsibility, accountability, and authority. To ease understanding, I interpret the pure dictionary definitions for two of these terms as they apply to our situation. I won't present my argument for these interpretations here, but I do offer a brief version as an endnote.[1]

> **Responsibility**—For our purposes, I define the term as a commitment to do or to perform work.

Responsibility is a *doing-ness*—more formally, a commitment to do or to perform work. For example: A purchasing agent accepts the responsibility of making sure she gets the right vendor for a contract; a marketing-communications manager accepts the responsibility to develop appropriate advertising for a product launch; or a ship's captain accepts the responsibility to get a ship from the Persian Gulf to Newport News, Virginia. Responsibility, as I've defined it, occurs before and during the activity. Responsibility is sharable—the project team shares the responsibility to perform the work of the project.

True responsibility comes from within. It's not just delegated; it must be accepted.

Now let's define accountability.

> **Accountability**—Accurate, timely reporting

Most dictionaries use the term **answerable** somewhere in their definition. The term has a negative connotation. This instills fear, which is both undesirable and not technically accurate. Consider a project manager who has just finished a failed project. The project manager is called in front of the governing board and asked why the project failed. The only (politically correct) answer the project manager can offer is, "It was my fault." Now imagine that the same project manager has just completed a successful project. When called in front of the governing board and asked why the project was successful, the project manager's only (politically correct) response can be, "I had a great team." No wonder people are afraid of accountability.

Note that, in both cases, the project manager was being accountable. In both situations, it's the project manager standing in front of the governing board answering the question, but the cause was directed to two different entities. Where someone points the finger cannot be the definition of accountability.

True accountability is simply accurate, timely reporting.

When a problem occurs in a project, the project manager should be the first to hear about it directly from the task performer who discovered it. That's accountability.

For our model, we strictly define the term as accurate, timely reporting. True accountability also comes from within—I don't need anybody's permission to be accountable.

Now let's address authority.

> **Authority**—The right and power to command, enforce laws, exact obedience, determine, or judge.[2]

True authority requires both power and permission. Here, I do need permission.

With our base terms defined, I can now define ownership. When you own something—it's yours. You can do with it what you choose. You can sell it, break it, lose it, store it, get it dirty, or give it as a gift, all without anyone's permission, consideration, guidance, or restrictions. For our model, the definition of ownership is as follows:

> **Ownership**—The synergistic integration of responsibility, accountability, and authority

The pure definition of ownership is unqualified authority as described above. However, in an organization, we cannot isolate authority from responsibility and accountability. For example, you wouldn't delegate authority unless individuals demonstrate that they are responsible and accountable. They work in unison and, ideally, in equal balance.

Graphically, they form an equilateral triangle. As one side grows, so must the other sides. As one side shrinks, so must the other sides. To make the model complete, we need one more element: success. People can demonstrate responsibility, they can demonstrate accountability, and you can give them authority. But if they are unsuccessful, their level of authority will shrink. I symbolize this with the circle surrounding the triangle in Figure 6.3.

Figure 6.3   Ownership model

For the size of the triangle to grow, someone must accept more responsibility. Some level of failure is unavoidable. For example, a programmer might want to become a systems designer. His first attempt will likely be flawed. If that programmer is responsible and accountable, the flaws will be identified early, the programmer will learn faster, and the effects on the project will be minimal.

> **If you want authority from me, I'll tell you exactly how to get it. Demonstrate responsibility and demonstrate accountability, and I'll give you proportional authority. Just make sure you're reasonably successful.**

In projects, each work element and product is assigned an owner. When team members own a work element, they are responsible for making sure it gets done correctly, they must accurately report on progress and any issues or problems that might arise, and they have complete authority to make decisions regarding that work package. They determine the estimate, they determine the best approach, they evaluate and monitor the risks, they tell the project manager what they need to get the job done right, and they get the rewards or punishment for success or failure.

When I assign any role in a project, I also delegate ownership for that role. Role and ownership are virtually synonymous.

Roles within the Organization

In Chapter 2, "Project Management Framework and Structure," I introduced organizational roles within the project itself. I deliberately presented a narrow perspective to keep the discussion focused within the project. Here, I expand that perspective to include more of the organization: including the role of functional managers and executive managers so that we can successfully integrate project management into the organization's mainstream workflow.

Functional Management

Functional managers own resources. We can see from the previous example that this can be a very difficult task. We now understand that many functional departments' structures are based on business process, not projects. However, functional managers must provide resources for both their own internal processes and project work. They must ensure that the department contains enough personnel and that the personnel have the right skill sets. To supply both, functional managers must understand both the skills and the work demand of all projects they must support. Mathematically, you can see this illustrated in the following equation:

Functional Department Resource Demands

$$\frac{\begin{array}{c} Internal\ Process\ Demand \\ +\ Internal\ Project\ Demand \\ +\ External\ Project\ Demand \end{array}}{Department\ Resource\ Demand}$$

Functional managers can evaluate their own internal demand, but they must receive reports regarding the demands for projects spawned externally. When they understand the total work demands, they must contribute to project scheduling decisions to ensure that they balance their resources. During execution, they must receive reports regarding changes to the schedule so that they can adjust the workload of their staff accordingly.

Functional managers own the resources. However, when functional managers loan a resource to a project, they also loan their ownership.

When the staff member is on loan, functional managers should not assume that they can call the staff member back any time they want. Similarly, when the team member is done with the project assignment, the project managers must relinquish their ownership to the functional manager. The transfer to and from projects must be clean.

Resources are not the only point of contention between functional and project management. Functional managers sanction projects for their own use and purpose. These projects might include internal process-improvement projects, projects to develop new skills, quality measures, or new technologies that will stay within their own department. Functional managers must coordinate the goals of these projects with those of other initiatives. A marketing department that wants to acquire a new market-analysis software package must coordinate with the IT department to ensure that the new system will integrate with the current and future IT infrastructure. A finance department attempting to improve data collection must coordinate with all departments that supply the financial data. This is part of the purpose of the OGBS.

The roles of functional managers include:

- Provide sufficient staff for internal processes, internal projects, and external projects
- Train staff on skills required for project work
- Transfer staff ownership to project managers
- Receive and incorporate performance reports from project managers for performance reviews
- Communicate and coordinate internal projects with appropriate portfolio managers and portfolio designers

Portfolio Designers and Managers

Portfolio designers own, among other things, the portfolio resource plan and strategy. Therefore, they must accept resource needs from both project managers and functional managers, and work with them to perform the following tasks:

- Schedule projects based on the strategic plan and resource availability
- Establish criteria for a clean transfer between functional managers and project managers
- Aid functional managers and project managers with resource constraints

In organizations where project management is well established, portfolio designers and managers can schedule all project resources, alleviating the project manager of this burden. This is known as **centralized scheduling.**

Project Designers and Managers

Responsibilities of the project managers or project designers include providing accurate estimates for workload by skill set for the various projects. As we discovered earlier, the subject matter experts should provide this information.

> **These experts live within their own departments, so a natural communication link should exist between the project managers and functional managers.**

However, this link breaks down when the functional manager doesn't buy in to the project or when the projects are estimated long before they begin. Project and portfolio designers often scope out a strategic or creative project and then submit their findings to the portfolio managers or executive management. The decision to accept or reject the project might come much later and often without warning, putting the functional manager into a resource bind.

Allocation is only one part of the complete picture. When staff members are assigned to a project, they (should) stop reporting to their "normal" boss—the functional manager—and start reporting to the project manager. The functional manager loans out ownership of the individual to the project manager. The functional manager has little visibility in the staff members' performance. Therefore, we must create a mechanism to enable project managers to report the staff members' performance to the functional managers. We must also ensure that sufficient communication occurs between project managers and functional managers about the staff members' transfer between project and functional work.

The roles of project designers and managers, therefore, include:

- Provide accurate estimates for skill requirements to portfolio designers and managers
- Work with functional managers for daily resource allocation
- Report staff performance on project work to functional managers

Executive Management

In addition to defining, communicating, and ensuring the coordination of strategic projects, you, as an executive manager, must provide both the culture and the infrastructure to properly coordinate workloads, resources, and project objectives across the organization. In addition, you must provide both doctrine and guidelines to create a working framework for such coordination. You own the culture, infrastructure, and goals for the organization.

Organization Alignment Constructs

The sections that follow describe teams, committees, departments, and similar structures designed to help coordinate projects throughout the organization. These include the following:

- Steering committees
- The program management office (PMO)
- The project management department
- The chief project officer (CPO)
- Gate review teams

Steering Committees

Steering committees take many forms. For this discussion, I define a steering committee as a committee that is chartered to manage all projects within an organization or sub-organization (department, region, and so on), and that consists of all leaders of that (sub)organization.

Steering committees have demonstrated significant success during the past few decades. They don't require any reorganization; simply create a team or committee of all the managers at a particular peer level and their immediate boss, as illustrated in Figure 6.4.

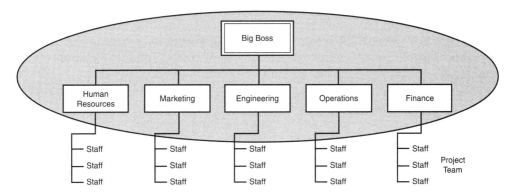

Figure 6.4   Steering committee

You can define steering committees at any level of the organization. They can also be developed with or without formal authority—many develop as grass roots initiatives.

One purpose of the steering committee is to get the functional managers working together as a team for the benefit of the organization and for projects. Interestingly, strong side benefits emerge from steering committees:

- All functional managers (FM) are aware of all projects.

- FMs can help schedule projects to effect better resource balance.

- PMs are less burdened from organizational politics.

- FMs work as a team to the benefit of the organization, instead of as enemies fighting over turf and resources.

Steering committees break down silos. They create a team of managers working for the benefit of the organization instead of waging political turf wars. Some politics will still exist, but steering committees can significantly reduce it.

Steering committees also greatly reduce the political issues facing project managers. I previously mentioned that project managers must handle all stakeholders, regardless of rank or position within the company. Many of these stakeholders will be high in the organization and might actually want to sabotage a project. When a steering committee exists, it can handle a significant portion of these problems, enabling the project manager to focus on the mechanics of the project itself.

Responsibilities of the Steering Committee

For our purposes, the steering committee owns the portfolio within its purview. Some projects are mandated by higher levels within the organization; others are created or sanctioned by the committee for its own purposes (and supported by the OGBS). For example, a national electronics wholesaler might divide its organization by geographic region. The steering committee for the northeast region would be responsible for all strategic initiatives spawned by corporate headquarters and its own projects to improve operations within the region. Similarly, the steering committee for the database management group of an IT department would be responsible for handling all IT projects and its own projects for restructuring and maintaining the databases.

The primary roles for the steering committee include:

- Determine resource needs for all projects within the portfolio
- Work with higher-level portfolio managers to balance resource demands
- Select or reject projects in the portfolio for its own purposes
- Schedule projects to balance resources
- Review the progress of all projects within the portfolio
- Handle portfolio-level problems (For example, when the mix of projects overwhelms one of the departments, the steering committee can readjust project schedules or authorize hiring contractors.)

Steering Committee Makeup

The only requirement for creating a steering committee is that it must include all the managers at a particular peer level. Ideally, their immediate boss should also be included; however, if the boss is out of touch because of geographical or political issues, or is just incompetent, the committee usually can run fine without this person.

Problems arise when someone within the level is excluded. The committee then must make decisions with false or missing information, and the excluded individual feels slighted. Political turmoil is inevitable.

Forming a steering committee not only changes the organization; it also changes the culture. Therefore, steering committees take time to become effective, typically 12–18 months before they become truly productive. Be patient and work through the issues; the results are worth it. You can significantly reduce the start-up period by properly chartering the committee; clearly defining its role, responsibilities, and authorities (yes … ownership); and ensuring that all members have buy-in on the process.

The Steering Committee as Portfolio Designer and Manager

In our context, the primary purpose of the steering committee is portfolio management. The committee addresses portfolio management at the strategic level, not the tactical level. The steering committee reviews the portfolio's progress and adjusts the schedule or workload to balance resources and improve efficiency. A person, team, committee, or group must develop and roll up resource requirements for proposed projects, develop schedule proposals, communicate and disseminate the decisions of the committee, manage the daily issues across the portfolio, and implement the directives of the committee. A PMO, the project manager department, or a designated portfolio design and management group can perform this role.

The Program Management Office (PMO)

The program management office (also sometimes called the project management office) is another very broad topic within project management, probably one that deserves its own book. This section presents a very brief introduction.

PMOs grew from two distinct origins. The first is large multiyear programs, consisting of multiple projects. Many large-scale government contracts employ this architecture. The prime contractor acts as the PMO and subcontracts much of the work to outside vendors.

The second origin began as project management started to become a recognized discipline. Originally, project managers had little or no support, and few people really understood it. Project managers in this era had little training and faced organizations optimized for business processes, not projects. For self-preservation, project managers formed their own groups to handle whatever problems they collectively faced. Some tools they used included sharing lessons learned, defining a consistent and successful methodology, managing vendors collectively, handling internal political issues, and balancing resources across the project mix.

Today, PMOs still hold both definitions. If you are handling the former scenario, you are already familiar with such PMOs and organizational alignment is not an issue. I address the latter scenario here.

Originally, PMOs were considered temporary. They were created to solve whatever problem needed to be solved, such as developing a project methodology that could be consistently used throughout the organization, or evaluating project management software tools. When the problem was solved, the methodology developed, and the tools selected, the PMO could dissolve. However, as time progressed, people realized that some issues continued in perpetuity. After all, the methodology needed to grow and change with the organization, and new project managers needed training on how to use the tools. PMOs then found a happy and permanent home in the organization.

Responsibilities of the PMO

The PMO has a tactical focus. It works in the field, handling issues on behalf of the project managers or the portfolio designers and managers. As stated earlier, it can also be the implementation arm of the steering committee. The roles and responsibilities might change among different organizations. Here are common responsibilities many PMOs undertake:

- Develop and continuously improve the project methodologies

- Implement the decisions of the steering committee or portfolio managers

- Submit collective resource requirements for the portfolio designers

- Define training programs for project managers

- Receive status reports from project managers; summarize and communicate status to steering committees, portfolio management, or executive management

- Translate business objectives into project requirements (This activity is best done by business analysts, but PMOs frequently perform this task when organizations lack such functions.)

- Mentor and help project managers

- Help balance resources across projects on a daily basis

- Help balance risks across projects

- Maintain budgets and finances

- Receive and handle problem escalations

- Handle political problems facing project managers

- Hire and fire project managers (This is unusual, but some PMOs do this.)

- Evaluate tools such as project management software tools

The PMOs can be quite busy. If they don't perform these activities, the project managers are left to handle these issues individually, which is inefficient and prevents consistency.

Structure and Makeup of the PMO

Because PMOs solve different problems for different organizations, they exhibit a wide variety of structures and makeup. One common structure is for the project managers to simply meet on a regular basis to address collective issues. More formally, they (or senior management) might select a chairperson for the committee: the program management officer or even a chief project officer (CPO). Frequently, PMOs might have rotating personnel. If an organization has 12 project managers, the PMO might consist of a program management officer and three project managers on a six-month or one-year rotating basis. When done right, this provides consistency yet enables new ideas to enter the group.

PMOs can also manage distributed or virtual teams. You can create a central PMO that is located in the corporate headquarters, and each division, office, or region might have a liaison physically on-site. The liaison doesn't need to be a full-time role—simply a seasoned project manager loyal to the organization who plays the role of a PMO member when necessary.

Executive and midlevel management are frequently encouraged to participate in PMOs. Their representation enables the PMO to stay focused on the organization and gain input from a broader group. Executive management is the primary client for projects, and midlevel management is critical for project success. Their contribution can be invaluable. Again, executive and midlevel representation can be on a rotating basis, as appropriate.

The only key to successful structure and makeup is common sense. The PMO will be ineffective if it's too large or too small, if it has too much input from too many sources, or if it doesn't receive enough input. If will also be ineffective if you, the executive manager, do not support its decisions. Ideally, the PMO will include some of your best project managers. They are subject matter experts, so let them do their work.

Other Duties of the PMO

Because of their position and charter, PMOs can take on many other duties for the benefit of the organization. For brevity, I address only two: communication and turmoil.

Communication

Many executives don't speak the language of project management. Similarly, most project managers don't speak the language of executive management. PMOs are in the right position to act as a translator. They can translate executive decisions into project objectives. They can also accept detailed project statuses, roll them up, and communicate the summary to executives in terms you understand.

> **PMOs can also filter unneeded and potentially confusing communication between the two groups.**

Politics and Turmoil

I once consulted a company that had merged with several of its competitors in a very short period of time. Although the executive managers were quite competent, they were overwhelmed by the unexpected diversity of the cultures they were trying to integrate. One of the merged companies was projectized, another ran more as a family, and a third was very process and leadership driven. The resulting conglomerate would have overwhelmed even the most experienced executive managers. The organization needed to stabilize new product development (among other things), and the organization's management needed time to adjust to the new conglomerate.

We constructed a PMO, headed by a seasoned project manager, who had the president's support. At each company, we assigned a liaison primarily for communication and reporting.

We needed to capitalize on the diversities, yet develop some level of consistency and coordination across the new product mix. We had one more (then unspoken) duty: to protect senior management from the daily issues facing the project managers, and to protect the project managers from several overwhelmed senior executives. When the company became stabilized, the PMO could resume its normal duties.

The Project Management Department

Many organizations create a separate department for project management. This department acts both as a service organization, offering project management services to the other departments, and as the implementation arm of the strategic planning committee or steering committee for strategic projects.

Responsibilities of the Project Management Department

The project management department performs similar functions to the PMO. It usually owns and manages the methodologies, offers a defined training curriculum and career path for project management, defines the skill sets needed for project management in the organization, and hires and fires project managers.

Project management departments typically don't prioritize projects or translate business objectives into project requirements, although they can perform such duties.

Structure and Makeup of the Project Management Department

Construct the project management department similar to any other department in your organization. One warning: Because the department effectively controls most large projects, the department head can become very powerful. If your project management department head is not loyal to the company or plays a lot of political games, you'll have a negative rippling effect through the organization.

Phase Gate Review Teams

The concept of **phase gates,** introduced in Chapter 3, "Project Definition and Planning," has been around for many years. To review, a **phase** is a management interjection, not specifically a work breakdown structure element. Phases are installed to aid the project manager by breaking down the project into smaller, more manageable pieces (similar to chapters in a book); and to give executive management (portfolio manager, sponsor, steering committee, and so on) an opportunity to reevaluate the project's position in the portfolio. At the end of each phase, the project manager presents the current status of the project to portfolio management and makes a recommendation on whether to continue the project into the next phase. Portfolio management confirms completion of the phase and makes a go, no-go, or hold decision regarding the project.

Phase reviews need not be conducted by executive management or even portfolio management. Many organizations create gate review teams to review nonstrategic projects.

These might include creative, opportunistic, mandatory, or consequential projects, or any combination. The team's makeup depends on the type and size of the projects for review.

I once consulted a research-driven organization that used gate review teams to review new product development projects. These projects spawned from research and the company needed to determine whether the products would be viable. The purpose was to eliminate projects that exhibited high risk and low returns. Interestingly, the initiative was spawned by the engineers and scientists themselves. They realized that they were trying to get so many products to market that none was actually making it there. After a short time, senior management gained buy-in on the initiative and began to support it.

Responsibilities of Gate Review Teams

Gate review teams should select projects for inclusion in the portfolio, and review progress of active projects to determine whether they should be continued, held, or terminated.

Structure and Makeup

Although the structure and makeup of gate review teams might vary, one consistent rule should apply: Ensure that all key stakeholders are represented in the team.

A chemical research–based company that wants to use gate review teams to select viable products should include: one representative of executive management (such as a vice president), to ensure that the products align with the overall organizational direction; a representative of the legal department, for patent infringement; someone from marketing, to evaluate cost, sales, and profit analysis; an engineering member, to determine whether a production line is feasible and cost effective; an operations person, to evaluate the production viability; and someone from purchasing, to determine raw materials cost and availability.

An IT department might implement gate review teams to manage infrastructure projects. These kinds of projects typically are invisible to executive management, yet they have a significant impact on the overall organization. Their complexity increases when advancing technology interferes with a changing suite of applications. Here, an appropriate gate review team might include the CIO (chief information officer) and representatives of the key departments within IT, such as database management, networking, and security.

The Chief Project Officer

The concept of the CPO is relatively new, and more organizations are beginning to embrace it. Recall from Chapter 1 that projects are the primary tool in an organization to effect change. Their impact is significant, and if projects fail, the cost to the organization can be excessive. Installing a C-level position designed specifically to manage project management can have a very positive impact on the organization's overall operations.

As with all C-level positions, the CPO defines the overall objectives and characteristics of project management in the organization. This person also represents project management to the rest of executive management.

The CPO also has a support staff. The exact makeup depends on many variables but can include any combinations of the previously described structures: PMO, gate review teams, steering committees, and so on.

Summary

Organizations' cultures, structures, and infrastructures must accommodate a variety of work, including projects, processes, operations, and research. Each organizational structure exhibits benefits and problems. As an executive manager, you must design the organization to accomplish all work.

In this chapter, I presented several common structures, teams, and committees successfully employed to overcome deficiencies in performing project work. The concepts that you decide to implement will depend on many factors, including your target markets, management style, desired culture, and existing infrastructure.

In the years I've been working as an employee, consultant, and trainer, I have seen many different types and permutations of organizations. The key to success lies less in the structure and more in the formal delineation of roles and responsibilities. True ownership—having a person, department, team, or group that is completely responsible, and accountable, with full authority—forms a cornerstone for defining the organization. Ensure that each project, process, and deliverable has an owner, and your organization will be fine, whatever its structure.

Table 6.1 allows you to rate how well your company integrates project management at the organizational level.

Table 6.1 Organizational Alignment Checklist

Performance Item	My Organization's Performance High ← → Low				
The organizational structure supports smooth transfers of decisions, information, products, and personnel among departments for both process and project work.					
The roles in my organization are clearly defined and supported by management.					

Performance Item	My Organization's Performance High ⟵ Low				
Ownership is properly allocated to each role within the organization: ■ The employee accepts responsibility for the role. ■ The employee reports on work status accurately and timely. ■ The employee has authority needed to execute his or her role.					
Functional managers' budgets include funds to handle process workloads, intraproject workloads, and interproject workloads.					
Functional managers delegate employee ownership to project managers when they loan the employee to project work.					
Project managers properly return ownership of loaned staff to the functional manager when their assignments are completed.					
Project designers accurately determine project workload plans in advance to permit effective planning.					
An organizational entity exists to select projects for inclusion in the portfolio.					
An organizational entity exists to integrate process and project workload demands into a comprehensive plan.					
An organizational entity exists to schedule projects based on strategic need and resource availability.					
An organizational entity exists to monitor, track, and adjust the project portfolio.					

7

Process Alignment

P receding chapters focused on aligning projects with the strategic plan and with the organization's structure. Successfully integrating project management into the organization requires one more challenge: aligning project work with the ongoing work of the organization.

In this final chapter on alignment, I take a work focus by examining project management as a part of normal business processes, to further help you seamlessly integrate project management into the organization. Additionally, if you already incorporate techniques to continuously improve your business processes (such as business process reengineering, continuous process improvement, or Six Sigma), you can apply them to your project management processes.

Viewing project management as a set of business processes is not a new concept. Major standards organizations, including the Software Engineering Institute (SEI) and the Project Management Institute (PMI), support and promote this concept through their standards. Recall that the PMI standard presents project management as a suite of 42 processes spread across five process groups. SEI developed a project management maturity model (a rating system to determine the capability of an organization to manage a project) based on this concept. Chapter 1, "The Goals of Project Management," introduced both of these standards.

However, this chapter's objective goes well beyond examining projects as business processes. Projects are frequently viewed as interruptions and distractions from the normal business routine. As such, project managers frequently have difficulty obtaining resources, getting answers to questions, and holding on to the resources they do have. Conversely, organizations that successfully integrate project management take the viewpoint that projects are not ancillary to what we do; they are an integral part of what we do.

The Paradox

In the previous chapter, "Organizational Alignment," we examined the difficulties of running projects in the process-oriented organization. I stressed that process constitutes the normal business routine and that projects are unique, disrupting the normal routine. This has not changed. Projects come and go. You encounter periods of high workload and quiet periods. However, projects follow a consistent pattern, a methodology. Neither the industry nor the technology matters. It doesn't matter whether you're building a ship that drills for oil in the ocean floors, creating a new drug, or moving an office—you manage the project the same way.

For example, regardless of industry or technology, every project is chartered, either formally or informally. Some organizations call it a charter; others call it a capital appropriation, or a work order. But someone, somewhere sanctions the project work.

Every project has a set of goals to achieve. You might call them requirements, business objectives, specifications, or stakeholders' needs. The project manager needs to gather and understand them to be successful. Every project needs a work plan, resource allocations, estimates, tracking, change control, and closure. These can be formal, informal, written, spoken, or implied.

> **When an organization standardizes project activities, communication and workflow become easier and more efficient, conflict lessens, and management simplifies.**

The Two Faces of Project Management

As with all business processes, project management has two faces: the one that looks within and the one that looks outward, as shown in the Venn diagram in Figure 7.1.

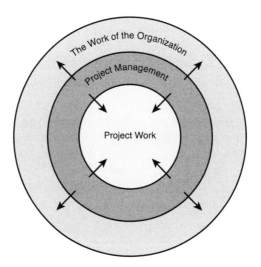

Figure 7.1 The two faces of project management

The inward-looking face manages the work of the project. This is the topic of many other books and seminars, including the *PMBOK® Guide.* Our focus is the face looking outward. Each project lives within the organization. Each activity in a project lives among other organizational activities. Our goal in this chapter is to examine those interfaces, successfully integrating project work with the rest of the organization's work.

Impeding this new viewpoint is the concern that project management has its own jargon. However, this issue is only cosmetic because…

> **…project management very closely mimics classical business process management, and vice versa.**

Precedence diagrams look remarkably similar to standard process maps, the WBS is essentially a hierarchical process chart, and resource allocation and activity costing are virtually identical.

Our objective then becomes presenting project management in a light that mimics more classical business process management, enabling it to integrate in a way familiar to you. To achieve this primary goal, we define the following detailed objectives:

- Integrate activities with ongoing operations
- Highlight where process interfaces take place
- Smooth the transfer of decisions, information, products, and personnel to and from project management
- Develop consistency in planning and executing projects
- Improve project management using classical continuous process improvement

Because our primary objective is aligning project management with the rest of the organization, we focus more on those interfaces between project management and other ongoing activities and less on the internal PM processes. I assume the roles listed in Table 7.1.

Roles and Responsibilities

The previous chapter illustrated the variations that can exist with roles and responsibilities. To aid the discussions in this chapter, Table 7.1 shows the assumptions regarding process ownership and roles and responsibilities.

To this standard list, we add one new entity: the change control board (CCB). The CCB is a committee that consists of key project stakeholders. Its function is to review project changes and change requests, determine their validity and benefit to the project and organization, and accept or reject the change.

Table 7.1   Key Roles for Project Integration

Party	Responsibility
PMO	We assume that the project management office (PMO) owns the project management process (methodology).
Project designer	The project designer is responsible for defining the project at the organizational level, satisfying the client and aligning the project with organizational needs.
Portfolio designer	The role integrates the project with the rest of the portfolio.
Project manager and team	The project manager and project management team define the project at the project level and implement the project.

Core Concepts

First, I present the framework and structure for our process integration model. Then I use the project framework presented in Chapter 2, "Project Management Framework and Structure," to identify the specific interfaces between project work and other organizational work.

Input-Process-Output-Trigger (IPOT)

In this chapter, I use the classical input-process-output-trigger (IPOT) process mapping method, shown in Figure 7.2. As our focus is integration and alignment, I stress the interfaces with project management instead of the internal processes. We examine the inputs into project management and the processes and people that supply those inputs. We also examine the outputs of project management and the people and processes that receive those outputs.

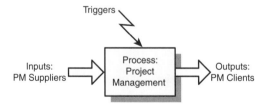

Figure 7.2   Input-process-output-trigger (IPOT) diagram

Inputs: The PM Suppliers

Inputs into the project management processes come from other processes, including external processes. For example, the strategic planning process might provide the business objectives for the project. Functional managers supply resources to the project. On this input side of the chart, project managers or project designers are the client, and the other process owners are the vendors. Project managers must let them know what they need to get the project done.

Process: PM Methodology

The process (sometimes referred to as the methodology) is internal to project management. I present these at the conceptual level to help you understand the interfaces. The *PMBOK Guide* and other publications offer definitions for these procedures. SEI's Capability Maturity Model Integration (CMMI®) standard presents goals for processes. Each standard presents a slightly different perspective.

Outputs: PM Clients

Outputs from project management become inputs to other business processes. This perspective is the reverse of inputs: The project management team is the vendor, and the other process performers are the clients. For example, project managers publish status reports and resource utilization reports that functional managers use in their resource planning. Project managers also supply actual costs used in the project to accounting, to maintain accurate cost analysis for the organization. The project manager's job is to provide their clients with what they need to get their job done. In project management, this is commonly called a **stakeholder analysis.**

Triggers

Triggers are events that imitate a process or a step in a process. Triggers within project management are commonly well defined and usually not problematic in most organizations.

Metrics to Measure Progress: Project Quality

When you establish project management as a normal business process, you can follow normal process quality techniques for managing project management. I am not discussing the quality of the client's deliverables created by project management; instead, I'm referring to the quality of the processes used to create the deliverables.

As with all business processes, you can establish metrics to see how well each of the subprocesses or steps is doing over time, by department, or by project type. One of the simpler and more common sets of metrics comes from a technique called **earned value.** Chapter 8, "Project Cost Management," discusses this technique, so I don't belabor this discussion here.

Managing the Interfaces

I previously presented the concept that project management primarily involves managing the critical interfaces between the project and its environment. Now that we've examined the roles and responsibilities, let's examine how to manage the project interfaces. I define project management as a five-step business process at a high level, and I focus on how each step interfaces with the other activities in your organization.

As a consultant, one of the key elements I find missing in many business process definitions is the concept of a "deliverables-based exchange." Recall from Chapter 2, that work produces products or services that achieve goals. It is these products or services (termed **deliverables**) that transfer between the processes. These might be tangible items, such as reports, documents, or forms. They might also be less tangible, such as updates to a database record or simply an e-mail indicating an approval of an action. Either way, it's the deliverable that transfers.

Familiarity among departments tends to breed less formal exchanges. Furthermore, as processes change, the exchange tends to become even less formal. For a normal business process, this practice is more acceptable because both sides devise workarounds to accommodate the changes. The repetitive nature of the processes enables them to get into the habit of the workaround—it becomes an unwritten procedure.

However, projects are unique and can't afford such informality. Projects are not repetitive, and the exchanges of both decisions and information must be more clearly defined and more rigorously followed.

**Successfully implementing project management depends on clearly
defining the deliverables for decisions and information exchanges
between the project management processes and other ongoing processes.**

For clarity and to promote formality, all information and control exchanged between project management steps and the other organizational entities is defined as process deliverables. Many deliverables are well defined in existing standards (including PMI), but others are defined more generally. In your organization, these deliverables should be defined jointly by the provider, the recipient, and the process owners. When this occurs, project management integrates nicely into the organization. Successful conditions for process integration include the following:

- Process products (deliverables) are the key interface articles.
- Products must contain all items needed for downstream processes, in both content and format.
- A stakeholder analysis can be used to start defining the interfaces.
- Most interfaces are codified in the project communication management plan.
- Think of project management as a business process, using the input-process-output-trigger (IPOT) method to help align it with other business processes.

Project Management Process Steps

Now, let's look at the major steps included in projects and where they interface with the rest of the organization.

Overall Process Flow

Here I use the process flow model that I presented in Chapter 2, which closely aligns with the PMI standard.[1] Because our goal does not involve formally defining internal project management processes, I take some liberties to facilitate understanding and reduce clutter. Differences between this model and the standard are noted where appropriate.

Figure 7.3 illustrates our model. Each box represents a high-level project management step. Deliverables are used to transfer information and decisions between steps. Note that Manage and Build are performed simultaneously. This division highlights the distinction between doing the project work and managing the project work. Also note that the Manage stage can reactivate the Plan step when changes occur.

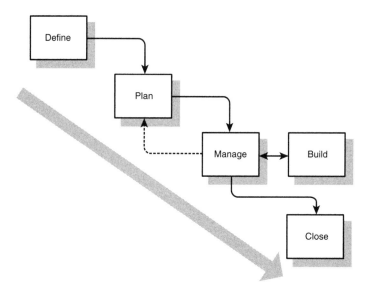

Figure 7.3   Overall process flow

Define

The first step in any project is to define the project. This step begins with the original project stimulus and ends with the project being accepted and sanctioned, put on hold, or rejected and discarded. The primary product for this step is the project charter (see Chapter 2). Figure 7.4 shows the IPOT diagram.

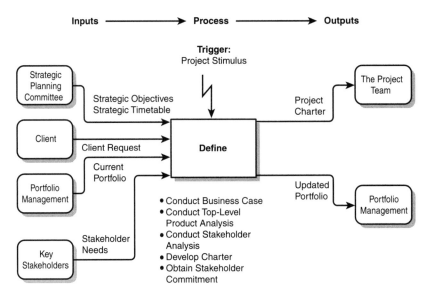

Figure 7.4   Define process IPOT diagram

Purpose

The purpose of this process is to define the project at the organizational level: ensuring that the project aligns with organizational objectives, and determining the organization's approach to providing funding and resources to the project. Another goal for this step is to obtain buy-in from all key stakeholders on the project.

Triggers

Many triggers can activate the Define process. These are the project stimuli. As an executive manager, you might want to define formal avenues for submitting project ideas, to prevent spurious projects from spawning and absorbing important resources. The process for submitting project ideas might be part of this process or part of other processes, such as strategic planning or market strategy processes.

Inputs

Primary inputs into this process originate from four sources: the strategic planning committee, the client, portfolio management, and the project's key stakeholders.

Strategic Planning Committee

Project management interacts with the strategic planning committee either to perform projects on behalf of the committee or to ensure that other projects align with the plan. The strategic planning committee usually meets on a regular basis to define or revise the organization's strategic plan. With a well-written plan, project and portfolio designers need little, if any, interaction with the committee itself. Direct interaction might include: the project or portfolio designers reporting on the progress of the portfolio, obtaining approval of a project with marginal alignment, or receiving project ideas for inclusion or consideration for the strategic plan.

Client

The **client request** is the primary interface between the project designer and the client. This interaction between project designers and clients has been one of the most difficult areas of project management. When poorly done, this interaction produces ill-defined projects, which almost inevitably fail. The request should include a general description of the work and, more important, specific and measurable characteristics of the final products. In Chapter 2 and Chapter 3, "Project Definition and Planning," I call these **requirements** or **exit criteria.**

Many books, articles, tools, and procedures are available now to assist project and portfolio designers with this interface. This becomes a critical interface for both the client and project management. Whether the client is internal or outside the company, spending time to define this process interface improves the probability for project success.

Portfolio Management

Project designers must successfully integrate their project with the current portfolio to ensure that the project aligns with organization objectives and to schedule the projects based on resource utilization and strategic needs.

This interface works well when the portfolio managers are familiar with project management practices. The portfolio manager can work with the project manager and functional managers to schedule the project and balance resources across the portfolio base. The portfolio manager might also adjust the project scope to better align it with organizational objectives, to prevent overlap with other projects, or to fill in gaps created by other projects.

This critical interface usually can be performed through formal or informal meetings. A well-documented and up-to-date portfolio document can also be a great aid.

Other Key Stakeholders

In an ideal organization, stakeholders' needs align with organizational objectives (such as with the OGBS). If your organization is less than ideal, stakeholder requirements might unduly expand, reduce, or even conflict with organizational objectives. Therefore, the Define process must have a resolution mechanism either to enable cost and schedule to expand, or to control stakeholders' needs. The portfolio manager, portfolio designer, project sponsor, steering committee, or anyone with a high enough authority and appropriate strategic knowledge can perform this function.

Project designers usually collect stakeholders' needs through formal and informal meetings or interviews. Project managers refer to the action of collecting and analyzing stakeholders' needs as conducting a **stakeholder analysis.**

Subprocesses

The subprocesses within this step involve a business analysis and stakeholder analysis, designed to determine the benefit of the project compared to the cost (in monetary, human, and nonhuman resources) and risk. I presented these in more detail in Chapters 2–5, and key steps are listed in Figure 7.4. When complete, these processes produce the project's business case and charter.

Outputs

The primary output of the Define process is the project charter. This document contains or references all project scope, schedule, resources, cost, and risk issues for the project at an executive level. For most organizations, this document is an executive summary of the business case. When executed, it becomes the formal authorization for the project and formally assigns the project manager. This authorizes the project manager to expend organizational resources (human, nonhuman, and capital) on behalf of the project. Charters might be large or small, formal or informal, but they must be complete.

The other output for this process is the updated project portfolio showing the inclusion of this new project.

Plan

This process is the busiest for the project management team. The team collects all the information needed to determine the project success criteria, to define all the work, to determine work estimates, to align resources, and to handle risks. Therefore, this step involves the most interfaces with the rest of the organization.

The quality of the Define process determines the ease of performing these processes. The Define process involves higher management levels. The Plan step involves subject matter experts that report to those managers. If the project and portfolio designers successfully obtained buy-in from those managers in the Define process, the project management team will get the resources needed to develop a successful plan. Otherwise, the project management team will have difficulty obtaining sufficient resources, and the plan will be inadequate.

One of the barriers in this step is that many functional managers and subject matter experts view this work as interruptions instead of productive work. In such cultures, project managers collect information by interrupting functional managers and subject matter experts, instead of using formal planning and designing techniques. In these cases, project planning is less process oriented and is performed more ad hoc.

Each department should work with the project management office (or other owner of the project management processes) to establish its own process to support project planning.

The result is less work, more consistent results, and improved plans. Lessons learned and continuous process improvement can help develop these processes.

Figure 7.5 shows the IPOT diagram for the Plan process. The information each department needs varies by department. For this diagram, I include functional managers and their subject matter experts as a group and describe the information they generally need.

This diagram is simplified. The project team, functional managers, and key project stakeholders are (or, at least, should be) heavily involved in creating the plan; they aren't just recipients of the final plan, as Figure 7.5 illustrates.

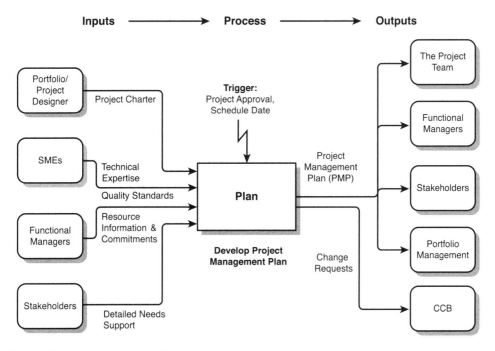

Figure 7.5 Plan process IPOT diagram

Purpose

The primary purpose of the Plan process is to ensure that the actions taken in the project produce the intended product or results, and to ensure that the project participants have clear direction. The project management plan (PMP) defines these issues. The PMP can be large or small, formal or informal. It must contain everything that the project management team and project participants need to get the job done right the first time.

In my practice, I see that most PMPs are less robust than needed. Organizations that are new to formalized project management should overdefine their projects instead of underdefining them. Underdefining can cause project failure, potentially costing you excessive time and money; overdefining costs you only a little time and money, but it increases the probability of a successful project. Also, overdefining establishes a cleaner benchmark for continuous improvement.

Trigger

This step is triggered when the project is sanctioned and activated. The project is sanctioned when all appropriate stakeholders sign the project charter. The step can be retriggered with approved changes.

Inputs

Primary inputs into Plan come from four sources: the portfolio and project designers, functional managers, their subject matter experts, and other key stakeholders. I address each in the following sections.

Portfolio or Project Designer

The portfolio or project designer creates the project charter—the primary driver for this step. They provide the charter, giving clear direction to the project management team.

Functional Managers and Their Subject Matter Experts

Collectively, the functional managers and their subject matter experts (SMEs) provide the greatest amount of information and resources for this step. The functional managers support the project by committing appropriate technical experts, providing standard processes from within their department, and providing defined quality standards for their work. The SMEs become part of the project team to design the products (or services), provide quality standards, and determine the components needed to build the products. The processes they use should coordinate with the PMO to satisfy both their specific discipline and project management. In summary, key inputs for this group include:

- **Resources**—Functional managers supply resource information and commitments for both project planning and execution.

- **Technical expertise**—SMEs define the technical design, work package definitions, estimates, and procedures.

- **Quality standards**—Functional managers supply preexisting quality standards for the project. The SMEs create the quality standards when formal quality standards don't exist or when the project requires quality standards that differ from the norm.

Stakeholders

Other key stakeholders remain involved in this process to offer more detailed needs and requirements. As the project evolves and the environment around the project changes, stakeholders often change their needs. Stakeholders and project managers must conscientiously retain the project's original goals when handling these issues.

**A well-defined and supported change management
process is mandatory during project planning.**

Subprocesses

Many subprocesses are involved in this step. Referencing the 4th edition of the *PMBOK Guide,* 20 of the 42 processes are included in their project planning process group. Key issues include the following:

- Each department should define appropriate subprocesses to support project planning. These should include resource allocation and commitment, and technical planning and design.

- Well-defined and -supported change management is mandatory to prevent scope creep and to keep from distorting the project scope.

- Subprocesses should include quality standards (usually defined in existing standards documents).

- Stakeholders must support the planning subprocesses to ensure efficient and timely execution.

Outputs

The primary output of the planning step is the project management plan. The product or system design is also an output, but I excluded it here because it's a technical issue. At a minimum, the PMP should include the following:

- Resource needs and commitment
- Work plan, including schedule
- Risk plan and analysis
- Procurement plan
- Communication plan
- Cost plan
- Scope documents (the characteristics of the products or services)
- Quality plan

This step inevitably generates changes. Project change management is well documented in many books, and I summarize it in Chapter 3. For our purposes here, change requests flow into the change control board (CCB). Its function is to determine whether the change is appropriate and to approve or reject the change. This mechanism helps retain the project's original scope.

Build

In our model, the Build process is primarily a technical issue. The job of the project manager and project management team is threefold:

1. Acquire the right resources (usually the ones committed during planning).

2. Ensure that those resources know their job as defined in the PMP and design documents.

3. Keep obstacles out of their way through stakeholder management.

The project manager and project management team also have two other jobs during the Build phase: risk management and change management. For our model, we handle all change requests in the Manage step that follows. Figure 7.6 illustrates the IPOT diagram for the Build process.

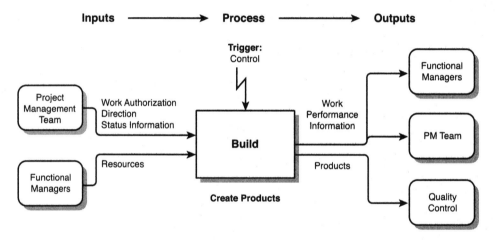

Figure 7.6 Build process IPOT diagram

Purpose
The purpose of this step is to build the products, create the results, or perform the services in the project.

Trigger
The trigger for this process comes from the Manage process through work authorizations.

Inputs
Two sources provide inputs into this step: the project management team and functional managers. These inputs include the following:

- **Work authorization**—The project management team authorizes the start of work.

- **Direction**—The project management team offers direction to the team.

- **Status information**—The project management team offers timely and accurate status information to the team.

- **Resources**—Functional managers offer resources to the team to perform work.

Subprocesses

Using the WBS, the project plan defines the actions taken in the Build process. Chapter 3 describes the WBS. The key difficulty with this step is the allocation (and reallocation) of resources. In a matrix organization, functional managers have the strongest control over their resources and can withhold them from the project with relative ease. This is one of the key reasons projects suffer delays. All functional managers should support the project at the appropriate level. Otherwise, executive management should intervene to ensure that the project receives appropriate staff. Processes should be in place to transfer resources between functional managers and the project team, and to escalate issues when problems arise.

Outputs

The outputs for this step are work performance information and the outputs of the project work (deliverables or products):

- **Work performance**—Work performance reports are offered to the supervisors of the project team members and the project management team itself.

- **Products**—Products, both interim and final, are sent to quality control to determine whether they conform to project scope requirements.

Manage

The primary goal of this process is to ensure that the right things are getting done in the right way. The project manager and project management team are responsible for the Manage process during project execution.

Figure 7.7 illustrates the IPOT diagram for this step. To improve clarity, this presentation is slightly different from the PMI version. PMI allocates the monitoring and controlling process group to the entire suite of processes, including initiating, planning, and closing.

Purpose

The purpose of this step is as follows:

1. Authorize the work steps.

2. Evaluate project performance and compare it to the plan.

3. Approve or reject changes and change requests.

4. Adjust the plan when needed.

5. Communicate status, plan changes, and forecasts.

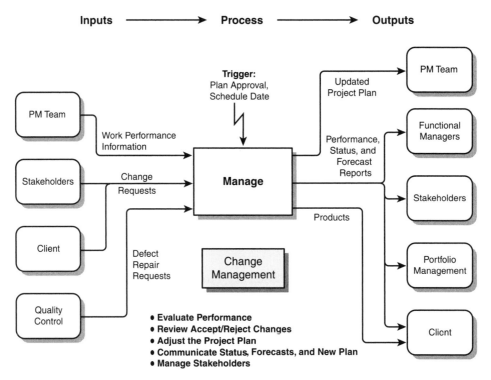

Figure 7.7 Manage process IPOT diagram

Trigger

The trigger for this suite of processes is approval of the project plan and work start authorization from the portfolio manager.

Inputs

The primary inputs for this step are work products, work performance information, and quality control reports. Change requests are also inputs, and virtually any stakeholder can initiate them. For simplicity, I summarize the inputs here.

- **Work performance**—The Build step provides work performance information to evaluate progress against the project plan.

- **Change requests**—Change requests are evaluated to determine their impact on project cost, schedule, final products, and project results. This information is then fed into the change management system for approval or rejection. Approved changes can cause replanning.

- **Quality control reports**—The reports compare the product evaluation against the requirements.

- **Defect repair requests**—The quality control department evaluates the products against requirements to determine whether a repair is warranted. This information is fed into the control processes to enact repairs or to initiate transfer of the products to the client.

Subprocesses

The project management team continuously monitors and tracks the progress of the project work. It determines team performance and product development, and produces status reports, work performance reports, and forecasts.

When changes occur or are requested, the change management process determines the disposition of the change. This decision is usually made by the CCB, which consists of key project stakeholders, the project sponsor, and the project manager. Changes in the project usually require the project management team to adjust the project plan, resulting in plan updates.

When the project work completes, the project management team can transfer the final products to the client.

Outputs

The primary outputs for this step are progress reports, work performance reports, and forecasts. Each stakeholder or group of stakeholders might receive different versions or different content, but they are all designed to accurately communicate progress, issues, problems, and resolutions. Although needs change across departmental boundaries, each department's needs should remain consistent across projects; therefore, this step is an ideal candidate for process definition. A typical list of reports includes the following:

- **Performance reports**—Performance reports are useful for functional managers who want to evaluate their staff's performance during the project. These reports are used for employee evaluations and other HR functions. They are also used to determine when staff can transfer onto or off the project.

- **Status reports**—Current status reports summarize resource utilization and project progress.

- **Forecast reports**—These reports provide forecasts for resource utilization and project activities.

When changes occur, the project management team develops and issues plan updates or, when appropriate, revisions of the entire plan.

Finally, when all work completes, the project management team can transfer the final product to the client.

Close

In our model, the Close process begins after the client has accepted the final products. Therefore, the process is primarily administrative: ensuring that the team has met all requirements, delivered all the deliverables, and captured and stored all archives. This step is also the last chance to capture accurate and timely lessons learned for process improvement. Figure 7.8 illustrates the IPOT diagram for the Close step.

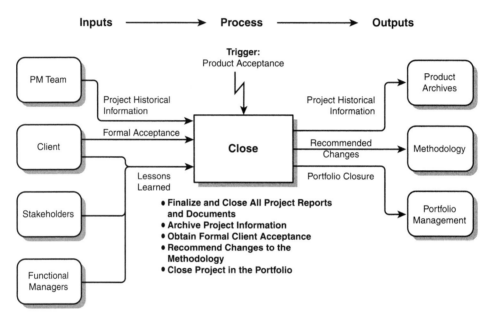

Figure 7.8   Close process IPOT diagram

Purpose

This process ensures that all project activities and requirements have been satisfied, final project historical information has been captured, and final lessons learned have been analyzed and captured.

Trigger

The primary trigger for our model is client acceptance of the final product(s).

Inputs

The project management team collects a variety of information from many sources during the Close process. For simplicity, I group this information into three categories: historical information, formal acceptance documentation from the client, and lessons learned information. The benefit of this information—and, therefore, the amount and format for the information—depends on organizational circumstances. The PMO, portfolio managers, and senior management should determine what information is appropriate and define processes to collect it efficiently.

My experience, both in the classroom and with consulting, reveals that organizations new to formalized project management tend to capture lessons learned, but no follow-up process takes place to implement changes. These lessons are extremely valuable in the early stages of project management development; but with no follow-up, they are lost to history.

> **Define the process to capture, review, and implement**
> **organizational change based on lessons learned in the**
> **early steps of implementing project management.**

Brief descriptions for these inputs include the following:

- **Historical information**—The PM team provides project historical information for lessons learned and archival purposes.

- **Formal acceptance**—The client formally accepts the final products and results for the project (this is an input and the process trigger).

- **Lessons learned**—All parties involved in the project should offer lessons learned in the form of survey information, complaints, and other communications. They can also participate in facilitated lessons-learned sessions. Client involvement is also recommended if the relationship allows.

Subprocesses

The subprocesses involved in this step are designed to ensure that all project activities have been completed, to capture final archive data and outstanding lessons learned. The project management team feeds this information to the PMO or process owner to determine whether improvements are warranted.

Outputs

PMI refers to the primary outputs for this Close process as **organizational process assets.** These outputs have different levels of value in different organizations. At a minimum, lessons learned should always be captured and forwarded to the business process owners, and actual resource utilization should be captured and archived to help estimate future projects. Key outputs include:

- **Project archives**—Maintained for future planning, especially estimating.
- **Recommended changes**—Recommend changes to the methodology. This is sent to the process owner (classically the PMO).
- **Portfolio closure**—Update the portfolio to reflect the closed project.

Continuous Improvement

After you have established project management as a normal business process, you can continuously improve it using classical techniques. The continuous process improvement activity is its own process, with inputs, process, outputs, and triggers. The process owner (usually the PMO) should perform this step.

Triggers

Continuous improvement for project management should be performed regularly (quarterly or semi-annually). This enables the PMO to gather information from several projects and review them collectively. The process also might be triggered at the end of a major project or if a project fails. Use this trigger when you need the information to be fresh in everyone's mind.

Inputs

Inputs for improving project management can come from any stakeholder at any time. The wise project management team establishes habits and procedures to capture this information during the life of the project. Key improvement information includes the following:

- **Lessons learned**—These are gathered continuously throughout all projects and funneled at appropriate times to the process owner for inclusion in the next review cycle.
- **Change orders**—Changes, whether unpredicted or predicted (as risks), represent potential process improvements.
- **Inspection results**—Results of quality inspections and audits indicate where your strengths and weaknesses lie. Use them to guide improvement.
- **Complaints**—Complaints captured either formally or informally are excellent sources for continuous improvement. Confront and cherish them; ignoring them does not make them go away.

Processes

The PMO regularly reviews collected information. It conducts root-cause analysis for changes, defects, lessons learned, and complaints to determine whether changes to the processes are appropriate.

Where appropriate, the processes are updated and redistributed. This might also require changes to training curriculum, standards documents, and other business process support functions.

Outputs

The primary output for this process is the updated methodology or suite of processes. Associated communication, revised training programs, recommended retraining, and other support materials might also be generated.

Summary

Project work is not ancillary to an organization; it's an integral part of it. Viewing projects as a normal business process helps integrate it into the organization, smoothes the interfaces between project activities and ongoing activities, and improves overall organizational efficiency. Creating a deliverables-based interface between project work and ongoing work further enhances overall efficiency.

Table 7.2 helps you determine how well your organization integrates project management as a normal business process.

Table 7.2 Process Alignment Summary Checklist

Performance Item	My Organization's Performance High ←——————→ Low				
Project management is institutionalized by standardizing the interfaces between project work and ongoing organizational work.					
The transfer of decisions, information, products, and resources between project work and ongoing organizational work is standardized.					
The transfer of decisions, information, products, and resources between project work and ongoing organizational work occurs through well-defined deliverables.					
Roles and responsibilities of all stakeholders that interface with projects are well defined.					
A process exists that formally sanctions and authorizes the project.					

(continues)

Table 7.2 Process Alignment Summary Checklist (continued)

Performance Item	My Organization's Performance				
	High ← → Low				
A process exists to plan the project sufficiently for success.					
Each department has a defined process to aid project planning.					
A process exists to build the project's deliverables.					
A process exists to manage project work.					
A process exists to formally close out the project.					
Lessons learned are not only captured, but processed to prevent repeat mistakes and to improve overall project quality.					

8

Project Cost Management

I begin Part III, "Project Management Oversight," by introducing project cost management. A sound **project cost management system** is a strategic tool for the executive manager for three reasons:

1. It helps manage projects as investments.

2. It helps evaluate project management at the organizational level.

3. It offers tools that aid in strategic outsourcing.

For the first objective, the link between cost management and investment management is obvious: We want to maximize our investments by minimizing costs. The second benefit is less obvious. Successful project management involves many issues beyond cost (such as staff efficiency and process improvement). However, formal project cost management offers tools to track and evaluate those other aspects. Finally, cost management becomes the cornerstone for developing a comprehensive and easy-to-implement outsourcing strategy. For these reasons, project cost management deserves its own chapter.

For those of you who might want to scurry away in fear of a lot of dry, tedious math, you can relax; put on your fuzzy slippers, sit back, and read. The recognized standard for project cost management is called **earned value management** (**EVM**), or simply **earned value** (**EV**). And although it does contain some interesting equations, I reserve the heavy math for the advanced project and program managers. However, buried deep within EVM is a concept that easily can be described as serendipitous: the work package (yes, the very same work package defined in Chapter 3, "Project Definition and Planning," and the very same work package that we exploit for strategic outsourcing in later chapters).

Also serendipitously, EVM offers three additional benefits:

1. It can track and manage both costs and progress across multiple projects, programs, and even the portfolio.

2. It is a primary aid in determining root cause for project management issues.

3. It's compliant with the Sarbanes-Oxley act[1], which is required for fiscal project tracking.

Aside from a few minor annoyances, EVM offers excellent benefits for executive project management and oversight.

The goal of this chapter is to describe a project cost management system that is realistic and achievable for your organization, and that offers the following benefits:

- Supports fiscal responsibility (including Sarbanes-Oxley)

- Accurately tracks project costs

- Quickly identifies troubled projects

- Promotes, supports, and tracks projects as capital investments

- Promotes, supports, and tracks a balanced portfolio

- Adds flexibility to the organization work flow and resource usage

- Provides support to your planning and estimating activities

Roles and Responsibilities for Cost Management

A successful project cost management system is the result of a collaborative effort.

A successful project cost management system requires collaboration from executive management, financial management, technical and functional management, and project management.

Executive management wants to ensure that the portfolio supports organizational objectives, meets cultural and regulatory requirements, and offers benchmarks for process improvement and organizational oversight. Executive management is responsible for establishing the doctrine that drives the project budgeting and cost management processes, and for ensuring that financial management and project management comply with that doctrine.

The financial management department needs to achieve fiscal compliance and responsibility. A successful project budget and tracking system must integrate with other budgeting processes and easily map into the organization's accounting and financial reporting systems.

Project managers hope that the budgeting process reduces administrative red tape while offering sound planning and tracking tools. Through the PMO or other appropriate committee, project management collaborates with executive management to ensure that the system is pragmatic and aids the project Plan, Manage, and Build processes. Project management also uses the cost management system as a key metric for measuring continuous process improvement initiatives.

Technical and functional managers are collaborators because they provide time, cost, and resource estimates for the work packages. Executives and project managers then negotiate these estimates, and, eventually, functional managers make commitments to the plan. Functional managers are also concerned with how projects affect their budgets.

Table 8.1 summarizes cost management responsibilities.

Table 8.1   Roles and Responsibilities for Cost Management

Executive managers	Responsible and accountable for establishing the high-level doctrine and goals of the system.
Finance managers	Work with the project management department to establish the mechanics of the system itself. They are also responsible for ensuring that the system complies with Sarbanes-Oxley, organizational doctrine, and other fiscal requirements.
Project managers	Includes project designers, portfolio managers, and portfolio designers who implement and use the system to monitor and track projects and programs. They also use the system to conduct root-cause analysis for continuous process improvement.
Functional managers	Want to tie the cost of project activities back into their budgets, to justify resources and balance their own department's budget.

Developing a Cost Management Doctrine

Executive management is responsible for defining the doctrine and high-level objectives for the cost management system. In this section, I offer key areas to guide you when reviewing or defining your doctrine and objectives, which includes earned value concepts.

- Regulatory compliance
- Support for organizational financial policy
- Support for project investment strategy
- Life cycle costing
- Support for strategic outsourcing
- Support for key organizational infrastructure systems
- Support for project managers
- Level of rigor

Regulatory Compliance

The project cost management system must comply with local, state, and federal financial tracking and reporting requirements. This includes mandatory compliance with the Sarbanes-Oxley act; Securities and Exchange Commission (SEC) regulations; federal, state, and local income tax reporting and tracking; and all other regulations that are forced upon the organization.

The system must also support regulations imposed through optional programs such as grants, compliance with voluntary policies to improve corporate image, and compliance for certifications.

**Earned value management complies with all known
U.S. governmental regulations, including Sarbanes-Oxley.**

Support Organizational Financial Policy

The project cost management system should support and complement the overall organization's financial management policies and procedures. This includes budgeting, cost tracking, and chargeback systems.

In my experience as a consultant, one of the key reasons projects have difficulty getting resources is the undue burden functional managers bear to support projects. In many organizations, project activities take valuable resources from the functional manager without compensation. A fair system enables the functional managers to charge back the cost of their resources to the project, using a process such as activity-based costing (ABC).[2]

The following considerations are helpful in developing a sound project cost management doctrine:

- Work packages tie costs directly to activities and products:
  - As a result, they directly support key management tools such as ABC.
  - Clients and other stakeholders clearly see the results of invested resources.
- Work package costs should be charged back to the project:
  - This helps balance the functional department's budget.
  - It justifies hiring staff or consultants for departments that bear excessive project work.
- Earned value supports ABC.
- The system should provide complete, accurate cost accounting.

Support for Project Investment Strategy

One key theme in this book is that projects are financial investments. Therefore, the project cost management systems should support this notion. Project cost management systems should perform the following:

- Accurately allocate the true cost of investment analysis to the project.

- Accurately track the project costs and cost variance to determine the continued viability of the investment.

- Support the capital investment requirements for the organization.

- Define work packages to improve project tracking:

  - Progress is measurable and provable, not speculated.

  - Independent evaluators can measure progress in consistent ways.

Life Cycle Costing

Life cycle costing is a technique that requires managers to consider the full life cycle cost of a capital purchase (such as a large machine or computer) when planning.

Janet's IT Project and Life Cycle Costing

Janet is an IT project manager charged with planning a major server upgrade. While investigating replacement servers, she finds two vendors whose products meet her organization's needs. Servers from Acme Computer Systems (ACS) will cost her $50,000 to purchase and install. Servers from ACS's competitor, Total Computer Systems (TCS), will cost $75,000 to purchase and install.

However, Janet knows that TCS's maintenance and licensing contracts are generally more attractive: ACS's maintenance and licensing fees will cost her company $2,500 per month, and TCS's costs will be $1,150 per month.

After consulting with subject matter experts, Janet concludes that the useful life of the system is four years. During the four years, the total cost from ACS's computers will be $170,000, and TCS's total cost will be $130,200. She submits her project plan to include TCS servers.

However, Janet's company views IT as overhead, tries to cut costs where possible, and doesn't employ life cycle costing policies. Janet's management just cut her project budget severely, forcing her to go with ACS's servers.

In this example, lack of forethought and appropriate policy forced Janet's hand. She had to go with the cheaper short-term cost solution. However, this will cost her company more money over time. Short-term cost savings sometimes justifies longer-term costs; however, in general, the following holds true:

> **The project cost management doctrine should support life cycle costing and avoid punishing project managers who purchase more expensive items to achieve long-term savings.**

Strategic Outsourcing

The cost management system should support the strategic outsourcing policies and procedures. Fortunately, earned value offers information needed to decide whether work packages should be outsourced or done in-house (the classic **make–buy** decision). The quality control metrics placed on work packages enable project managers to outsource them easily and quickly during the project if plans change.

This approach also establishes a set of benchmarks that enables executives to compare the work done by internal departments to outside solutions. For example, an IT department might ask for bids to develop a software module by outside vendors. Project managers can then create in-house estimates and compare results. If the analysis frequently determines that software development should be outsourced, the IT department might need restructuring.

> **This technique enables executive managers to determine whether internal departments are well managed, properly structured, and properly funded.**

Therefore, the cost management system should support make–buy decisions for strategic outsourcing and support benchmarking for the performance of internal departments.

Support for Key Organizational Infrastructure Systems

A properly developed project cost management system offers these benefits, which should become requirements for your cost management system:

- The systems must align with process and operational work:
  - ◆ Project budgeting and tracking should integrate with the normal budgeting and tracking systems.
- Project budgets and costs should tie to the organizational chart of accounts.
- The system should enhance accuracy.
- The system should enhance future cost estimating.
- Functional managers' resource contributions must be accurately reported, to justify resource levels for their own work and justify adjustments to their resource pool.

Support for Project Managers

Project managers also benefit from earned value concepts. The project cost management systems should take advantage of these benefits:

- Accurately determine true progress, not speculative progress.
- Supply critical information for root-cause analysis for failed or troubled projects.
- Support trade-off decisions among time, cost, and scope:
  - ◆ Project managers might employ value engineering[3] to work packages.

- Project managers might find faster or less costly alternatives to building the work package product.

■ Offer PMs the ability to outsource work packages easily and quickly.

Level of Rigor

Our discussion of a cost management model involves a relatively high level of rigor. Appropriate departments (such as PMO and finance) should determine the right level of rigor for project cost management. Many organizations that are experienced in project management define different levels of rigor based on the type and size of projects. Work with your finance department and the project management group(s) to define an appropriate level of rigor for your project mix.

The Foundations for Earned Value Management

Further discussions require a basic understanding of earned value management (EVM).

Earned Value Management

The name **earned value (EV)** originates from its core concept that each project has a value. In earned value management, we deem that the value of a project is its burden cost. Although the true value is likely greater than the cost, this value is both speculative and immaterial to EVM's purpose; therefore, it's not considered. If we deem that the value of a project is its burden cost, then the value of each work package in a project is worth its burden cost. As a work package completes, we "earn" its "value" toward the project. These values then become the basis for project cost and progress tracking.

At any point in time, the project plan tells us which work packages should have been completed. The sum of their estimated burden costs gives us the **planned value (PV).** The work packages we actually completed by that date tell us our EV. The difference between the two values tells us whether we're behind or ahead of schedule.

If your project consists of landscaping four separate areas of an office complex, you might define one work package for each area and estimate their burden cost. The project team might determine that each area should take one week to complete, as shown in Figure 8.1.

At the end of the first week, our plan tells us that we should have completed work package (WP) area 1 and that our planned value is $5,000.

Let's assume that at the end of the first week, we successfully completed the work package for area 1 and earn its value ($5,000) toward our project. We are on schedule. In EV terms, we say that our schedule variance is zero because our PV is equal to our EV.

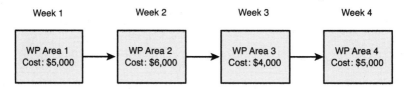

Figure 8.1 Simple EV example

Now we determine the actual cost to do the work. For this example, let's assume that it actually cost us $4,900. We're under budget. In EV terms, we say that we have a positive cost variance because our actual costs are less than our PV.

This means we are on schedule and under budget (by $100).

Work Packages, the WBS, and the GBS

Recall from Chapter 3 that the work breakdown structure (WBS) decomposes the high-level activities into smaller activities called work packages: a unit of work that produces a well-defined piece of a product or deliverable. Also recall that the goals breakdown structure (GBS) defines the measurable characteristics (quality control measures) of the products of those work packages. Finally, earned value establishes the burden cost of each work package.

> **The intersection of cost, quality, and work firmly defines the work package.**

At this point, we can roll up the cost of work packages to determine the cost of each product or deliverable produced in the project. Later, we'll see that this eases strategic outsourcing.

Developing the Project Budget

This section presents executive management concepts for developing project budgets.

Budgeting Concerns for Executives

This section offers key concepts to aid executives in developing budgeting policies that satisfy the expectations and requirements of key stakeholders. Specifically, we examine the following:

- Budgeting for internal resources (internal resources are *not* free!)
- Budgeting for the cost of managing the project
- Risk contingency allocations
- Profit considerations

- Privacy considerations
- Tax considerations

Internal Resources Are Not Free

In my consulting practice, I frequently discover an interesting notion: Internal resources are free. (Yes, I've actually heard seminar attendees use those exact words.) They present this argument: "These people are already on our payroll; their costs have been accounted for in the department budget. Therefore, it doesn't matter what tasks that they do…they're already paid for."

Consider these examples of this fallacy.

The information technology manager identifies the costs of a project by listing hardware, software, facility upgrades, and outside services. The costs of the internal staff needed to evaluate, select, install, manage, and roll out the project are conspicuously missing.

The engineering manager viewing a production line extension project documents anticipated costs for material, equipment, and external contract services. The costs for internal staff engineers to design, develop, test, implement, and operate the new system are, apparently, free.

Project costs must include internal resource costs, costs for procured goods and services, and ancillary costs, such as travel, overhead, and vendor management.

True project cost includes the cost of internal resources.

Let's assume that I can assign a resource to one of two tasks. One task offers a high return on investment; the other has a low return. Common sense dictates that management should allocate the resource to the high-return activity. Additionally, if you are managing projects as investments, then 1) you must allocate the total, true cost to the investment, and 2) if you can get the same or better result from an outside supplier, you are doing the organization a disservice by not outsourcing. You should also consider the number of employees you'd have if you outsourced all your project work—a very viable strategy.

In this book, we seek to optimize resource utilization, not in the sense that resources are busy all the time (a relatively unimportant metric, as we will see later), but in the sense that they are allocated and perform the most valuable actions available. The cost of internal resources must be allocated appropriately.

Cost of Project Management

The costs associated with project management are generally applied as a separate line item in the project budget: It is a separate work package or set of work packages. Whether management decides to outsource these work packages (such as hiring a project manager consultant to run the project) or keep it in-house, some level of oversight should remain in-house and be budgeted accordingly. Another way to budget the cost of managing the project is to include it in the overhead factor. This is less desirable because it tends to be less accurate.

> **Project costs should include the cost of project management as separate work packages or line items.**

Project Risk

A senior manager once asked me how my project planning was progressing. I indicated that my plan was almost complete; I was just doing final adjustments and allocating risk contingency to the plan. He stopped me midsentence saying, "Wait a minute, Bender, what do you mean by risk contingency?"

> I responded, "You know, allocations for time and money to deal with unexpected events or when things go wrong."
>
> "No, no, Bender," he replied, "we believe in success-oriented scheduling. Nothing ever goes wrong—that's why we hired you."
>
> I was smart enough not to say anything, but I definitely thought, "Well, if you're going to compare me to a deity, I should at least get a raise."

In formal project management, two kinds of reserves exist: project reserves and management reserves. **Project reserves** are included in the baselines and available to the project managers at their discretion. Project managers develop this **contingency** from known risks.

> **Projects should include reasonable risk contingency for both time and money.**

In addition, executive management maintains **management reserve.** These reserves are for "unknown unknowns," or projects that get hit with a lot of bad luck or have bad project managers. Management reserve is part of the project budget but not part of the project baseline—project managers need to ask for it. This creates an additional check-and-balance to monitor projects. When done properly, management reserve spent on one project should be reimbursed by unused contingency from another project.

Profit Allocation

Many organizations that perform projects for outside clients prefer to embed profits into their cost structure. The project budget then becomes the sell price to the client. This is a common method when project services are sold as time-and-materials contracts, in which each hour a project team member spends on a project is billed to the client. It is also useful for internal projects, in which activity-based costing is employed and each department is considered a profit center.

However, this doctrine removes (or, at least, reduces) the performing organization's capability to separate profits from costs. This restriction might impinge on nonmonetary value tracks, such as customer relations, corporate image, or new technology development. For example, an account representative might want to offer a small project at burden cost or even at a loss, to develop the business relationship or for future business. Using the true burden cost offers a more accurate picture of the investment.

> **Separating profit from the cost structure gives the project designer flexibility in choosing nonrevenue value tracks.**

Salary Banding

Seminar attendees and clients frequently express the concern that project managers shouldn't know people's salaries.

Salary banding is a popular mechanism to allocate costs of human resources while maintaining stricter security. If your human resources (HR) department establishes salary ranges for particular job functions, then the project management team can use the average cost for a particular job function or title. Then they don't need to know the actual salary of an individual.

If the salary range of a level-2 product marketing manager is between $45,000 and $65,000, the project management team can comfortably assign an unburdened cost of $55,000 for all resources with that job title. HR and finance might present the salary band with an overhead rate multiplier or might just supply the fully burdened cost for each band.

Tax and Government Aid Considerations

Taxes are complex issues that the finance group usually handles, and the details are beyond the scope of this book. Our requirements for developing a sound budgeting system demand both accuracy in cost allocation and support for projects as capital investments; therefore, we cannot ignore the tax considerations.

Project teams make many decisions that affect taxes. They select capital equipment, which might be fully deducted under Section 179 of the tax code, or receive investment tax incentives. They might hire or conduct training, which can be subject to tax breaks or direct aid from various government agencies.

As senior executives, you want project teams to take advantage of such benefits when making these decisions.

**Your project cost management doctrine must enable
projects to benefit from such tax and aid considerations.**

Furthermore, you might want to develop benefits and rewards for project managers who take advantage of such benefits. Tying life cycle costing with tax benefits provides your project manager with a comprehensive cost and budgeting strategy that will save your organization money.

Computing Work Package Costs

Accurate project budgets include all cost aspects of a work package. After all, the cost of purchasing gummy bears is not restricted to the price of the product. You must also take into account the cost of fuel to drive to the store, the time of the purchaser to go to the store, and the cost of quality control to make sure that the purchaser acquired the right amount, type, and freshness of the gummy bears.

The finance department should offer the appropriate breakdown for cost allocation in cooperation with project management. For our simplified approach, let's define three categories derived from the project manager's perspective: cost of the project team, cost of internal services, and other expenses. For our model, total work package cost is calculated as shown here:

$$\textit{Total Work Package Cost} = \sum \textit{(Internal Resources} \\ \textit{+ Internal Services + Other Expenses)}$$

First, I address the cost of the project team.

Internal Resource Costing

Most internal human resource costs are based on either salary or hourly wage. Most organizations have a multiplier to convert salaries or hourly wages to fully burdened costs, commonly called the **overhead rate.** This rate prorates the cost of such items as health insurance, allocation for utilities (such as lighting and heating), allocation for rent (such as floor space), and other allocations that the financial group establishes across the wage base.

A staff member's cost to the company is calculated as follows:

$$\textit{Fully Burdened Cost = (Salary x (1 + Overhead Rate))}$$

This is the **fully burdened cost** for the resource and is expressed in units of time (such as $75.32 per hour).

Our goal for project management is to establish the true, accurate cost of each task or work package in the project. Chapter 3 offers basic concepts for estimating tasks. Those estimates are based on the effort that a staff member actually expended on the activity. The cost incurred by the staff member on this activity is the fully burdened rate times the effort expended, not in calendar time, but in actual dedicated effort for the task. The sum of all resources applied to the activity becomes the internal labor costs for the activity.

$$Internal\ Resource\ Costs =$$
$$\sum (Fully\ Burdened\ Costs)\ \text{for all staff}$$

Internal Services Costing

As with many business processes, projects use services commonly available to the rest of the organization, such as reproduction and graphic design. Clearly, these services are chargeable to the project and should be included in the project budget. As with any client–vendor relationship, an organization can offer these services based on a certain unit of time (such as $50 per hour for production services) or on a fixed-price basis (such as $450 for producing 20 copies of the final project report). As in any client–vendor relationship, the service provider can fix-price a service only if it's well defined—something the project team should do anyway. In addition, both executive management and the project team prefer the fixed-price method. This method aligns with activity-based costing practices and enables the project management team to compare costs and services between internal and external offerings, increasing the project manager's flexibility in developing the project's deliverables.

Other Expenses

The project budget must include all costs associated with the activities, including the following:

- Travel costs
- Shipping and stocking costs
- Additional insurance needed for the project
- Quality control costs associated with the project
- Cost of other internal services not otherwise allocated
- Cost of external services, including consulting and outsourcing
- Any other associated costs

Developing the Cost Baseline

We now have the necessary building blocks to develop a project cost baseline. Again, we take a work package focus. Project managers develop the WBS using a top-down approach, ultimately creating the work packages. You can roll back up the cost of the work packages to establish accurate project budgets. I use this concept to develop the project budget using these three steps:

1. Determine work package costs
2. Develop a time-phased budget
3. Develop the completed cost baseline

Project Cost Baseline

The final result of project budget analysis is the project cost baseline. PMI defines the project cost baseline as the time-phased cost plan. The WBS does this intrinsically by rolling up work packages into phases. We explore the concept of phases in greater detail in subsequent chapters. For this chapter, it is sufficient to understand that phases essentially are a collection of work packages.

As part of their normal activities, the project management team puts the work packages in a logical sequence (see Figure 3.4, Sample Critical Path, in Chapter 3). This establishes the budget in both a phased and a time perspective.

The result is a cumulative cost-line graph, also known as an "S" curve because of its distinctive shape. Figure 8.2 shows the cumulative amount of money that the project should spend over time.

Phase Gates

In classical project management, projects undergo formal senior management reviews at the end of each phase. At those reviews, go or no-go decisions determine whether the project should continue. Essentially, this is a funding issue—the project cannot proceed if funding is not approved.

With this approach, executive management formally sanctions a project management team to proceed into the next phase of a project. This formally funds all areas of the next phase, but no further. When executive management authorizes a phase, the project manager can use internal resources according to the project management plan (and as promised by functional managers), issue purchase orders, and sign contracts on behalf of the project.

Reconciling Project Phases with Financial Cycles

One final concern for fiscal tracking is that project work packages don't always start or end on nice, even fiscal period boundaries. Senior managers, the financial department, and the PMO should work collaboratively to determine appropriate reporting and data collection processes to handle this situation.

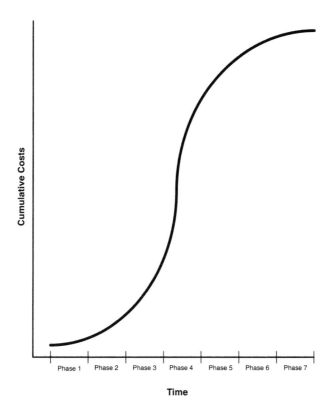

Figure 8.2 Project cost-line graph, or "S" curve

A well-defined project plan offers a list of work packages that should be completed by the end of a financial cycle. This milestone can provide a savvy financial department with all it needs to handle this concern without sacrificing the project's phases.

Managing Project Costs

After the project starts, the project manager and finance group have the primary responsibility for project cost management and tracking. They must report progress periodically and escalate exceptions as they occur. The project communication plan describes how to escalate the exceptions. In this section, I describe how to detect them.

Project Cost Management Basics

We are now ready to start tracking project costs. Serendipitously, this mechanism also enables us to track actual schedule progress. First, we examine the three schedules needed to determine progress; then we discuss how to track the progress using earned value.

The Three Schedules

Tracking involves three metrics or schedules:

- **Baseline**—The formal, official, originally sanctioned plan, plus approved scope changes

- **Actuals**—The amounts actually expended on behalf of the activity, work package, phase, or project

- **Current plan**—An updated plan that includes all changes (not just approved scope changes)

As the project unfolds, the project management team gathers actual results and compares them to the current plan. The team continuously adjusts the plan to account for internal project changes. The project management team analyzes the variances to determine whether corrective action is required. Extreme variances demand escalation and exception reporting, as defined in the communication plan.

Tracking Costs with Earned Value

Remember that EV is based on the concept that a project is worth its burden cost. Therefore, each work package is worth its burden cost. As we complete a work package, we earn its value toward the project.

Based on this principle, EV employs three metrics for variance detection. Note that these acronyms have recently changed from the original Department of Defense (DOD) standard for EV from the 1960s:

- **Planned value (PV)**—The total value of all work packages that should have been completed to date

- **Earned value (EV)**—The total value of all work packages actually completed to date

- **Actual cost (AC)**—The actual cost to complete the work packages to date

For an ideal project that is exactly on time and on budget, PV, EV, and AC all are equal. For our discussion, we add one final metric:

- **Budget at completion (BAC)**—The expected total cost of the project.

Let's look at another example.[4] We examine a simple project consisting of three work packages, labeled A, B, and C. The project team estimates that each work package should take one month to complete. For this example, we assume that the tasks run sequentially. The burden cost (and, therefore, the value) of work package A is $5,000, work package B is $10,000, and work package C is $5,000. The total project budget is BAC = $20,000. Figure 8.3 shows the precedence diagram for this simple project.

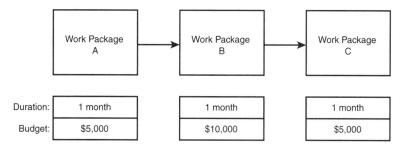

Figure 8.3   Earned value sample project

Let's assume that we complete work package A on time. At the end of month 1, we show $5,000 of earned value. We also capture the actual cost of the task and enter that in AC under the first month; let's assume that it's $4,800.

At the end of month 2, we're only 80 percent of the way through work package B. The question arises, "How much value have we earned?" In this situation, the answer is $0. Because we haven't completed the work package, we don't earn its value. Although the EVM standard does allow for partial completion under some conditions, we earn a work package's value only when it's completed (commonly known as the 0–100% rule in EVM) in this book.

For the rest of the chart, let's assume that we complete work package B in month 3 and that its actual cost was $11,000. We complete work package C in month 4, and its actual cost was $4,800. This yields the information in Table 8.2.

Table 8.2   Earned Value Table

| | Month | | | |
Metric	1	2	3	4
PV	$5,000	$15,000	$20,000	
EV	$5,000	$5,000	$15,000	$20,000
AC	$4,800	$4,800	$15,800	$20,600

Reporting and Exception Detection

Although we might use Table 8.2 for reporting purposes, you can graph the numbers for improved presentation. Figure 8.4 shows a common single-project graph. This graph plots the percentage cost and schedule variance on a periodic basis. For completeness, I offer the equations for the percentage variances here:

$$Cost\ Variance\ Percent = \left(\frac{EV - AC}{EV}\right) \times 100\%$$

$$Schedule\ Variance\ Percent = \left(\frac{EV - PV}{PV}\right) \times 100\%$$

The equations are deliberately designed to be graphed. One key and sometimes confusing concept of earned value is that when it's graphed, up is always good and down is always bad. Although this depiction might seem childish, when tracking an earned value–cost variance graph downward, one instinctively thinks that costs are reducing; however, the opposite is occurring. Table 8.3 illustrates this concept.

Table 8.3   Earned Value Variance Analysis

	Variance % < 0	Variance % = 0	Variance % > 0
Cost variance %	Over budget	On budget	Under budget
Schedule variance %	Behind schedule	On schedule	Ahead of schedule

For completeness, we add control limits to the graph. The purpose of the control limits is to signal when the project is in trouble. Classically, when the cost variance percentage or schedule variance percentage crosses the inner control limit, the project management team must take corrective action. If either variance percentage crosses the outer control limit, the project manager must escalate the issue to senior management. The location of the control limits varies among organizations and project categories.

In Figure 8.4, the cost variance has decreased (meaning that the project is costing more than expected). The cost variance percentage crosses an inner control limit. This forces the project management team to take corrective action through problem solving, root cause analysis, or some other technique. We see in the following period a slight increase, indicating that the corrective action might be taking hold and reversing the severe downward trend. If the trend had continued, it would have eventually crossed the outer control limit, forcing the project management team to escalate the issue to the PMO, steering committee, sponsor, or other senior management representative.

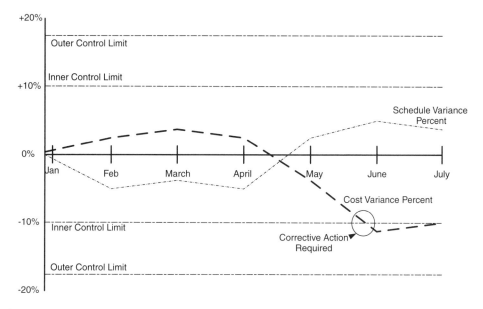

Figure 8.4 Earned value control limits graph

Conclusions and Summary

Executive management views projects as capital investments. Successful investment analysis requires accurate cost management and portrayal. In this chapter, we examined classical budgeting techniques and expanded upon those to create the building blocks needed for prudent investment management. These building blocks also enable executive management to accurately track project and program progress and conduct root-cause analysis for issues as they arise.

Additionally, these building blocks conform to contemporary regulatory compliance requirements, including Sarbanes-Oxley, and advanced organizational management techniques, including ABC.

In the next chapter, we expand upon these building blocks to develop a comprehensive capital investment–oriented project portfolio. These same tools also afford project managers greater flexibility in project planning, scheduling, and cost management.

Use Table 8.4 to rate how well your organization manages project costs.

Table 8.4 Project Cost Management Summary Checklist

Performance Item	My Organization's Performance				
	High ⟵			⟶ Low	
The project cost management system supports regulatory compliance, including Sarbanes-Oxley.					
The project cost management system supports organizational financial policy and procedures.					
The project cost management system supports the organization's project investment strategy.					
The project cost management system includes life cycle costing.					
The project cost management system supports the organization's strategic outsourcing strategy.					
The project cost management system supports key organizational infrastructure systems.					
The project cost management system supports project managers.					
The level of rigor is appropriate for different classes of projects.					

9

Project Oversight

We have seen that project planning can be an involved process. Project objectives must successfully integrate with strategic objectives, and projects themselves must integrate with both the ongoing business process and the organization. This chapter presents tools to help you ensure that these activities are working properly and that project management is improving in your organization. At the executive level, you want to ensure that the following hold true:

- Projects achieve the executive-designed goals that take the organization toward its vision:
  - ◆ Portfolios include a suite of projects and programs that take the organization in a unified direction as designed in the organization's strategic plan.
  - ◆ Project objectives and plans conform to the organization's values and culture.
- Project management integrates with the organization:
  - ◆ Information flows smoothly between projects and other ongoing business processes.
  - ◆ Resources move smoothly between projects and other organizational activities.
  - ◆ The workload is balanced throughout the organization, maximizing efficiency.
- The processes that develop projects support these objectives and continuously improve:
  - ◆ Processes are compliant with internal and external regulations and requirements.
  - ◆ Processes support and promote a healthy organizational culture and information and resource flow.
  - ◆ Processes are efficient, achieving the project goals with a minimum of waste.
- Project managers have sufficient skills, guidance, and tools to develop and maintain successful project plans:

- Project managers have sufficient training, tools, time, and guidance.
- Project managers have access to needed subject matter experts.

As the environment changes and the projects unfold, you also must ensure that you confront and handle changes to projects and the environment to retain continued quality.

Designing an oversight system to meet these goals initially might seem daunting. Fortunately, the discipline of project management handles a significant portion of this oversight. Our job is to ensure that those systems are in place and to cover areas that the project management discipline does not include.

The Three Perspectives of Project Oversight

When we take the viewpoint that projects are an ongoing business process, we realize that we can manage them similar to any other ongoing process. Two tools are at our disposal to achieve this: **quality control** and **quality assurance.** Again, I take some liberties to ease understanding and to reduce clutter.

Quality control focuses on the product, making sure that the products created by the project meet their specifications and requirements. Quality control involves inspecting, testing, demonstrating, analyzing, and evaluating the products to make sure that they conform to the client's requirements. At the executive level, let's refer to this as **product quality**.

Quality assurance focuses on the process that made the product: It ensures that the processes and procedures (both the project's and the technological methodologies) are performed correctly. Quality assurance isn't concerned with the product or result, but with how the product was made. If we are installing an engine on a jet's wing, quality assurance makes sure that the engine was always level while it was hoisted to the wing, that the mounting flanges were aligned when the engine met the wing, and that the fasteners were installed properly, to ensure a tight assembly while preventing overstressed components. We must rely on the process to make sure that the engine doesn't fall off during the stress of flight.

Similarly, if we are developing the goals of a project, we want to make sure that the goals breakdown structure was performed correctly and the component designs include the right specifications. Therefore, when we combine them into the final product, we want to know that the product will work and meet its goals. Furthermore, we want to make sure that we don't overspecify the components, creating waste. As with the jet engine example, we rely on following a defined process to ensure quality.

Most quality assurance processes focus on product generation. At the executive level, we need to take this one step further. In addition to ensuring that the processes create the right products, we want the managerial aspects of project management to run well, such as communication, efficient use of resources, and proper change management, to name a few. Let us refer to both these technical and managerial aspects as **project quality**.

The project management discipline addresses both quality control and quality assurance, reducing the executive's effort in oversight. As an executive, you are responsible for defining and enforcing the doctrine that ensures these actions are taken, and then the organization's quality control and quality assurance departments perform the actions.

The third area executives must cover is ensuring that the projects' objectives align with the organization's vision, mission, value statements, quality statements, and strategic plan through the OGBS. This provides three perspectives for oversight (also portrayed in Figure 9.1):

- **Product quality**—Making sure that the products or services produced by the projects meet requirements. Quality control validates product quality.

- **Project quality**—Evaluating the execution of the projects, to ensure proper product development, proper resource utilization, interproject communication, and other key aspects that make projects correct and efficient. Quality assurance validates project quality.

- **Link to executive team**—Maintaining the link between the projects and executive management, making sure that executive management supports the projects' goals and that both product quality and project quality are being achieved.

Figure 9.1   Project oversight

Bottom-Up Approach

Previously, I presented concepts for defining the organization, communicating strategic objectives, and developing clear project objectives. These are all top-down activities. Executives define the organization's vision, mission, values, and quality statements (the organization definition statements) and promulgate those down through the OGBS so that the employees perform the right actions and build the right products.

Conversely, monitoring and controlling begins at the lowest level of the organization. Consider programmers writing a software module. Once the programmers know what to write, our responsibility becomes making sure they write it correctly. We inspect both the process used to write the module and the module itself. We accumulate the results of those inspections into reports that combine with reports from other modules. These reports are summarized, travel up the organization, and ultimately reach your desk. These are all bottom-up activities. Therefore, I present this chapter from the bottom up so that you can see how information and quality management ultimately lead to project oversight.

The Responsibility of Project Oversight

Chapter 4, "Strategic Alignment," presents several options for developing a project oversight group, committee, or team. A complete oversight system might employ more than one group or department. Therefore, you should develop the roles and responsibilities through a collaborative effort among yourselves (as executive managers), the project management group, the quality department, and the functional managers. I present three classical approaches here.

One common architecture uses the steering committee to define, select, and monitor project progress from an executive level, providing the linkage to the executive team. The steering committee selects projects to include in the portfolio, ensures that these projects align with and support the organization, and continually tracks projects as the environment and projects change. They also define the doctrine for both quality assurance and quality control, but delegate detailed oversight to the program management office (PMO). The PMO doesn't necessarily conduct the quality control or assurance activities; it just makes sure that they happen.

Other organizations use a portfolio management department linked to the strategic planning committee to ensure executive linkage. Here the portfolio designers and managers maintain project alignment. Such organizations might employ a chief project officer (CPO) to provide a clear communication path between the portfolio managers and the executives. Quality assurance and quality control are separate organizations which may report to the CPO or separate quality group.

You also might use a separate functional department of project management to oversee project and product quality. This can be dangerous because you're putting the fox in charge of the henhouse, but this can work in the right cultures.

Assigning roles and responsibilities for specific oversight functions depends on the existing organizational structure and culture and the types of projects you do.

Product Quality—Quality Control

Product quality (quality control) begins with the most detailed level of the project. Although this is arguably the simplest of the considerations for project oversight, it is the core of the oversight activities. When product quality management doesn't start with the smallest component, quality management becomes flawed, at best.

Consider our jet engine again. The engine itself might contain a few dozen fan blades designed to push air through the engine. If one blade is flawed—for example, it weighs more than the rest—the engine will be out of balance and eventually will rip apart. Therefore, each blade must be properly inspected to very tight tolerances before it is assembled into the engine.

We see from this example that we can't just inspect the final product, we need to inspect the components that make up that product. Let's look at a software system. If we fail to inspect each component before we integrate the system, the errors will be difficult to both find and fix. If we inspect each component, we can remove many of the errors, significantly reducing the problem.

Product quality management is a technical issue and is usually subject to organizations' quality control department; however…

> **…executive management is responsible for establishing
> the quality control doctrine and level of discipline.**

We present those aspects of product quality management that are needed to develop appropriate doctrine and level of discipline.

Requirements Definition

The quality control process starts with solid requirements. I addressed their characteristics and development in earlier chapters. However, remember that requirements are measurable and verifiable characteristics of the products or services of the project. The client, in conjunction with the project or portfolio designers and other key stakeholders, defines the requirements. Requirements must have these qualities:

- **Measurable**—We can quality-control them.
- **Complete**—Nothing is left out; they are the complete set of requirements.
- **Specific**—No ambiguity exists.

Most products are built from separate components, which are eventually integrated into the final product (service or result). If the components are flawed, the final product must also be flawed.

**The key to successful product quality control
is to begin with the lowest-level components.**

In earlier discussions, I presented the concept of the work package: the unit of work that produces a well-defined component of a deliverable. I also presented the concept that the work package must be so well defined that the organization can outsource it for a fixed price contract. Here I rephrase that stipulation to say that the organization can quality-control the results.

To illustrate the importance of this concept, let's consider a computer system development project. For simplicity, let's eliminate the hardware concerns and work strictly with the software development. The primary product of the project is the software system. To build the system, the subject matter experts develop software components called modules, each performing well-defined functions. The system's design document identifies these functions. The goals breakdown structure (GBS) identifies measurable specifications for these functions. For this example, let's assume that the team defined the GBS well: Specifications for each module are thorough, measurable, and specific. Now let's consider two separate scenarios: 1) The project doesn't have appropriate product quality control procedures, and 2) the project has appropriate product quality control procedures.

Example 1: Systems Integration Without Product Quality Procedures

Systems component developers begin by complying with GBS specifications and making sure that their components meet those specifications. This continues until the project comes under stress. Time, resource, cost, and technical stresses pressure the developers to hurry through development and to cut corners. Because we lack product quality control, the work package owners submit their components to the system's integrators without external quality evaluation.

The project continues apparently on time and on budget. The work packages are being completed on time and within resource constraints. Work package owners declare success, truly feeling that the cut corners are unimportant. The project proceeds as planned until the integration phase.

During the integration phase, the cut corners manifest themselves. Component A doesn't properly interface with component B. However, the problem is not quite that simple. During integration, hundreds of components combine into the system. The cut corners don't reveal themselves in nice, clean, well-codified error messages; they reveal themselves in a hodgepodge of mishaps, crashes, and strange results that are virtually impossible to trace.

Management now needs to make a decision: Ship the flawed system on time, or spend undeterminable time and money to fix the bugs?

Many cultural divides begin here: Staff and management claim that they want quality, yet they bypass quality to give in to immediate and short-term pressures.

Managers say one thing; but under stress, they do another. In this example, it's interesting to note that the time lost in finding and fixing the bugs is far greater than the time saved by not inspecting the components. Inspection would have quickly identified a majority of the bugs, and the bugs would have been fixed more quickly because the design was still fresh in the developers' minds. By waiting until system integration, the team now needs to spend extra time locating and resolving the bugs. This process becomes more complicated because the original developers are likely no longer on the project—and if they are, the design is no longer fresh in their minds.

Now let's examine the same scenario with appropriate quality control.

Example 2: Systems Integration With Quality Control Procedures

Systems component developers begin by complying with GBS specification, making sure that their components meet those specifications. This continues until the project comes under stress. Time, resource, cost, and technical stresses pressure the developers to cut corners.

Because we have product quality control procedures in place, the quality control group catches the problems at the first work package that doesn't meet its specifications. Quality control demands that the team fix the problems. Although the team begins to feel stress imposed by the demands, the cost to repair is small (relative to the first scenario). Forced to comply with quality control, developers feel frustrated and, perhaps, some anxiety. Some adjustments in both attitude and schedule might occur at this point. With proper leadership, the team adjusts and quality becomes the norm. The team develops a culture of quality. This change in attitude causes the team to focus on "getting it right the first time."

During the integration phase, the team sees the reward. Although no one expects the system to be error free, the errors that do occur are both simple and identifiable. The result is an integration phase that flows smoothly; errors are quickly identified and resolved.

> **Projects that incorporate sound GBS practices**
> **combined with sound product quality control practices**
> **run faster, better, and cheaper than those that don't.**

Successful project execution demands sound product quality control:

- The GBS develops component-level specifications that are measurable, verifiable, and quality controlled.

- Work packages are not accepted until all specifications are verified through approved quality control procedures.

Note that when project teams meet these two conditions, they can outsource work packages for a fixed price.

Creativity and Entrepreneurship

Some believe that rigorous quality control can squash creativity and even entrepreneurship. The discipline of project management not only allows for these, but also offers tools for creativity and entrepreneurship in different stages of projects. Research projects, discovery stages, prototyping, and other tools enable subject matter experts to experiment and try out different scenarios to achieve the project's goals in its early stages. However, at some point, sound project methodologies demand that the team choose a design and identify the requirements for the product. These requirements and specifications must be quality controlled.

The team can even implement late discoveries through the project's change management system.

Responsibility for Quality Control

Because many cultures attempt to skimp on quality when under stress, a group outside project management should conduct the quality control and quality assurance procedures. The lowest level at which the project team leadership and quality team leadership should intersect is at the project sponsor level. In many companies, quality control and quality assurance report directly to the president—an architecture I personally prefer.

Project Quality—Quality Assurance

Project quality evaluates whether the project is executed the "correct" way. It answers the question, "Did the project team follow the doctrine, process, and procedures?"

Unlike product quality, which focuses on technical issues, project quality involves two aspects: a technical aspect and a management aspect. Each discipline involved in the project incorporates technical procedures for executing work. For example, accountants have procedures for auditing finances, engineers have procedures for designing machines, and product marketing managers have procedures for conducting focus groups.

Additionally, project quality includes a management aspect: We must ensure that the project manager and project management team perform their work correctly.

For the rest of this section, I focus on the latter aspect, with the understanding that the discussion applies equally to the technical aspects of the project.

Roles

Developing and executing a successful project quality management system requires a working knowledge of project management. Therefore, the group most commonly called on to perform this oversight is the PMO. Furthermore, the PMO usually defines the processes and procedures for project management—they *own* the methodology. They can then receive reports, lessons learned, and project metrics to evaluate their procedures and offer continuous process improvement.

Although other executives, such as the project sponsor, can perform this function, different sponsors manage their projects differently, which yields inconsistencies. Politics among the project sponsors also affects organizational efficiency.

> **As with product quality control, executive management is responsible for establishing the doctrine and level of discipline employed in project quality.**

As an executive manager, you are more involved in this aspect than in quality control. Your job involves receiving reports from the portfolio and program managers regarding their actions to further ensure compliance.

Project Quality Management Actions

If you already have established methodologies in place, overseeing project management is neither tedious nor difficult. The job of oversight is two-fold: 1) to make sure that the project manager is doing his or her job and 2) to ensure that the methodology is sound. To achieve these goals, we define four key actions:

- Establish appropriate project quality metrics
- Conduct regular reviews and reporting
- Communicate both up and down (hierarchical reporting)
- Communicate exceptions through exception reporting

Establish Appropriate Project Quality Metrics

Project quality, similar to product quality, demands appropriate metrics.

Metrics are a key element for successfully tracking management functions to prevent politically motivated or distorted reports.

As described in the previous chapter, earned value management (EVM) offers excellent metrics for project quality oversight. You can find the remaining metrics in the OGBS or balanced scorecard. Remember that the organization's goals begin with the organization's definition statements and are broken down using a balanced scorecard or OGBS approach, described in Chapter 5, "A Framework for Strategic Alignment." These combine to provide metrics for both the technical and managerial aspects of project quality.

When problems arise, standard root-cause analysis, problem solving, and other traditional methods can identify the cause of the problem area. These result in change requests, which are tracked through the standard project change management system. When the root cause is the methodology itself, the PMO is notified so that it can implement appropriate changes.

Regular Reviews and Reporting

When we inspect a product, we must wait until the product is finished to inspect it. However, monitoring the work is an ongoing activity. Therefore, regular quality reviews are mandatory in most situations—and are certainly mandatory for outsourced projects or work packages. Progress and quality reporting should also be performed regularly.

Reports should concentrate on three quality areas: concerns within the organization performing the project (the **performing organization**), concerns within the client's organization, and concerns within the boundary between the two.

Reports don't need to be long or formal: Five minutes per project is fine for most situations in which methodologies are strong and staff is well trained. If these components are lacking, a proportional increase in reporting time occurs. Large-scale, high-visibility, or complex projects can also take longer.

Hierarchical Reporting

Regular reporting also provides a consistent communication path up and down the organization. This enables executives to communicate changes in the organizational environment, project situation, or other key issues to project managers; it also enables project managers to funnel key issues to executive management. Depending on organization size, project size, organization structure, and methodologies, hierarchical reporting might span several layers.

A formalized process for communicating progress throughout the organization helps enforce oversight, ensures that project managers stay on top of their projects, and prevents issues from falling through the cracks.

For example, project managers might report directly to the PMO on a semimonthly basis. The PMO might summarize the status of all the projects, along with resource utilization and project scope issues, to the portfolio manager(s) on a monthly basis. The portfolio manager might summarize and report to the strategic planning committee on a monthly or quarterly basis.

In later chapters, we examine how you can use EVM to roll up project and program status for higher-level management and for communicating key issues.

Exception Reporting

A problem that affects the portfolio or strategic plan should be escalated immediately instead of waiting until the next status report. In the previous chapter, I presented how you can use EVM to initiate an exception report up the chain. Similar mechanisms placed at the right areas ensure that key issues reach the right person in time to correct any problems.

> **A well-designed and staunchly followed problem escalation plan is a key factor in project oversight.**

Linkage to Executive Team

I have addressed two of the three aspects of oversight: product quality–quality control, and project quality–quality assurance. In this final section, I address the last aspect: linkage to the executive team.

I once conducted a seminar for a research-driven company. During the project scope presentation, one attendee raised his hand and told me that his project had been going on for ten years. I asked him when he expected the project to finish, and he indicated that he saw no end in sight. Needless to say, he wasn't happy when I told him not to share that with his manager—if I was his manager and heard that, I'd terminate the project on the spot. This "project" had gone on so long that it was no longer a project—just an ongoing, useless activity. Clearly, this project had lost its way.

Although this might be an extreme example, run-on projects are still quite prevalent in both industry and not-for-profit organizations. A run-on project is one that just keeps going. It might have had an original estimate of six months, but after two years, the project is still active.

Several issues cause run-on projects, including ill-defined objectives, unachievable objectives, constantly moving objectives (usually caused by ill-focused executives), and just bad project management. The previous sections regarding project oversight handle the latter of these items. This section handles the first three. More specifically, our goals for this section include the following:

- We're making money (or demonstrating fiscal responsibility).

- We're achieving our strategic goals.

- We're following our values and supporting our culture.

Additionally, this section covers how to handle constantly changing objectives: the dynamic portfolio.

Our Assets

Let's consider the following assets:

- **The project charter**—The charter contains the business-level objectives that link the project directly to the strategic plan. The charter also contains the project constraints (conditions under which executive management will undertake the project) and project risks.

- **Project change management**—The process to evaluate changes that may affect the goals or constraints defined in the charter.

- **Project methodology**—The methodology includes defined policies and procedures for executing the project that conform to and support the goals of the organization. Ideally, this methodology incorporates the concepts presented in the previous two sections.

What We Do

Two mechanisms exist for ensuring proper linkage between the project and executive management. The first is management by exception. This method assumes that no news is good news; no regularly scheduled reviews occur, and we simply track the project through the change management system. This requires that the executive team be properly represented in the project's change control board (CCB), through a sponsor, representative of the PMO, or steering committee liaison. Although this is a viable method, it should be attempted only when a solid change management process is in place and staunchly followed, to keep from missing scope changes or keep a politically savvy manager from sneaking inappropriate scope changes into projects.

The more common method is to schedule executive-level reviews at strategic points within the project. These key milestones might include the following:

- Regular calendar events (monthly, for example)

- Key work packages

- Major deliverables (if not at a phase end)

- Project phases

The most common milestone review is project phases.

Phases and Phase Gates

Project evaluations at the end of a phase are frequently called **phase reviews** or **phase gates.**

> **The purpose of phase gates is to evaluate the project at the executive or portfolio level and determine whether the project should continue, be terminated, or be temporarily held.**

Note that phases are not purely part of the work breakdown structure (WBS), but are a structure superimposed on the WBS to provide this function. History has taught us that project phases should terminate when any of the following conditions occur:

1. At the completion of a major deliverable
2. At a point where executive management should review and evaluate the project
3. At a convenient stopping point in the project plan

At the end of each phase, the project management team presents the project to the portfolio management body (such as the steering committee, portfolio managers, or project sponsor). This presentation is designed to answer two questions:

1. Are we truly at the end of this phase?
2. Should we continue to the next phase?

The answer to the first question is mostly a technical answer. Product and project quality control should have evaluated and approved the deliverables before the phase gate review. However, one question still remains: "Do the deliverables achieve the objectives for which they were designed?" This is a business analysts' question, which demands an answer for the review.

The second question is more involved. In its purest form, it demands that the project be reevaluated and reapproved for inclusion in the portfolio. Consider these conditions:

- Has the business environment changed enough to invalidate the project charter's objectives?
- Will the project achieve the objectives defined in the charter?
- Does a better alternative exist for achieving those objectives?
- Has the portfolio changed sufficiently to require resource redistribution?

The results of this analysis enable the governing body to terminate the project if the objectives are no longer valid or cannot be met, or if a better alternative exists. The governing body might temporarily halt the project to redistribute resources, evaluate alternatives, or wait for a change in the business environment. Finally, the governing body might continue to the next phase of the project.

Common places to end phases are at the completion of the following deliverables:

- **Business case**—This is classically the first phase of most projects, when the portfolio and project designers determine whether the project is feasible, whether it can achieve its goals, and what resources are required.

- **Requirements**—The primary product for this phase is a complete requirements document that outlines all technical and business requirements. The project team determines the project's feasibility for review by the executive team.

- **Top-level design**—This is the first time that the project's design is fully defined and estimated. Therefore, it is a convenient place to make sure that the products designed will achieve the goals and that the original estimates and constraints are still viable.

- **Prototypes**—Prototype development also is a common place to terminate phases. The prototype enables the clients, executive management, and business analysts to evaluate the prototype to ensure that it will meet business needs. Appropriate prototypes include proof-of-concept prototypes, client approval prototypes, and production prototypes.

- **Detailed design**—This is commonly the last point at which the organization can terminate a project or hold it before project execution. Execution is the most costly part of the project, absorbing the most resources and spending the most capital.

- **Development**—The project team has finished creating the components, but they aren't yet integrated.

- **Integration**—A phase ends upon successful integration of all components into a cohesive system.

- **Final products**—Phases also commonly terminate with the completion of the project's primary products (services or results). Although most of the money and resources have already been spent by this point, prudence demands a final check before the organization commits those products to the marketplace or its clients.

This mechanism exhibits many benefits; perhaps the most important is that…

> **…phase gate reviews enable executives to maintain control of their organization from the top, where it belongs.**

The PMO or other governing body can handle the detailed oversight; you are responsible for giving this group the authority and tools they need. When you've done that, your job gets much easier.

Summary

Project management oversight involves three perspectives: product quality, performed by the quality control department to ensure that the products meet their requirements and specifications; project quality, where the quality assurance department and PMO make sure that the project team performs the right actions; and projects linked to the executive team, which ensures that the two previous perspectives are defined and performed, and ensures that the projects support the organization's strategic plan.

Project management oversight involves defining doctrine and the level of discipline to be performed in both quality control and quality assurance. It also demands that executives get reports on projects, to keep the processes on track.

Finally, executives need to ensure that the projects', programs', and portfolios' objectives align with the organization—incorporating appropriate organizational changes, excluding inappropriate changes, and focusing on the organization's vision. Table 9.1 allows you to rate your organization's project and product quality systems and doctrine.

Table 9.1 Project Management Oversight Rating Sheet

Performance Item	My Organization's Performance High ◄——————— Low				
The executive team has defined the doctrine and level of discipline appropriate for quality control to ensure that products conform to their designed requirements.					
The executive team has defined the doctrine and level of discipline appropriate for quality assurance to ensure that project activities comply with organizational policy and direction.					
Both quality control and quality assurance begin evaluations at the lowest levels and progress hierarchically up.					

(continues)

Table 9.1   Project Management Oversight Rating Sheet (continued)

Performance Item	My Organization's Performance				
	High ←			→ Low	
A formal communication strategy is in place to report on the progress of projects, programs, and the portfolio.					
The communication strategy includes an exception reporting mechanism that quickly communicates issues and changes to the appropriate governing body.					
Metrics are in place to verify that the processes and actions taken in projects comply with the organization's culture and definition statements.					
Metrics were created using a defined process, such as a balanced scorecard or organizational goals breakdown structure (OGBS).					
The executive team regularly reviews the objectives included in the portfolio and strategic plan.					

10

Project Management Oversight

The previous chapter examined techniques to ensure that projects are executing correctly. As an executive, you develop the overall goals and doctrine for project oversight, then you delegate this responsibility to some organizational entity (such as the PMO or quality assurance). Your responsibility is to make sure that the organizational entity is doing its job using the techniques addressed in that chapter. Specifically, you want to ensure that 1) each discipline under your responsibility performs at its peak and that 2) the organization's culture promotes growth, quality, and success.

In this chapter, I present mechanisms to enable you to track how well the discipline of project management is performing as a whole throughout the organization, eliminating the guesswork, speculation, and politics. For this task, I expand the concepts presented in the previous chapter by applying them to a multiproject environment. Using these techniques, you can look at project management from all aspects—size, department, region, and so on—to identify problem areas for root-cause analysis and take advantage of best practices.

I also present tools to address an issue that many executives often overlook: the organization's culture. Executive management defines the organization's culture, whether consciously or unconsciously. If middle managers or staff skimp on quality, cut corners, pad estimates, or circumvent procedures, it's because executive management either intentionally or accidentally created the culture that promotes such activities. These issues affect every project manager's ability to succeed.

Fortunately, project management offers excellent tools to help you address both cultural and systemic problems within the project management discipline: change management and earned value. The first two sections of this chapter help you identify problem areas and best practices using these techniques. For the last section of this chapter, I offer a brief presentation on continuous process improvement as it relates to project management.

Change Management as an Executive Tool

I addressed basic project change management procedures in Chapter 3, "Project Definition and Planning," and Chapter 7, "Process Alignment." The procedure is not difficult, just unpracticed. Recall that the project manager first documents the change. The project team then evaluates the change against the plan, determines alternatives, and determines the cost and schedule impact of implementing the change; and then presents the information to the Change Control Board (CCB) for approval or rejection. In this chapter, we look at how to use the results of this procedure to identify project management and cultural issues.

Project change management is primarily a control and monitoring tool. As a monitoring tool, the project manager can track changes within a project to identify and address technical issues. When we roll these up across multiple projects, we can identify cultural and systemic issues.

For example, I once took over a project that was in trouble; the previous project manager had left in disgrace. I asked the team to show me the project change order forms and the change log. They indicated that they didn't have any forms (which I discovered was one of the root causes of the problem), but the previous project manager did keep a change log. The log was unsophisticated—simply a list of change requests, handwritten on loose-leaf paper in a three-ring binder. I found entries written in crayon (really). The crayon entries didn't bother me or slow me down—the problem with this project jumped right off the page. We had a client who was out of control. The page was full of client-requested changes, most of which had never been implemented—primarily because they had fallen through the cracks.

It only took a few well-placed questions to find the problem. The root cause was a project manager who was trying too hard to please the client. He'd accepted change requests and tried to do them all. But they'd come so fast that he couldn't keep up, and he'd lost control of the project. If he had completed the standard change control forms, he would have had to confront the cost and schedule impact of the changes, which might have saved the project.

This project manager was not alone. In this company, this practice was not limited to one project manager—it was cultural. The organization was so focused on making the client happy that it neglected to control its projects. Interestingly, the result was very unhappy clients.

Although I could save this project, executive management needed to address the cultural problem—a concept they found very difficult.

Change Management Responsibilities

Successfully implementing change management involves several groups within the organization.

Executive Management

Executive management is responsible for two aspects of change management. The first is creating the change management doctrine. The "Critical Concepts for Change Management" section addresses key concepts for creating this doctrine. The first doctrine you should create is the one that enforces the change management procedure. This might be the most difficult doctrine you create—not because it's technically difficult, but because it forces the discipline on even the highest-level managers—including yourself.

Chapter 3 identifies change management as a simple process that is often unpracticed for cultural reasons. Even the most basic courses teach new project managers proper change management. However, managers are forced to abandon those procedures when an executive (such as the vice president) demands a change but doesn't want to be bothered with procedures; the executive wants it done without changing the deadline or cost. In this simple act, the vice president has derailed the project's cost, schedule, and work plans; derailed any projects or other work that share resources with this project; devalued the change management procedure; and promoted an "anything goes" culture.

There are times you will need to bypass procedures.
This, however, should not be the norm.

Your second responsibility to the change management process is to define the areas that you want to track, as identified by your organizational goals breakdown structure (OGBS), balanced scorecard, or similar structure. This tells the PMO how to set up metrics that help you monitor the organization.

The Program Management Office (PMO)

The program management office (PMO) usually owns and maintains the project methodology (processes), including the change management process. The PMO should ensure that the procedure captures the information you need for tracking and that the procedure is followed correctly.

The Project's Change Control Board (CCB)

Each project and program should have a change control board (CCB). Chapter 7 defines the CCB as a committee that reviews changes in a project (or program) and determines whether they should be implemented, rejected, or modified. This committee should reject a change request if that change does not benefit the organization. I present the evaluation criteria in subsequent paragraphs.

Portfolio Management

Some changes might have effects beyond the project or program. For example, project managers might discover that some technical issue prevents them from meeting some requirements. This also means that some strategic objectives might not be met. When this occurs, the portfolio designers must review the change against the rest of the portfolio to see if another project can satisfy those strategic goals.

Changes such as this aren't always negative. Let's say a project team discovers some technical breakthrough, and the team can either complete the project early or accomplish more than originally planned. Again, the portfolio management team should review the change to determine the best course of action: whether to apply the newly freed resources to some other troubled project or to expand the scope of this project.

Project Manager

The project managers are responsible for enforcing change management within their projects. This is more difficult than you might expect because it frequently pits the project manager against the client (who wants a lot of changes for free, instantly), stakeholders (who want a lot of changes for free, instantly), and executive managers (who also want a lot of changes for free, instantly).

Project managers who enforce proper use of the change management system are often accused of not being team players or loyal employees.

> **A project manager who enforces proper use of the**
> **change management process *is* the team player.**

It's the project manager who bypasses this process that adds to the chaos within the system and within the team.

Critical Concepts for Change Management

A few critical concepts are needed for successful change management. These concepts were presented earlier in this book but are elaborated here to offer perspective and serve as a review.

The Project Charter Is a Contract

The project charter is the document that links the project to the organization. Each project charter is a puzzle piece that interlocks with other project charters to form a comprehensive portfolio designed to achieve strategic objectives. This design begins at the highest level of the organization in the strategic plan. Changing a charter can have a very broad effect on the organization's strategy.

The charter is also a contract between executive management and the project manager. The project manager agrees to create deliverables or perform services that achieve the goals identified in the charter within the time and cost identified in the charter. Executive management agrees to provide the project manager with the needed resources and support described in the charter.

The charter is the one document in a project that does not change. Therefore, changes within a project are bound by the charter. The CCB should reject any changes that would expand the project past the boundaries identified in the charter or reduce the project's scope to prevent the team from achieving the charter's goals.

Some conditions violate this rule. If these occur, the portfolio managers and designers must be part of the decision-making process to preserve the portfolio's structural integrity.

Change Management Is the Gatekeeper for Project Scope

The change management process is a gatekeeper or filter. It is designed to enable good and beneficial changes to pass through to the project and prevent bad and nonbeneficial changes from affecting the project.

Executive management, a portfolio designer, or a steering committee initially selected this project because the benefits it provides outweigh the costs. Each change affects both the benefits and the cost; therefore, each change must be evaluated using the same or similar criteria.

> **Changes that don't provide sufficient benefit-to-cost ratios
> should be rejected; those that do should be approved.**

Quality Assurance and Quality Control Provide the Checks and Balances

Quality assurance reviews the project team's work against the procedures, including the change management procedures. Quality control also reviews the products of the work against the requirements. Both of these actions serve as checks and balances against the change management procedure.

When the CCB approves requirement changes, it must communicate the changes to quality control so that it can test the products against the new requirements.

Jim's Blue Cell Phones

Jim is the project manager leading a project to develop a new cell phone for his company's cell phone product line. Jim is responsible for only the phone's development; other project managers are handling production, logistics, and marketing. The product requirements state that the phone should be offered in three colors: black, silver, and red. Jim is just finishing his design phase and already has paint sample prototypes developed. Jim is on a very tight deadline to get the phones out by the end of September for the holiday season.

Janet is the product marketing manager. In a casual lunch with a colleague, she learns that blue has been a very popular color among high school students. She neglected to include high school students in her original studies. Realizing her mistake, she goes to Jim and demands that he add the fourth color as fast as he can.

Janet is well connected with several senior managers and isn't afraid to use her clout when needed. Under pressure, Jim bypasses the change control process and goes directly to his people to get them working on the fourth color. The impact to Jim's development project is negligible; however, the production line was designed for only three colors, raw material purchases will need adjustment, and marketing materials require changes.

Bypassing procedures in this company was not unusual. And although quality assurance and quality control are strong in the production areas, they are weak in the project areas, so the event went undetected for some time. The production line design was approved and raw materials were already ordered when Janet discovered that the line was set up for only three colors. Production, engineering, purchasing, and marketing scrambled frantically to add the fourth color.

The change delayed the announcement for the new phone, losing an estimated 30 percent in sales for the season.

In this example, we can trace back the root cause for this change to Janet's missing a significant demographic in her marketing research. She used her clout to try to remedy the mistake. Her attempt to bypass procedure wasn't inspired by greed or deceit—just a rational desire to fix a mistake quickly in a culture in which she has clout and bypassing procedures is routine.

If quality assurance and quality control were strongly supported in project management, either would have caught the change early. Quality assurance could catch the mistake while conducting a routine audit of the purchasing procedures for Jim's project when they discovered a requisition for blue paint samples. Quality control could catch it when they were asked to inspect a blue prototype. After the change was caught, the change control procedure and CCB would need to make sure that the other project managers (from marketing communications, production line design, and inventory control) were involved in the initial decision to determine whether the change could be done in time to meet market demand.

A Summary of the Change Management Process
- Project change control is neither complicated nor difficult; it just must be followed rigorously.

- All changes must align with and be beneficial to the performing organization.

- All changes must be within the boundaries of the project charter.

- Change evaluations include all aspects of the change, including time, cost, and impact on other projects and work.

- Change evaluations must involve appropriate stakeholders.
- QA and QC act as checks and balances to the change management system.

Change Management As an Executive Tool

In an ideal world, you would expect the following capabilities from your organization's project management system:

- Project managers are superb planners.
- The staff members know their jobs and do them.
- Project clients know what they want.
- The external environment is predictable.
- Personnel move into and out of projects seamlessly and flawlessly.

If all these capabilities existed, projects could not only run efficiently, they'd run without change. Changes occur whenever your organization falls short on these capabilities, incurring delays and inefficiencies. Therefore, we use change management to evaluate the organization's culture, effectiveness, and efficiency.

I am not promoting that organizations run with machinelike precision. Spontaneity, inspiration, creativity, and experimentation should be encouraged. And although we don't expect our people to be perfect, we can use change management as a tool to identify problem areas for process improvement.

For example, imagine that you receive notification that a project manager declares a two-week delay for a deliverable. You ask her about the delay, and she indicates that her two top resources were pulled off her project for two weeks to go to Oshkosh, Wisconsin, to handle a client that's been complaining about their delivery (unrelated to her project). These staff members were on the project's critical path and have particular expertise needed for their tasks. She also indicates that this occurrence isn't unusual.

You decide to examine the change notices for several projects that were late. Under investigation, you discover a pattern of top-level people being pulled off projects to handle client issues. You also notice that the problems fall into the same technical area. You investigate the quality control reports for this area, but it reveals no particular problems with quality.

You examine the human resource records for this area and discover an unusually high turnover rate. Because you're well schooled in management by wandering around (MBWA),[1] you stroll through the area and quietly observe several staff members apparently working hard, with many papers and books strewn about their cubes; others seem to be quite relaxed.

This example demonstrates how change management can help you identify functional managers who are not doing their jobs. Several of their staff have taken it upon themselves to get things done, and others are enjoying the lack of management and collecting a paycheck for little work. Morale is low, turnover is high, and the few good workers are constantly pulled in too many directions.

Trends in change management are excellent for locating cultural issues and technical and management issues. If staff is being pulled in too many directions, if clients and other project stakeholders frequently change their minds on project requirements, or if quality control is lax, you discover it in the change management metrics.

Consider this simple process for establishing change management metrics for reporting purposes:

1. Identify change categories that track to organizational and strategic objectives, and identify categories that help you locate the source for the change.

2. Make sure that project managers rigorously capture accurate change information. This is standard procedure for any formalized methodology.

3. Capture sufficient current-state data to establish a baseline. Roll up and summarize data by category and source across the portfolio. Act on any obvious issues that you discover during this period.

4. Identify problem areas and root cause.

5. Adjust the strategic plan, project management doctrine, processes, or other areas to relieve the problems.

6. Monitor positive and negative trends.

7. Use metrics and trends to identify noncompliance and cultural issues. Use this information as inputs into your continuous process improvement procedures.

Charting the results in Figure 10.1 produces excellent trend information. Figure 10.1 shows the percentage of change requests for different categories of the entire portfolio. Two categories show significant change over time (both displayed as solid lines). Scope definition is trending downward, indicating that the organization is improving its ability to define scope. Resource changes are trending upward, indicating that resource issues are becoming a problem. The cause might be simply a work overload, a political situation, or the way resources transfer among project managers and functional managers. A root-cause analysis would reveal the core problem.

Also notice that vendor issues are decreasing over time, indicating that your organization is improving how it handles vendors.

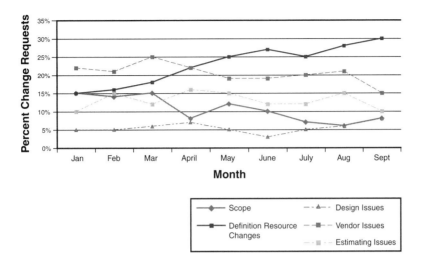

Figure 10.1   Portfolio change requests by category

Managing the Project Environment

This chapter's primary objective is to find tools and techniques for evaluating and improving how the organization manages projects as a whole. In this section, I present key factors for evaluating the project environment, and then I identify the source and cause for undesired performance. In the next section, I present the basic concepts for continuous improvement.

Evaluating the Project Environment

You can use two key sources for evaluating the project environment. The first involves tracking change request and change orders, as presented in the previous section. The second is our old friend EVM (earned value management).

Multiple Project EVM Roll-Up

EVM is an excellent method for tracking the project environment. Earned value is specifically designed to be rolled up and decomposed. Not only can we roll up the EVM numbers for a department, group, region, or any other combination of projects that we want, but we can also decompose EVM numbers by any means we want and then roll up the decomposition. For example, you can examine how well the engineering department in the Northeast compares to the vendors used in the Southwest for company-wide product-development projects.

Figure 10.2 shows a histogram using earned value metrics (cost and schedule variance percent) for a portfolio. Note the classical and desired bell-shaped curve for both cost and schedule variance. Most projects are within 20 percent of plan with only a few going out to 30 percent. A good PMO investigates and fixes these projects, which reduces the spread of the graph. This graph, however, doesn't reveal any major or cultural issues as long as the PMO is allowed to do its job.

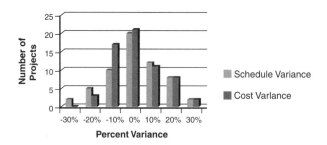

Figure 10.2   Earned value portfolio graph

A skewed graph in either cost or schedule indicates a problem in that area. Consider the graph in Figure 10.3. The schedule variance still exhibits the nice bell-shaped curve, but the cost variance is skewed to the left. This organization is good at time estimating and management, but it lacks skill in cost estimating and management. This issue might require executive management's help. The issue might be cultural or there might be a systemic problem within project management. Again, root cause analysis would reveal the problem.

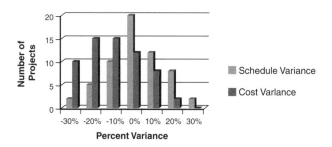

Figure 10.3   Portfolio histogram with cost variance skewed left

Portfolio Stoplight Graph

This graph employs the classical stoplight color-coding system that many project managers use for status reports. The colors are red (project in trouble), yellow (project having difficulty but not in trouble), and green (project running according to plan). The graph plots the number of projects in each category over time. Figure 10.4 shows the preferred trend:

The number of troubled projects (red) is decreasing, and the number of on-time, on-schedule projects (green) is increasing over time. This shows an executive management team and PMO that are doing their jobs.

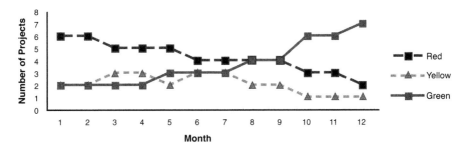

Figure 10.4   Portfolio stoplight graph

Determining Root Cause

The next step in improving the project environment is to identify the root cause of issues. We exploit our original sources of information—change management—to achieve this goal. First, we examine a pareto diagram from the change request metrics to help us focus on which problems to solve, and then we use EVM to help pinpoint cause.

The Change Management Pareto Diagram

In the previous section, I presented a chart that identifies trends using change management as our primary metric. For this section, you look at a snapshot of that chart to see which problems cause the greatest number of change requests. This is frequently called a **pareto diagram.** Using a bar-chart format, rank categories from highest to lowest, and then add a cumulative line for convenience. Figure 10.5 illustrates a change request pareto chart.

Figure 10.5 indicates that vendor issues, implementation, resource changes, estimating issues, *and* scope definition issues account for more than 80 percent of change requests. You can create similar charts to determine changes with the greatest impact on time, cost, quality, vendor relations, and so on.

Using EVM for Root-Cause Analysis

When you've identified the set of problem areas, you can use EVM as a tool to help identify the root causes. Figure 10.6 tracks components of the earned value numbers against a calendar. The project manager for this project maintained separate EVM numbers for the four categories shown (in-house staff, contractors, outside vendors, and capital expenditures). Note that the in-house staff shows negative variance, but the contractors and vendors maintain a positive variance. This indicates that the project manager relies heavily on the contractors and vendors to get the project work done. They are compensating for in-house staff that is falling behind.

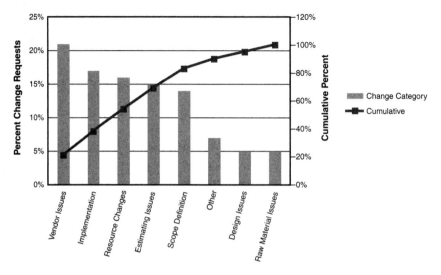

Figure 10.5 Change request pareto chart

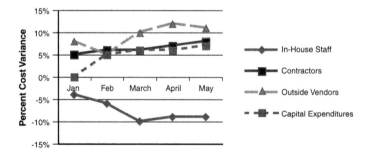

Figure 10.6 Cost variance by cost category

Improving the Project Environment

The tools presented in the preceding sections help identify where problems exist. The results of these analyses feed a standard continuous process improvement cycle for the project management methodology, enabling the discipline to improve over time.

Roles and Responsibilities for Project Management Improvement

Each organization must examine its own structure, culture, goals, and strategy to determine the appropriate roles and responsibilities. Table 10.1 illustrates a standard project management tool called a resource assignment matrix (RAM), to illustrate some typical roles and responsibilities you might use for continuous project management improvement.

Table 10.1 Project Management Improvement RAM

Stakeholder Task	Task Owner	Executive Management	Chief Project Officer (CPO)	Program Management Office (PMO)	Strategic Planning Committee
Define the goals of project management	CPO	C	RA	P	C
Define the project management methodology	PMO		C	RA, P	
Track performance	PMO		C	RA, P	
Recommend improvements	PMO	I	C	RA, P	I
Implement, communicate, and roll out updated methodology	PMO	I	I	RA, P	I

Legend:

RA: Responsible and accountable   **I:** Must be informed

P: Task performer   **C:** Must be consulted

For this model, the CPO defines the project management goals by consulting executive management and the strategic planning committee. This action ensures that project management aligns with the organization. The CPO delegates methodology ownership to the PMO. To ensure that the methodology remains aligned with the organization, the CPO must be consulted on all methodology actions. The PMO owns the methodology, and recommends and implements changes after consulting with the CPO. Executive management and the strategic planning committee must be informed of all methodology actions. It's necessary to provide checks and balances and generate senior management support for methodology changes.

Note that responsibility and accountability are inseparable using my legend. Also note that the task owner is always responsible and accountable.

IPOT Map

Figure 10.7 presents the IPOT diagram for continuous process improvement of project management.

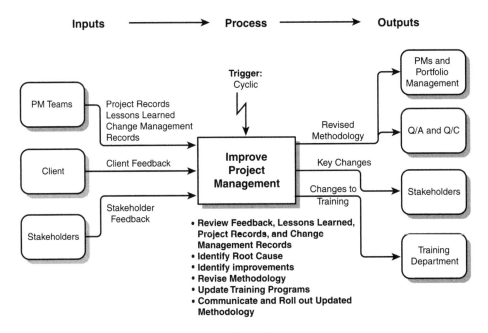

Figure 10.7 Continuous process improvement for project management

Process Inputs

Key inputs for the process originate from the following:

- **Project management teams**—Provide key project metrics from earned value and other project records, change management records, and lessons learned sessions

- **Client**—Offers feedback both during and after the project through complaints, compliments, and surveys

- **Stakeholders**—Offer direct feedback similar to the client

The Process of Improvement

The project methodology owner (usually the PMO) accepts and accumulates all the input information. At regular intervals, the committee reviews the results, determines which improvement areas will have the greatest impact, and performs a root-cause analysis to determine the true cause of problems or source of improvements. From this analysis, they identify specific improvements or changes to the methodology, ensuring compliance with internal and external regulations, organizational definition statements, the strategic plan, and organizational culture.

Process Outputs

When the revised methodology is ready, the PMO must roll out the changes to all affected groups. This includes communicating the changed methodology to existing project and portfolio managers and their teams. The quality assurance and quality control groups must also be notified so they can monitor based on the new methodology. The PMO must also communicate key changes to project stakeholders, including functional managers, executive managers, service departments, and others. Finally, the training department must modify training classes based on the new methodology.

Process Trigger

The PMO usually performs this process on a cyclical basis. If you're new to formalized project management, you might do this quarterly. Less mature methodologies tend to be less complex, which eases analysis, but they also require more frequent modification.

As your methodology matures, your review cycles can be longer. More mature methodologies require a more detailed analysis. However, they have fewer problems and require less frequent updates. Mature methodologies might require only annual reviews.

Summary

Executive management plays a key role in making sure that project management supports the organization. Using existing and well-defined procedures, executives can develop a simple structure to monitor and track how the organization manages projects, handles problems, and improves project management over time. These key tools include earned value management (EVM), change management, and standard continuous process improvement technologies.

Successful project management also requires both executive direction and oversight. It is your responsibility to define project management's role within the organization, to provide organizational structure and resources to succeed in project management, and to make sure those resources are doing their job. Table 10.2 provides the executive checklist for managing project management.

Table 10.2 Managing Project Management Summary Checklist

Performance Item	My Organization's Performance				
	High ⟵———————— Low				
Project management's goals are defined and communicated.					
Project management's goals align with organizational objectives.					
Project management's goals align with the preferred organizational culture.					
An organizational entity owns the methodology.					
Key metrics are in place to roll up multiple projects to examine project management as a whole, including earned value management and change management.					
Metrics help find the root cause for problems and target improvement.					
The process improvement process is well defined and followed.					
Key stakeholders have a way to communicate improvement suggestions in the improvement process.					
Clients have a way to communicate improvement suggestions in the improvement process.					
Pareto charts or other tools enable the methodology owner to determine the most important issues to address.					

11

Projects as Capital Investments

T he purpose of any project is to add value, and the value must outweigh the project cost. This is the basic concept for this chapter.

The value doesn't need to be purely monetary. Consider a project to finish a basement. Although you certainly hope to add real value to your house, you recognize that the financial value added will likely be less than your investment. The additional value comes from enjoying the basement while you live in the house.

Organizations are no different. Not-for-profit organizations' goals are not monetary (presumably). For-profit organizations recognize the need to invest in the organization's culture—to develop mores that inspire honesty, hard work, respect, and personal growth. You also recognize that many projects offer financial benefits that might be difficult to quantify. Information technology (IT) infrastructure projects often fall into this category.

This discussion leads us back to the balanced portfolio: a portfolio designed to cover all aspects of the organization. A stable, balanced portfolio demands that we consider all goals for a project before work begins. We recognize that changing our mind midstream is highly disruptive and inefficient, not only at the project level, but also at the portfolio level.

The Basement Remodel Project

Let's continue our basement remodeling project example. Your primary objective is to have a place where you and your spouse can relax without disturbing the rest of the household. As the owner and primary user of the basement, you want it to be attractive, useful, and easy to maintain. You also want to add value to the house, which might require more expensive side molding and wall coverings. You want the basement finished by Thanksgiving because it's your turn to host the family Thanksgiving dinner.

Satisfied with your project's scope, you complete your project plan. You estimate that the project will take two months (well before Thanksgiving) and cost about $7,000 (within your budget). You get a home equity loan for $10,000 (including a bit of mad money).

Satisfied with your plan and finances, you purchase materials and start to build walls.

While discussing the project with a friend, you discover that adding a home theater will significantly increase the value of the house. The increased home value and increased usefulness are enough for you to add the theater to your basement remodeling project. This new addition requires you to change some walls you've already built, add some sound-proofing and internal wiring, and reapply for your permits. Between redesign, rework, and added materials and equipment, your project will now take four months and cost $14,000. The schedule is tight but doable; you'll need to add another $4,000 out of savings, but you deem that the added value is worth it.

With winter looming, you call your furnace service vendor to do the annual service. After winding their way through the ongoing construction several times, they inform you that your ten-year-old furnace is still usable but is very inefficient and will need replacement in a year or two. Certainly, it would be less expensive and less disruptive to do it before construction finishes. With the increased cost of fuel and improvements in furnace technology, you decide to include a furnace-replacement project to your basement renovation portfolio. You halt construction until the new furnace is in. Thanksgiving is no longer an achievable target and you are well above your budget. Although the furnace company gave you a low-interest loan, adding those payments to your home equity loan payments puts you above your monthly budget for the next year.

Worse, the demands of the holidays will significantly impair your ability to complete the basement. Your original two-month, $7,000 project will now take nearly ten months and cost more than $20,000.

This example demonstrates how scope can increase in a project when you have not considered all aspects in advance. If you had considered all aspects at the beginning of the project, you would have included the furnace and home theater in your project plans, the loan (albeit higher) would have been sufficient to cover all the costs, and the project would have been done by Thanksgiving.

Now imagine what can happen to projects in a complex business environment.

This chapter and the two that follow present concepts to help ensure that each project adds value to your organization and that the portfolio is balanced—ensuring all organizational values, goals, and strategies are handled. From an investment perspective, viewing a sound, balanced project portfolio provides several important benefits:

- The investment strategy approach streamlines capitalizing projects, not only for planned projects, but also for unplanned opportunities.

- A balanced portfolio addresses all the organization's needs. This prevents false starts and offers comprehensive organizational support.

- A balanced portfolio enables you to virtually stop reprioritizing projects. This also eliminates priorities du jour and political infighting for schedules and resources, enabling resources to focus on completing defined tasks.

- A balanced portfolio enables you to spread projects over time. This smoothes resource loadings, improves productivity, and encourages executives to ration capital in terms of value tracks, not crises.

- A balanced portfolio enhances resource predictability, improving overall strategic and tactical planning.

A Basis for Sound Project Investment Strategies

You cannot develop a sound project investment strategy using a glib approach. At a minimum, you should understand key aspects of project investment strategies, basic cost management, and concepts of common financial management tools. Also, as an executive, you affect multiple projects, not just one. Therefore, you should understand basic concepts for portfolio management.

This section presents core concepts needed to develop sound investment strategies. This list is not exhaustive, but highlights key areas I find missing in most organizations. I introduced some of these concepts in earlier chapters; others are new:

- Project investment concepts
  - Establish true project costs
  - Align project with value tracks
  - Balance risk and reward
  - Integrate project results into operations
- Cost management tools
  - Life cycle costing
  - Activity-based costing (ABC)
  - Cost of quality
- Financial investment tools
  - Return on investment (ROI)
  - Discounted cash flow (DCF)
  - Net present value (NPV)
  - Internal rate of return (IRR)
  - Modified internal rate of return (MIRR)

- The balanced portfolio
  - Eliminate dynamic reprioritization
  - The infinite resource pool
  - Continued balancing

Project Investment Concepts

Project management continues to mature as a discipline and handles many investment concepts well. However, in my practice as a consultant and seminar leader, I see many organizations missing the four key concepts presented in the following sections.

Establish True Project Costs

It might seem both extreme and cold, but each individual, project, pen, pencil, and keyboard in the organization must support the organization's objectives. In particular, the net benefit or value of every human resource in an organization should be greater than the fully burdened cost of that resource. If not, the resource should be let go to save the organization money—or perhaps the executive that issued and approved the requisition without a sound investment strategy should be let go. Either way, resource benefits should be greater than their cost.

Similarly, project benefits should be greater than their cost. The true cost of the project includes all individuals, pens, pencils, keyboards, and other items involved in the project. If individuals weren't working on this project, they could be working elsewhere. If this project adds no value, the individuals could be working on some other project that does add value. True project costs include all associated costs, including internal human resources.

> **Human resources are not free—they cost the organization
> real money. The project's budget must include
> their cost and all project-associated costs.**

Align Projects with Value Tracks

I previously addressed the concept that not all value is financial. In Chapter 4, "Strategic Alignment," and Chapter 5, "A Framework for Strategic Alignment," I presented the organizational goals breakdown structure (OGBS): a method for developing comprehensive objectives for all levels of the organization. The OGBS is similar to the balanced scorecard (BSC) presented by Kaplan and Norton. Both the OGBS and the BSC recognize the need for a holistic approach to an organization. Let's consider an OGBS implementation for the fictitious XYZ Corporation. For brevity, I restrict the OGBS presentation to the vision, mission, and four value statements, each simplified for clarity:

- **Vision**—XYZ Corporation is an international leader in high-quality widget innovation, production, and installation.

- **Mission**—XYZ Corporation develops state-of-the-art widgets of the highest quality for both industry and home use across the globe.

- **Value statements**—
  - Grow profitably through fiscal integrity
  - Develop as individuals, teams, and an organization
  - Pursue excellence in all that we do
  - Dedicate ourselves to our clients' success

When we continue developing the OGBS, we define tracks where value can flow up to support these statements, as illustrated in Figure 11.1.

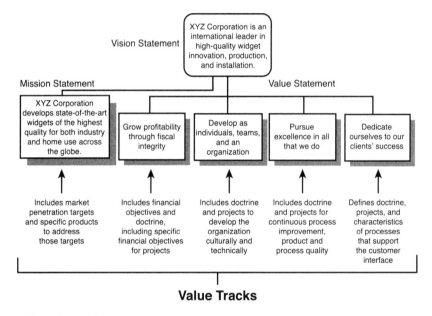

Value Tracks

Figure 11.1 Value tracks

Using the OGBS, we decompose these statements to define specific goals and projects for the organization. We codify these goals and projects in the organization's strategic plan. For example, our strategic plan might include a goal that 25 percent of all project managers be PMP certified by the end of the year. Such a project could support the "Pursue excellence…" value by improving project and product quality, the "Develop as individuals…" value by improving individuals' and project teams' skills, and the "Grow profitably…" value by improving the return on project investment through better management.

**The value track provides both portfolio and project designers
clear guidelines for establishing well-defined project objectives.**

In both the OGBS and BSC implementations, executive management must identify clear, measurable targets for each of these value tracks in the strategic plan.

Balance Risk and Reward

All portfolio managers are familiar with the concept of balancing risk and reward: The greater the risk, the greater the potential reward. By its nature, every project involves risk. Even the most sound project plan lives in a dynamic environment that threatens the project's success.

Because greater potential reward involves greater risk, our quest for a balanced portfolio demands a way of engaging in high-risk ventures without endangering the organization if those ventures fail. Fortunately, standard and well-developed project tools offer us the solution.

**Standard project management tools such as phase gates, prototyping,
and research projects enable organizations to engage in high-risk
projects while maintaining long-term portfolio stability.**

These tools enable us to develop a balanced risk management strategy. After executive management determines the level of creativity or risk they desire in the organization, the portfolio designers can balance project risk accordingly.

Integrate Project Results into Operations

One final area I find missing in many organizations involves the interaction between projects and other organizational activities including process, operations, and production. This is one area in which many project managers fall short.

**Project managers are responsible to include actions to transfer
project results to operations in their project plans.**

Even as the project unfolds, project managers and subject matter experts make choices that affect ongoing operations. This includes training staff on the new procedures, maintaining spare parts, updating operation and maintenance documentation, and impacting operating costs. However, because the ongoing operating cost is not part of the project budget, many project managers overlook this consideration. Life cycle costing is another tool organizations can use to address this issue as described in the next section.

Cost Management Tools

This section introduces useful cost-management tools for developing sound project investment strategies.

Life Cycle Costing

Life cycle costing is a cost-analysis method that considers the total cost of ownership, not just acquisition cost. For example, in our basement remodeling portfolio, you decided to replace your old furnace with a newer, more efficient model. Let's compare two different models. Model A is an inexpensive model that has a shorter useful life, burns fuel less efficiently, and costs more to maintain. Model B costs more to buy but has a longer useful life, is more fuel efficient, and costs less to maintain. At some point, the money saved in operational costs pays for the increased purchase price.

Facing tight budget concerns, a project manager would select the less expensive furnace (model A) to protect the project's budget because the project team isn't responsible for ongoing costs of operation. However, this might not be the least expensive solution over time.

Life cycle costing accounts for all costs associated with the purchase, including operating and maintenance costs throughout the item's useful life. Life cycle costing is generally the preferred cost-analysis method. The exception arises when an organization is in a cash-tight situation. In such situations, it might be more prudent to forego the longer-term benefits in favor of the shorter-term cash flow issue. The wise project designer or manager should consult the financial department to determine the best approach.

Activity-Based Costing

One common thread woven through this book is the serendipitous work package. The work package is a well-defined component of a deliverable, specific enough that the organization can outsource it for a fixed price. It's a unit of work that has a well-defined cost.

Activity-based costing (ABC) serendipitously employs similar techniques and features. Using ABC, a department determines the cost of performing a specific activity, such as hiring an employee or developing a page of an engineering drawing. The department then charges other departments that cost to perform those services, as if it was an outside vendor.

This approach offers significant advantages to a project manager. Without ABC, the project manager might need to go to the individual doing the work, establish an estimate for the time and cost, and then manage the work.

When the organization employs ABC, the performing organization has already predetermined the cost and time for the service. From the project managers' and project designers' perspectives, it's simply another work package. Appropriate subject matter experts can estimate a project's required level of services and cost it out. If a project requires an estimated 50 pages of engineering drawings, and the engineering drafting department charges $200 per drawing, the project manager simply adds $10,000 to the cost of the project. This process transfers the burden of resource management to the supervisors and functional managers, where it belongs.

The work package concept also interfaces nicely with financial systems that already employ ABC, easing the bureaucratic burden of both the financial department and the project managers.

Cost of Quality

When we examine quality from a purely financial perspective, we can easily establish the optimum financial solution to the problem of balancing quality, cost, and time. In our business operations, we add processes (and, therefore, cost) to embed quality into the project or product. These processes might include such steps as reviews, inspections, change management procedures, configuration management, and others. We categorize these steps as quality initiatives. Unfortunately, many executives view these as overhead. However, removing these steps creates several problems: one short-term and two long-term.

The short-term problem arises from inherent system errors, resulting in faulty products. These products now cost the company money through returns, repairs, and increased customer service costs. You experience increases in field personnel, spare parts, and shipping costs. At some point, the money lost in handling bad quality overshadows the money saved by reducing quality initiatives.

The (simplified) cost of quality then becomes

$$Cost\ of\ quality = \sum(Cost\ of\ quality\ initiatives)$$
$$+ \sum(Cost\ of\ nonconformance)$$

The two long-term problems exacerbate the issue. The first long-term problem is that the lack of checks and balances inherent in quality activities allows laziness in both personnel and processes. This results in an increased number of errors and reduced product quality. The second—and, perhaps, more important—of the two long-term issues is the loss of customers due to customer dissatisfaction.

We now can expand our cost of quality equation to read

$$Cost\ of\ quality = \sum(Cost\ of\ quality\ initiatives) +$$
$$\sum(Cost\ of\ nonconformance) + \sum(Loss\ of$$
$$productivity) + \sum(Lost\ profit\ from\ lost\ customers)$$

At this point, I must clarify the discussion by separating two concepts: quality and grade. Grade refers to the number and type of features in a product. A high-end product (high grade) might have many features, and a low-end product (low grade) might have few. However, each product would have equal quality if the number of defects is identical.

In project management, *quality* is defined simply as meeting requirements and specifications.

In a product-oriented company, the product marketing managers or other marketing subject matter experts determine the market niche and, therefore, product grade. However, the project manager has a clearly defined mandate: to ensure that the product meets quality standards by reducing or eliminating defects so that the product meets defined requirements. Shortcutting these steps results in products that don't meet market needs and in unmet sales and revenue targets.

The solution to the apparent dichotomy of time versus quality becomes defining the grade appropriate for the marketplace within the appropriate market window. Properly defining these values in advance of the project enables the project manager and team to develop the appropriate quality steps needed to meet the established requirements. However, their mandate has not changed; it remains: meet quality standards.

Your basement remodeling portfolio would have a very different grade if the basement was designed as a playroom for small children instead of an adult entertainment area. Regardless of the grade, you, as the homeowner, would be just as upset if a wall had to be rebuilt because a contractor failed to meet a particular municipal construction code.

Project Financial Analysis Tools

Before we examine formal methods for developing balanced portfolios, we need to establish a common set of tools: our base building blocks. This section offers common financial investment tools and methods for analyzing projects' financial benefits. We focus on return on investment (ROI), discounted cash flows (DCF), internal rate of return (IRR), net present values (NPV), and some of their variations. In this book, I offer a basic understanding and leave advanced issues to college professors and your financial group.

Return on Investment (ROI)

Return on investment (ROI) is arguably the most commonly used and easily understood financial investment measure. Its acronym also makes it easy to remember its calculation. Think of it as "return over investment." To calculate ROI, start with the net return (total money received minus associated costs), subtract the initial investment, and divide by the initial investment:

$$Return\ on\ Investment = \frac{(Net\ Return\ -\ Initial\ Investment)}{Initial\ Investment}$$

ROI is easy to calculate and offers a solid metric for evaluating the financial benefit of a project.

However, it is flawed because it doesn't take the time value of money into account. Therefore, ROI should be limited to projects that offer short-term benefits.

Some organizations use a variation on ROI; for example, return on total invested capital (ROTIC) was popular a few years ago. Other variations have been popular over time. Work with your financial experts to determine the best approach for your economic objectives.

Cash Flows

Typically, you undertake projects to produce a financial benefit to the organization. This benefit frequently lasts for a long time, usually several years. Let's refer to the project's cost (budget) as our initial investment.

Most financial analysts consider that the project's budget (the initial investment) is spent in the first period (a period is usually a year) and that the project's financial benefits extend for several periods.

Let's further refer to the series of financial results as cash flows, as Table 11.1 illustrates. For our example, let's consider a simple process improvement project: improving the workflow in the marketing, production, and distribution department. When complete, the improved process will result in less waste and lower production costs.

The project's sponsor assigns Jim as the project manager. Jim calls the marketing department and asks them to estimate the current process and distribution costs, along with how must work they expect to do during the next five years. The marketing department believes that the process cycle will last only that long (the useful life).

After consulting with experts, Jim and his team estimate the savings that the project should bring to the process. Jim forecasts the financial benefits that result from the project and creates Table 11.1.

Jim works with his subject matter experts and the client, and estimates that the total project cost will be $50,000; so at this point, the project's benefits outweigh the cost.

Discounted Cash Flow

Basic finance teaches us that present-day dollars are worth more than future dollars. If you deposit $1,000 into a simple interest-bearing account that paid 10 percent interest per year, you would have $1,100 at the end of one year. This means that $1,100 a year from now is worth only $1,000 today. So we must discount the future value of money to equal today's value by using this equation:

$$PresentValue = \frac{FutureValue}{(1 + DR)^n}$$

where

PresentValue—Value in present-day dollars ($1,000 in the example)

FutureValue—Value in the future ($1,100 in the example)

DR—Discount rate (10 percent in the example)

n—Number of future periods (=1 in the example)

Table 11.1   Project Cash Flow Table

Period	Item	Projected Cash Flow
1	Financial benefit for year 1	$20,000
2	Financial benefit for year 2	$40,000
3	Financial benefit for year 3	$50,000
4	Financial benefit for year 4	$30,000
5	Financial benefit for year 5	$20,000
Total:		$160,000

We must apply this principle to our cash flow table to establish the discounted cash flow. The finance department should determine the discount rate based on a combination of inflation, cost of capital, and other financial circumstances.

Jim asks his financial department for the discount rate. The finance department tells him it's 10 percent for the foreseeable future. He then computes the discounted cash flow as illustrated in Table 11.2.

Net Present Value (NPV)

Net present value (NPV) analysis is the same as the discounted cash flow analysis, except that NPV takes the cost of the project into account. Notice the addition of the project budget (initial investment) in Table 11.3. Also note that the initial investment is not discounted. We assume that it's spent in period 0, so we use present-day dollars.

Table 11.2 Discounted Cash Flow Table

Period	Item	Projected Cash Flow	Discounted Cash Flow
1	Financial benefit for year 1	$20,000	$18,181.82
2	Financial benefit for year 2	$40,000	$33,057.85
3	Financial benefit for year 3	$50,000	$37,565.74
4	Financial benefit for year 4	$30,000	$20,490.40
5	Financial benefit for year 5	$20,000	$12,418.43
Total:		$160,000	$121,714.24

Table 11.3 Net Present Value (NPV)

Period	Item	Projected Cash Flow	Discounted Cash Flow
1	Financial benefit for year 1	$20,000	$18,181.82
2	Financial benefit for year 2	$40,000	$33,057.85
3	Financial benefit for year 3	$50,000	$37,565.74
4	Financial benefit for year 4	$30,000	$20,490.40
5	Financial benefit for year 5	$20,000	$12,418.43
Total:		$160,000	$121,714.24
Minus initial investment:		($50,000)	($50,000.00)
Net present value (NPV):			$71,714.24

Our NPV for this project is $71,714.24, which means that this project essentially adds $71,714.24 in value to our organization.

The NPV analysis includes several benefits:

1. It determines the net impact (positive or negative) on the organization as a whole.

2. It accounts for the time value of money.

3. It offers a simple go or no-go decision.

If the project has a positive NPV, it adds value to the organization. If the NPV is negative, the project expends more in resources than it benefits. A for-profit organization should not accept a project with a negative NPV unless it expects significant nonfinancial benefits or is required by regulation.

The NPV also offers another benefit unavailable to other analyses. Finance can adjust the discount rate for both the project and for different periods. They can adjust the rate to account for long-term projects, projects exhibiting excessive risks, or other unique conditions. Financial managers can also adjust the discount rate to account for a specific project's source of funds. For example, if a project is funded by a combination of a stock offering, bank loans, and corporate bonds, finance can include the higher cost of capital in the discount rate. Such discount rates are sometimes called the **weighted average cost of capital** (WACC). Similarly, a company can increase the discount rate for risky projects to better balance the risk portfolio.

Internal Rate of Return (IRR)

The internal rate of return (IRR) is another project investment analysis tool. The IRR expresses the project's benefits in a percentage return format, similar to other financial investments. This method enables you to compare the project's IRR to a stock repurchase plan, potential acquisition, or other standard investment strategy. For example, a financial group might look to invest $1 million. Its options include buying tax-free municipal bonds, initiating a stock buyback, or authorizing a project. Let's assume that the municipal bonds offer a 12 percent return (tax adjusted), the stock is anticipated to grow at a rate of 18 percent per year, and the project exhibits an IRR of 25 percent. Based on the information provided, the financial department would invest in your project, assuming that the risk is tolerable.

Simply stated, the IRR for a project is the discount rate at which the NPV reaches zero. From the previous example, we see that if we increase the discount rate, the NPV drops. At some discount rate, the NPV reaches identically zero. Increasing the discount rate beyond that point results in a negative NPV. The discount rate at which the NPV reaches zero is the IRR.

This tool translates the project into a simple interest-bearing investment. Table 11.4 shows that the NPV calculation from Table 11.3 exhibits a 56 percent IRR.

Modified IRR (MIRR)

Modified IRR (MIRR) is becoming a more popular tool. The standard IRR calculation assumes that the positive cash flow is reinvested at a rate equal to the project's IRR. The MIRR calculation assumes that the positive cash flows are reinvested into the organization's cost of capital—usually a more realistic approach. The MIRR generally yields a slightly smaller result than the IRR calculation, primarily because most projects show a greater return than the general ongoing operation. If they don't, you probably shouldn't do them.

Table 11.4   Internal Rate of Return (IRR)

Period	Item	Projected Cash Flow	Discounted Cash Flow
1	Financial benefit for year 1	$20,000	$12,858.15
2	Financial benefit for year 2	$40,000	$16,533.21
3	Financial benefit for year 3	$50,000	$13,286.66
4	Financial benefit for year 4	$30,000	$5,125.26
5	Financial benefit for year 5	$20,000	$2,196.71
Total:		$160,000	$50,000.00
Minus initial investment:		($50,000)	($50,000.00)
Net present value (NPV):			$0.00
Internal rate of return (IRR):			56%

A Comparison of Project Financial Analysis Tools

Table 11.5 briefly lists the advantages and disadvantages of different financial analysis tools.

Table 11.5   A Comparison of Project Financial Analysis Tools

Tool	Primary Advantages	Primary Disadvantages	Comments
Return on investment (ROI)	Easy to calculate.	Does not account for the time value of money.	Good for short-term projects.
Cash flow	Easy to see long-term benefits.	Does not account for the time value of money.	Not a true picture for long-term projects or long-term benefits.

Tool	Primary Advantages	Primary Disadvantages	Comments
Discounted cash flow (DCF)	Provides accurate cash flow projections.	Doesn't include the project's cost.	Excellent for communicating benefits.
Net present value (NPV)	Presents an accurate projection of the project's value.	Discount rate might be unstable over time.	Excellent project-selection metric.
Internal rate of return (IRR)	Presents the project as a regular invest-ment.	Reinvests positive cash at the project's cost of capital, not the organi-zation's. It also can't account for risk.	Well known.
Modified IRR (MIRR)	Presents an accurate projection of the project as an invest-ment instrument.	Can't account for risk.	Excellent project-selection metric against other proj-ects and other investments.

The Balanced Portfolio

We require only three more concepts to allow us to develop our balanced portfolio: elim-inating dynamic prioritization as a resource-balancing tool, creating an infinite resource pool, and developing improved methods for continued resource and portfolio balancing.

Eliminate Dynamic Reprioritization

Chapter 4 presented an argument to eliminate (or significantly reduce) dynamic project priorities as a resource-balancing tool. We should prioritize projects to select or reject them, not to manage them. The primary difference is that when you select a project, you must support it. Dynamically prioritizing projects causes resource reshuffling, half-done activities, utilization inefficiencies, and other waste.

We select a project because it increases the value of our organization along one or more value tracks. When the project was selected, senior management—through the steering committee, PMO, or other authorized group—deemed that the project's value was bene-ficial to the organization. Delaying the project might reduce its value and increase its costs.

If the project is eventually abandoned, either overtly or through neglect, not only is the benefit lost, but the resources involved were also wasted and potentially demoralized.

Starving one project in favor of another creates waste.

Conditions to successfully select or reject a project include the following:

- Determine due dates by real business need, not arbitrary executive management political agendas or convenient ends of fiscal periods.

- Define and align project benefits with organizational objectives or value tracks.

- Project value must include true project cost, including internal resource cost.

- When a project is selected, support it with promised resources.

You should abandon projects only when their benefit-cost relationship becomes unfavorable. If you must abandon a project, do so cleanly.

The Infinite Resource Pool

Whether you track projects with earned value management (EVM) or some other method, the concept of the work package offers project and executive managers a distinct advantage: the ability to easily and confidently outsource project work. By definition, work packages are so well defined that the organization can easily outsource them with a fixed-price contract. This also means that the quality of the resulting product does not depend on the resource doing the work. This resource independence essentially broadens our resource pool to include any viable vendor.

The only other concern becomes cost versus time. When we start calculating the true cost and schedule for using in-house resources, outsourcing might be not only feasible, but prudent. This effectively gives the project managers and portfolio designers an infinite resource pool, enabling them to more effectively balance resources and achieve project schedules while addressing unexpected opportunities. I elaborate on this more in Part V, "Globalization and Resource Optimization."

Continued Balancing

Creating a balanced portfolio is the first concern. The next concern is continually balancing the portfolio in a dynamic environment. You need a mechanism to continually evaluate the cost–benefit relationship among projects within a portfolio, you need to quickly abandon projects in which the cost–benefit relationship becomes unfavorable, and you need a mechanism to take advantage of unexpected opportunities as they arise, without affecting other projects. The ability to embrace unexpected opportunities needs no additional tools if you can engage in that project without affecting other projects.

The tools to continually balance the portfolio are no different than those used to create it. Project portfolio designers and managers understand how to do this. The organization need only be diligent. Your job as executive manager is to ensure that they are trained, assigned the task, and supported by you.

Summary

Understanding project management and relating those core concepts to standard, accepted financial tools enables you to develop a suite of concepts to build a well-defined, structured, and value-based project investment strategy. The ubiquitous work package concept ties nicely with activity-based costing and cost of quality; ROI, NPV, IRR, and MIRR offer standard financial analysis tools to determine the true value of projects. They also enable us to compare projects to each other and to other investment strategies.

You can use Table 11.6 to help you evaluate your organization's ability to use projects as investments. In the next chapter, we integrate these concepts into cohesive investment strategies designed to maximize your investment dollars.

Table 11.6 Projects As Investments Summary Checklist

Performance Item	My Organization's Performance High ← Low				
My organization takes a value-added approach to project selection.					
Defined value tracks enable project and portfolio designers to identify project objectives that support the organization.					
Value tracks have defined and measurable targets.					
My projects successfully transfer their products into operations smoothly and efficiently.					
My organization has defined risk/reward analysis and maintenance tools.					
My project managers account for the cost of internal resources in their project budgets to provide an accurate picture of the cost of the investment.					
My organization defines both the grade and quality for the projects' products.					

(continues)

■

Table 11.6 Projects As Investments Summary Checklist (continued)

Performance Item	My Organization's Performance
	High ⟵——————⟶ Low
My organization has established financial analysis tools to determine the value of a project.					
My organization accounts for the long-term effects of projects using such tools as life cycle costing and the time value of money.					
Portfolio designers and managers are properly trained to construct and maintain the organization's portfolio in a dynamic environment.					
Executive management supports the portfolio designers and managers in their tasks.					

12

Developing a Balanced Portfolio

I introduced the concept of the balanced portfolio in Chapter 4, "Strategic Alignment." In subsequent chapters, I developed and presented additional concepts to aid in developing a portfolio. In this chapter, I expand upon those tools and concepts to develop strategies and doctrine for a comprehensive, balanced portfolio. I begin with a formal definition:

> **Balanced portfolio**—A balanced portfolio contains all programs, projects, and activities required to ensure the success of all strategic value tracks.

I divided this chapter into four sections. The first ("Themes and Concepts of a Balanced Portfolio") presents basic concepts and tools that you can use when balancing a portfolio. The second ("Basic Project Selection Methods") offers specific tools to select or rejects projects using a single criterion. The third ("Balancing a Portfolio") presents advanced techniques to optimize the portfolio using multiple criteria. The fourth ("Balancing Risk/Reward") addresses how to balance risk.

Themes and Concepts of a Balanced Portfolio

This section presents three themes regarding the balanced portfolio, including the effects of an unbalanced portfolio, suggestions regarding budgeting for different project types, and concepts to translate nonfinancial value tracks into financial benefits.

Effects of the Unbalanced Portfolio

Earlier I presented the analogy of a car's tires being out of alignment. There are two ways cars can go out of alignment: slowly over time or instantly from a specific event, such has hitting a pothole. Let's consider the former.

The former method suggests either a lack of understanding about cars, relative apathy, or nonstrategic thinking. In this case, the owner usually says he was just too busy to take the car in for alignment. This suggests that aligning the car was a low-priority item and that the owner was dealing with higher-priority items. Inevitably, after the damage has been done and at an inconvenient time, the owner must wrestle with the steering wheel, watch as the tires wear quickly and unevenly, and struggle to find the time to get the car in for alignment.

The problem now becomes operational: The owner finds it difficult to perform the simple act of driving.

**Failing to balance the portfolio causes projects
to drift toward operations instead of strategy.**

A strategic thinker would take the car in at regular, predefined intervals, eliminating the ill effects—and freeing himself to concentrate on more productive issues. If your organization is struggling to maintain operations and your staff is spending significant time handling emergencies or fire-fighting, the problem could be a lack of a strategic approach to developing a balanced project portfolio.

Budgeting for a Balanced Portfolio

Every organization employs its own financial strategy; I don't presume to guess at yours. Some concepts, however, are common. One concept is critical to budgeting for a balanced portfolio:

Project budgets must include all costs associated with the project.

Excluding any costs distorts the financial analysis required for true benefits analysis and, as we will see in the next chapter, removes flexibility. For this analysis, I use the project model I developed in Chapter 5, "A Framework for Strategic Alignment," which identifies mandatory, consequential, strategic, creative, and opportunistic projects. Let's first examine projects that reduce the available budget.

Mandatory and Consequential Projects

Recall that mandatory projects are those forced by regulatory agencies or circumstance (new regulations, union strikes, and so on). Recall also that consequential projects are those undertaken to resolve problems or issues. Both project types prevent the organization from losing value and, in general, should be done using the least-cost solution. This leaves the maximum budget for projects that increase value.

You can't always predict specific events or the effect they'll have on your project budgets, but you can identify trends. Go back into your project archives, determine which projects fall into these categories, and look at how much budget money they absorbed. If your organization is more than a few years old, you should have sufficient information to forecast expenditures for future periods. Insurance companies, for example, can develop trends for handling regulatory changes that occur annually. A simple analysis can help you predict even which states will change regulations year by year.

You should find similar trends for consequential projects. The project archives likely will show clear trends on problems and issues. If you've had quality problems with some of your products, you can see how many projects were undertaken to fix those problems, by product line or business unit. You can also see how many times you've had to send people into the field to satisfy an unhappy client.

You might face two problems when conducting this analysis. First, you might not have accurate archives. Many organizations trapped in an operational focus (dealing with issues day-by-day instead of strategically) typically don't capture such information. For example, can you determine how much engineering time your organization spent handling dissatisfied client generated issues last year?

Second, even if you have archives, you might not capture enough information about the events. For example, many organizations don't include internal personnel costs in their budgets, invalidating the analysis. However, you might be able to back into the information using time sheets or hours spent in a project by job title.

If information is simply not available, you can establish a baseline using surveys or interviews. Be careful to make the information accurate. Some people might not want to share true problems with executive management.

Whichever approach you prefer, a little information gathering should offer sufficient trends to help you establish a reasonable budget for mandatory and consequential projects.

Opportunistic Projects

Recall that opportunistic projects take advantage of unexpected opportunities. The opportunity could spawn from an external event or simply an idea that springs into someone's mind. Regardless, some opportunity exists and we want to capture it.

Theory holds that for-profit organizations do not need to allocate budget funds for opportunistic projects. This assumes that three conditions are true. Consider the following:

1. Developing the business case justifies the financial expenditure for the project.

2. The business case considers all cost, including internal resources.

3. The financial justification is based on the organization's cost of capital.

If these conditions are true, you can borrow the money. The only other considerations are how much you can borrow and risk, which I address later in this chapter. In practice, however, many organizations maintain a reserve which they can use for such projects.

Nonprofit organizations, however, might need to budget for such projects because many of these projects will not offer financial benefit. If your organization is financed through contributions (religious organizations, museums, and so on), you might be able to raise the capital through a fund-raising campaign based on the project's benefits. If you're on a fixed budget (for example, if you work for a government agency) or you don't have time to otherwise raise the capital, you need to allocate some percentage of your budget for such projects.

Strategic and Creative Projects

I group strategic and creative projects together for this discussion because they serve the same purpose: to achieve the goals of the strategic plan. Recall that their primary difference is that executive management (such as the strategic planning committee) defines strategic projects; staff members define creative projects. Therefore, if the strategic planners of a museum decide that they need to increase membership by 10 percent this year, they might offer a bonus to any employee who suggests an idea that the portfolio designers approve. Allocating some percentage of your strategic budget to creative projects builds camaraderie and loyalty. It also reduces your workload. For the rest of this discussion, I refer to both of these projects types as strategic projects.

The strategic projects are usually the highest-priority projects in the organization. They add clear and defined value to the organization, and they move the organization toward its vision. When properly defined and executed, they reduce the amount of money spent on both mandatory and consequential projects.

Classically, you allocate the budget that remains after mandatory and consequential projects to strategic and creative projects. It's easy to fall into a trap at this point. Many organizations take up their remaining budget and then "back into" the project definitions. Even worse, they define the strategic projects and force an unrealistic budget on them. Both of these approaches force project managers to limit the goals of the project based on the budget. This nearly guarantees that the projects won't achieve their goals, and you'll have wasted your strategic budget.

A better method is to solicit the support of the portfolio and project designers to identify projects to meet strategic objectives; that is, turn strategic projects into creative projects. Then have subject matter experts estimate the time and cost for those projects. One of three conditions will exist: 1) You have more than enough money, 2) you have the right amount of money, or 3) you have less money than needed. The first two need no further discussion. The latter forces you to make a choice:

- **Borrow the money**—If the project's financial analysis was done properly, it will add value greater than the cost, based on the organization's cost of capital. In other words, you'll borrow money at the cost of capital (say, 12 percent) and have an Internal Rate of Return (IRR) of, say, 56 percent. You'll be 44 percent ahead, risk and cash-flow issues notwithstanding.

- **Restructure the portfolio**—Attempt to achieve the same strategic goals with a different project mix

- **Adjust your strategic goals**—Your strategic goals might simply be too aggressive or may be ill-focused. For example, if you're spending too much money on consequential projects, you might want to focus more money on internal business development rather than new products. Review the goals and adjust them according to realistic assets.

Strategic Budgeting

Each organization is different. As an executive manager, you must work with your colleagues to determine an approach that satisfies your needs. Codify the results of that collaboration in the form of a portfolio doctrine. Consider these points:

- Use project archives to determine appropriate budgets for mandatory and consequential projects.

- Consider outside money sources for opportunistic projects.

- Properly fund strategic projects.

- Look for creative projects that satisfy multiple value tracks, balancing the remaining time and money.

Translating Value Tracks to Financial Benefit

Many nonmonetary value tracks translate easily into financial benefits in both for-profit and not-for-profit organizations. Concepts such as cost-of-quality enable project and process designers to achieve optimum financial gains regarding quality. Increasing customers translates to increased profits using predictable and easy-to-build models; efficient improvements translate into specific cost reductions.

Frequently, however, establishing these metrics is difficult and relies on assumptions, which must be both acknowledged and documented. One of the pervasive themes of this book relates to your responsibility to define a corporate culture tailored to your organization's vision. Certainly, an excellent culture is much more productive than a poor culture. So if you spend money on a project designed to improve your culture, the issue becomes establishing the productivity gain versus the investment capital relationship. Just because you might have difficulty establishing clear target metrics doesn't mean you should avoid the project.

I presented high-level concepts to resolve these issues with the goal breakdown structure, and I offer others in subsequent chapters. Norton and Kaplan's book *The Balanced Scorecard* offers additional, similar concepts. By some means, you must be able to evaluate projects based on their benefit relative to their cost. This is the basis and a necessary condition for a balanced portfolio.

Finally, when all else fails, you can compare projects using a benefit-cost ratio. If, for example, you are a museum and you want to compare projects that will increase membership, you can compare projects using a ratio such as new members/$1000 of project cost.

Establishing standard practices, aligned with the organization's portfolio doctrine for conducting these translations, further enables project and portfolio designers to properly select and reject projects.

Basic Project Selection Methods

We can now use our building blocks to develop simple methods for selecting and rejecting projects. Again, in this section, we strategically prioritize to select or reject projects, and we avoid prioritizing as an operational tactic. In particular, I present net present value (NPV) tables, internal rate of return (IRR) tables, and benefits/cost analysis approaches. I offer advanced topics as well, including risk analysis, research-driven projects or organizations, and IT portfolio generation, in subsequent sections.

NPV Tables

NPV tables are one of the simplest forms of portfolio project selection methods. The portfolio designer simply enters appropriate projects into a table and sorts the projects from highest NPV to lowest. The designer creates an additional column that contains the running total for the project budgets. The portfolio designer selects all projects above the point where the accumulated project budgets exceed the available funds. Table 12.1 shows a sample table.

Table 12.1   NPV Project Ranking Table

Project ID	Project Title	NPV ('000)	Budget ('000)	Cumulative Budget ('000)
1	Project A	$15,000	$10,000	$10,000
2	Project B	$12,500	$5,000	$15,000
3	Project C	$10,000	$7,000	$22,000
4	Project D	$9,500	$2,000	$24,000
5	Project E	$8,200	$2,500	$26,500
6	Project F	$7,250	$4,000	$30,500
7	Project G	$5,000	$4,000	$34,500

If this portfolio designer had a $25 million budget, she might select projects A–D, leaving the rest for opportunistic, creative, mandatory, and consequential projects. If the company historically expended approximately $3 million for these other projects, the strategic projects would be restricted to A–C, leaving $3 million for these other projects.

The difficulty with NPV tables is that using them can reject strategic projects based on budget. For example, if you had a $25 million budget and your strategic plan dictated that you needed projects A–F, you'd have to decide whether to borrow the money for projects E and F, restructure other projects to include the goals obtained by E and F, or postpone E and F until later.

IRR and MIRR Tables

IRR tables work identically to NPV tables, except that you sort the projects by decreasing IRR or modified internal rate of return (MIRR). Table 12.2 shows a typical MIRR project ranking table. Most organizations that use IRR or MIRR have a minimum value that they will accept for a project, for two reasons: 1) IRR/MIRR cannot account for project risk and 2) the projects must compete with other investment strategies, which could offer competitive returns.

Table 12.2 MIRR Project Ranking Table

Project ID	Project Title	MIRR	Budget ('000)	Cumulative Budget ('000)
1	Project A	240%	$10,000	$10,000
2	Project B	195%	$5,000	$15,000
3	Project C	120%	$7,000	$22,000
4	Project D	90%	$2,000	$24,000
5	Project E	85%	$2,500	$26,500
6	Project F	74%	$4,000	$30,500
7	Project G	56%	$4,000	$34,500

IRR and MIRR have an advantage over NPV: They make it easier to justify borrowing money for a project because they show the project's return in the same terms as the cost of capital. If you can borrow money at 12 percent, it's easy to justify a project with a 56 percent MIRR (again, risk and cash flow issues notwithstanding).

Benefits/Cost Ratio

Benefits/cost ratios are useful for selecting projects in which the direct financial benefits might be unimportant or difficult to calculate. These can include projects designed to improve the culture, reduce risk (assuming that well-established metrics are not available), improve processes in which activity-based costing (ABC) is not used, improve customer satisfaction, or other less-tangible benefits.

Benefits/cost ratios are also useful for not-for-profit organizations. A medical society might fund a project to determine best practices for dermatological disease or new oncology radiation procedures. A museum might want to evaluate a suite of project ideas designed to increase different value tracks, such as membership or school visits; churches might look to increase attendance at a particular service; and the police might want to reduce the number of speeders through a dangerous intersection.

Calculate the benefit/cost ratio by simply dividing the desired target metric by project cost. The target metric should map to the strategic plan or organization value statements. Then select the project(s) that achieve target objectives for minimum cost. The next section covers balancing the portfolio across multiple benefit tracks. Table 12.3 shows a benefit/cost ratio (BCR) table for a professional organization that wants to increase its membership.

Table 12.3 Benefit/Cost Ratio Table

Project	Estimated New Members	Project Cost	BCR (Members per $1,000)	Approach
A	15,000	$50,000	300	Free seminars
B	25,000	$90,000	278	Advertising campaign with mailings
C	20,000	$45,000	444	Webinar with give-a-way
D	22,000	$66,000	333	Local chapter membership drives

Balancing a Portfolio

Achieving an optimized project portfolio involves more than a strictly financial perspective. Our quest to balance the organization's portfolio and eliminate frequent project reprioritization demands a balanced suite of projects/programs that achieve all organizational objectives. Even for a for-profit organization, culture, internal process efficiency, future growth, employee loyalty, and many other aspects of the organization affect its capability to achieve its goals.

Two simple tools are useful for balancing projects across multiple objectives: balanced and weighted scorecards. More sophisticated models, including Quality Function Deployment (QFD) and House of Quality techniques are beyond the scope of this book.

Balanced Scorecards

Balanced scorecards (BSC) are tools designed to establish strategic objectives. The benefit of using a balanced scorecard for portfolio management is that the scorecard establishes a complete set of clear, measurable objectives for the portfolio designer. The portfolio designer can work with the functional managers, project managers, and business analysts to design projects that achieve all organizational objectives. The scorecard effectively becomes a checklist to ensure that the portfolio achieves all organization objectives.

The challenge with this technique involves distributing resources across the project mix. Some relatively minor objectives might absorb an inappropriate amount of resources. Simple experience improves resource apportionment in a balanced scorecard–driven organization. You can also use weighted scorecards and other techniques (presented next and in other texts) in conjunction with BSC to reapportion resources.

Weighted Scorecards

Weighted scorecards are valuable when projects offer multiple objectives. The portfolio designer creates a matrix in which the organization's benefits run down the left column and the projects run across the top. The strategic plan assigns a weight to each benefit based on its importance. The portfolio designer then determines the relative contribution for the projects for each objective.

This technique is analogous to the technique known in the 1980s as Quality Function Deployment (QFD) and currently known as the House of Quality technique in Six Sigma. One useful characteristic of these techniques is that they can be continuously decomposed into smaller units, just like the WBS and GBS. This enables the implementer to establish high-level organizational objectives, establish high-level projects and programs, and then decompose those to more detailed and specific projects and programs that map up to the strategic plans. Figure 12.1 shows a sample weighted scorecard.

Strategic planners and portfolio designers can then attach costs to each project and select the optimum set of projects.

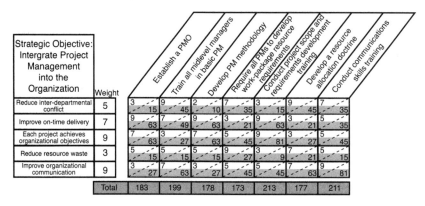

Strategic Objective: Intergrate Project Management into the Organization	Weight	Establish a PMO	Train all midlevel managers in basic PM	Develop PM methodology	Require all PMs to develop work-package resource requirements	Conduct project scope and requirements development training	Develop a resource allocation doctrine	Conduct communications skills training
Reduce inter-departmental conflict	5	3 / 15	9 / 45	2 / 10	7 / 35	3 / 15	9 / 45	7 / 35
Improve on-time delivery	7	9 / 63	7 / 49	9 / 63	3 / 21	9 / 63	3 / 21	5 / 35
Each project achieves organizational objectives	9	7 / 63	3 / 27	7 / 63	5 / 45	9 / 81	3 / 27	5 / 45
Reduce resource waste	3	5 / 15	5 / 15	5 / 15	9 / 27	3 / 9	7 / 21	5 / 15
Improve organizational communication	9	3 / 27	7 / 63	3 / 27	5 / 45	5 / 45	7 / 63	9 / 81
	Total	183	199	178	173	213	177	211

Figure 12.1 Weighted scoring model

Balancing Risk/Reward

All organizations, profit and nonprofit alike, struggle to balance risk and reward. As in any investment portfolio, a balanced project portfolio includes high-, medium-, and low-risk projects. Additionally, each organization wants to minimize its losses from risky ventures that won't succeed. The method for managing portfolio risk must allocate an appropriate proportion of projects and resources to the various risk levels, and then quickly cut losses on projects that will fail to achieve their goals. For this discussion, I present two techniques: research projects and phase gates:

- **Research projects** are short-term, inexpensive projects designed to evaluate risk, discover least-risky strategies, or determine the feasibility of high-risk project ideas.

- **Phase gates** are another method for handling risky projects. This method integrates nicely with the WBS structures presented in earlier chapters and enables executive managers to monitor and control high-risk projects with minimal organizational impact.

Research Projects

Research projects are useful for conducting early research on high-risk initiatives. Ideally, you should schedule research projects well in advance of the actual development effort—when you see new technologies entering your marketplace. You can also schedule research projects in the early stages of development projects, to handle unknowns or partially developed technologies.

As in all projects, research projects have well-defined deliverables. Deliverables are usually reports of the research results, prototypes, or mock-ups. These also can include feasibility studies, recommendations for strategies, or optimum technical solutions for technology projects. Research projects also must have clearly defined objectives. Unlike other projects, it is easy to continue research well beyond what is needed for a particular situation. Therefore, you must limit research projects by time and/or cost instead of by quality. Let's see how this might work.

Jason's Research Project

Jason is a project manager working for the program management office (PMO). The PMO wants to create a system to capture the actual time people spend on project activities, improve the reliability of project archives, remain compliant with the Sarbanes-Oxley act, and improve estimates for future projects.

Jason's project team is proficient in several databases and has selected one for this project. The database company, however, is issuing a new release of its product, including improvements in the core database engine and the human interface. The human interface is completely new and enhanced (according to the company). This leaves Jason with two risks: 1) His team doesn't know how to program in the new interface and 2) he's unsure of how the end users will react with the new interface.

He spawns two research projects. The objective for the first is to learn the best techniques for programming using the new interface. Jason assigns one of his team to this research project. The individual first takes a training class in the new product and then develops a defined set of prototype transactions that will be similar to the ones planned for the project. The objective: to discover through training plus trial-and-error the best techniques for programming using the new interface. The deliverable: the set of screens, the code behind the screens, recommendations, and the lessons learned in programming the transactions. The final project activity involves the researcher presenting his findings to the rest of the development team along with recommendations for both training and programming techniques.

Jason knows that the researcher can spend excessive time continually improving the techniques, so he sets a hard limit of three weeks and $10,000 for this research project. Wherever the researcher is when either the time or cost limit is exhausted, the project terminates and the researcher presents his findings to the team.

The second research project involves conducting a focus group on the developed screens. The group will include a cross-section of end users, who will evaluate the ease-of-use and efficiency considerations for the new interface. The project team can then modify the screens to see if the group likes the changes.

Again, this cycle can continue virtually without bound, so Jason wisely limits the project to three cycles. At the end of the third cycle, the team running the focus group must make final recommendations to the project team.

After the two projects complete, Jason can develop hard, measurable project requirements; fix the price and schedule for the project; and proceed virtually risk free.

Wisely developed research projects allow a savvy project or portfolio designer to separate the risky areas and address them safely.

The Phase-Gate Process

I first introduced phase gates in Chapter 3, "Project Definition and Planning." Recall that phases are not actually part of the work breakdown structure (WBS), but they are superimposed on the WBS to provide management-level project oversight. In this chapter, I exploit this concept to demonstrate how you can use phase gates to help balance your portfolio. One significant advantage of phase gates is that they enable you to try high-risk projects but then get out if the project fails. These steps outline the phase-gate process for this application.

1. **Allocate appropriate percentages of resources and projects to desired risk levels.** The strategic planners should establish risk levels and project apportionment based on organizational circumstances, market characteristics, senior management risk tolerance, and other factors. More aggressive organizations might include more high-risk projects; conservative organizations might include only a few—or even none. You can apportion projects by percentage of either portfolio budget or resources. You can delegate the responsibility to a savvy portfolio designer, the strategic planning committee, or the steering committee. For example, you might allocate 20 percent of your budget or resources to high-risk projects, 60 percent to medium-risk projects, and 20 percent to low-risk projects.

2. **Identify and address the riskiest aspects of the project first.** Portfolio designers should work with project designers to identify the aspects of the project that are most likely to cause the project to fail. These are frequently called *show-stoppers*.

   Project designers address these risky aspects early in the project. That way, if they cannot overcome the risk, they can terminate the project as early as possible, to move its resources to more beneficial projects.

3. **Establish clear time-phased objectives.** Employing project phases (see Chapter 3), the project and portfolio designers establish the first phases of the project to address these risky aspects. For each phase, the designers establish clear objectives that the project team must achieve to demonstrate that it has overcome the risks.

4. **Employ phase/gate reviews to terminate risky projects that don't meet their time-phased objectives.** At the end of each phase, the project manager reports on project progress to the appropriate committee (steering committee, portfolio managers, PMO, and so on). The committee evaluates the progress and terminates the project if it feels that the project won't succeed.

5. **Projects that survive have reduced their risk to a low level and can be managed as any other project.** After the project manager eliminates the risky aspects of the project, the project can move to a more standard development cycle. This does not mean that a project should stop having phase gate reviews. Such reviews should continue even as the project's risk reduces. The capability to terminate any project at a phase gate enables the organization to constantly monitor and balance its portfolio as circumstances change. In formal project management, projects also can be held temporarily, to address other opportunities or emergencies.

Figure 12.2 shows this concept. In the figure are four projects. The first (Project A) fails to pass its initial assessment, indicating that the subject matter experts decided that the project isn't worth pursuing. Project B passes its initial assessment. The project team attempts but fails to eliminate the highest-level risks. For project C, the project team eliminated the highest-level risks but failed to eliminate the medium-level risks. Project D passed all the risk-related phases and progressed into the standard product development cycle.

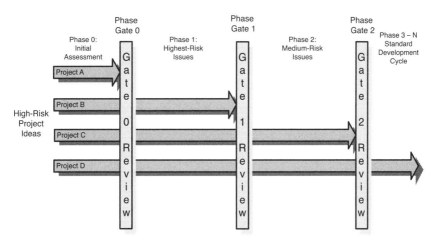

Figure 12.2   Phase-gate reviews

Example: Outsourcing Manufacturing Overseas

As an example, let's look at an organization that plans to move its manufacturing overseas.

Acme Manufacturing Company produces high-quality widgets. However, Acme can't compete with foreign imports on cost and is losing market share. Acme undertakes a project to move manufacturing to the Far East. The strategic planners establish clear objectives for the project:

- Reduce manufacturing costs (now to also include shipping) by 60 percent

- Maintain current product quality and tolerances

- Product order lead time not to exceed two months (allowing Acme to maintain only a two-month inventory)

Acme's standard process identifies Phase 0 as an assessment phase. The project designer conducts a quick assessment and determines that achieving the cost objective will not be difficult, but quality and schedule will. Acme further discovers that the country selection has as much impact on cost, schedule, and quality as the company within the country. The project designers establish the following phases:

- **Phase 1: Select country and determine feasibility of success.** This first phase has three deliverables. The first is the country that should present the greatest probability of achieving all the objectives. The second deliverable is a feasibility study that outlines the probability of achieving the objectives. The third deliverable is the plan to select a company.

At the end of Phase 1, the project manager can present the results to the appropriate committee. If the committee is satisfied that the project is viable, it can proceed to phase 2; otherwise, the committee terminates the project.

- **Phase 2: Create a short list of companies within the country and determine the feasibility of success.** Phase 2 now authorizes the project team to execute the plan to select a company. Phase 2 deliverables include a short list of potential business partners, a more detailed feasibility study outlining the probability for success, and a plan to select the partner and conduct final negotiations.

This approach isolates the risky items, enables the project and portfolio designers to address the items quickly, and allows senior management to control organization risk.

Summary

This chapter presents common techniques that you can use to develop a balanced portfolio. This list of tools is not exhaustive; you can use it alongside other tools and techniques that work for you. The only criterion to determine whether a tool is useful is to determine whether it helps you define and manage projects that increase your organization's value while minimizing resources. Table 12.4 shows the organizational evaluation matrix for this chapter.

Table 12.4 Balanced Portfolio Organization Evaluation Matrix

Performance Item	My Organization's Performance High ⟵————⟶ Low				
My organization takes a balanced portfolio approach.					
My organization has well-defined value tracks.					
My organization communicates these value tracks to the portfolio and project designers.					
My organization has techniques for justifying projects financially.					
My organization has techniques for justifying projects' organizational value but not their intangible financial value.					
My organization can prioritize projects based on multiple value tracks.					
My organization constantly tracks the progress of the portfolio, adding or cancelling projects as appropriate.					
My organization allocates an appropriate budget for all project types.					
My organization can identify and manage low-, medium-, and high-risk projects.					
My organization addresses risk up front to stabilize the portfolio.					
My organization sets limits for pure research and risky activities.					

13

Balanced Portfolio Techniques in Action

I n this chapter, I present several scenarios and suggest how to develop and maintain a balanced portfolio using presented techniques. There are as many different strategies to achieving a balanced portfolio as there are strategists. Each organization is unique, with a unique set of strengths and weaknesses. You need to select the set of techniques that's right for you.

This book is not a cookbook—it's designed to inspire.

Portfolio Management for Research-Driven Organizations

I once led a workshop for project managers and technical leads in project management at a large research-driven company. The attendees looked forward to the class because they were overworked and very few projects were successful.

In this particular class, I was told that the class would have to start late on the last day because the company was having a mandatory company-wide meeting. At the scheduled time, the attendees strolled into the training room, heads down in obvious dismay. I asked what happened at the meeting.

> "We have a new corporate edict," one participant told me. "All of us are to dedicate 20 percent of our time to pure research."
>
> Having spent some time with the group already, and understanding their current workload, I (hesitantly) asked, "Does that mean that they're taking away 20 percent of your other duties?"
>
> "No," responded the attendee. "That's why we're all so upset."

Balancing portfolios in a research-driven organization offers unique challenges. For our discussion, we must separate pure research from development research.

Pure Research

Pure research has no particular objective other than discovery. A scientist might mix two lipids and heat them just to see what happens, or an engineer might rub together two pieces of a material just to determine their coefficient of friction. Pure research is technically not a project in the modern sense. Each experiment might have an objective, but it has no (or vague) time and cost boundaries, and many experiments are performed purely for curiosity. These actions are necessary in any research-driven organization, but they must be limited and controlled.

A colleague of mine once presented me with a problem she was having with a client. The client was a start-up company with an excellent technology that improved renewable energy generation and improved energy efficiency in many fields. The firm hired her to help take the company to the next level. I took one look at the management team and told her she should cancel her contract and look for another client.

The management team was a group of technology experts; all had at least one Ph.D. to their credit—most had several. They weren't about to focus on the business; they were focusing on the technology. The company filed bankruptcy five months following this discussion, and my colleague was never paid for her work.

> **Senior management must constrain pure research by apportioning resources and time, and must maintain its focus on the objectives of the organization.**

Again, the secret to achieving a goal is to establish clear organizational metrics. For example, pharmaceutical companies incur significant research costs, in both pure and developmental research. One metric that might be appropriate for pure research is the amount of dollars spent on pure research verses the number of approved FDA products per year. This sends a clear message to the scientists—we're here to develop products, not run random experiments in a lab. In the drug companies' defense, the lag time between research and product approval can be many years.

> **Management must maintain a very strict discipline on research because failures could take years to manifest.**

Scientists' and researchers' objectives don't always align with the organization. Your job as an executive is to make sure the researchers maintain their focus and generate tangible products that support the organization. Scientists can turn into successful entrepreneurs, but this is very rare.

At some point, pure research might generate a viable idea for a product. At this point, the pure research stops and development research begins.

Development Research

Development research has objectives. For example, a drug company might want to design a protein that can be taken orally to help dissolve calcified blood clots in patients with deep vein thrombosis. Returning to our basement remodeling portfolio I presented earlier, you might conduct development research to determine the best home theater video and audio offerings and examine your soundproofing options before you commit to a home theater.

Development research is a high-risk activity. For high-risk projects, we must determine whether the project is viable while expending minimal resources.

For high-risk projects, address the greatest risks early in the project.

You do this using research projects, presented in the previous chapter. If you combine this technique with phase gates, you have a comprehensive strategy that enables you to embrace high-risk projects with minimum downside loss.

Research-Driven Project Strategy

Figure 13.1 offers a flow for addressing high-risk and research-driven projects.

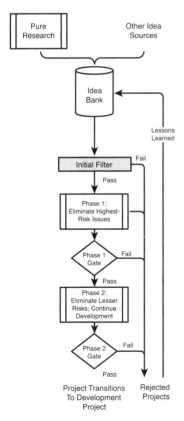

Figure 13.1 Research project flow

Idea Banks

Ideas banks are an excellent method for feeding ideas into the product development cycle. Pure research, for example, can pass product ideas into the idea bank, which then feeds the development cycle using the process defined next.

Initial Project Filter

A committee regularly reviews ideas in the idea bank and filters obvious rejects, including duplicates, ideas not aligned with organizational objectives, and ideas that were recently tried and failed. Ideas that survive this initial filter pass into the phase-gate process.

Phase Review Teams

Surviving projects enter the first phase of the development cycle. Employing concepts presented earlier, this first phase addresses the highest-risk aspects of the project first. Objectives for Phase 1 include resolving key show-stoppers. Activities might include:

- Conduct an initial patent search to prevent lawsuits
- Research technical production aspects to determine the risks and difficulty in producing the product
- Research the availability and cost of raw materials
- Conduct an initial marketability study to determine the potential market size and identify what customers would be willing to pay for the product
- Research the availability of a production facility and equipment
- Determine whether the product aligns with organizational objectives
- Research inventory, shipping, and handling issues
- Research regulatory issues

Because the project is heavily research oriented, we place clear boundaries on time and resources to maintain control. For example, Phase 1 might have a solid constraint of $10,000 and three weeks. If the project team cannot adequately address these issues within that period and cost, the committee terminates the project.

Phase objectives dictate the constituents of the phase review teams. For this example, the phase review team requires some representation from legal, marketing, senior management, technology, and production.

Projects that pass Phase 1 proceed to Phase 2. Phase 2 addresses lesser risks and elaborates on the work conducted in Phase 1. This phase might require a full patent search, high-level production line design, marketing business strategy, and so on. Phase 2 also necessitates creating a high-level project plan for development and product rollout, including costs by phase, key milestone schedules, and resource requirements. In this example, Phase 2 is neither research nor a formal project. The portfolio designer might negotiate with the project team regarding time and cost boundaries. Projects that pass Phase 2 then become normal development projects.

Portfolio Management for Nonprofit Organizations

For-profit organizations invest money to make more money. This simplifies project justification and funding. For-profit organizations can borrow money, sell stock, and issue bonds to fund lucrative projects.

Nonprofit organizations invest money for nonfinancial benefits. Funding options are more restrictive, and although money is not your primary concern, maintaining fiscal responsibility and apportioning funds to maximize organizational benefits is a concern (or, at least, should be).

Recall that *value tracks* are specific, well-defined areas where the organization intends to benefit. For example, a museum might choose to define three primary value tracks in this year's strategic plan:

1. Involve and cater to the intellectual community to generate notoriety, improve quality, and justify grants

2. Involve the local community and schools to generate exhibit traffic and community relations

3. Increase membership to generate exhibit traffic, support, and revenue

A synagogue might define value tracks for congregants, Hebrew education, and global charities. A state governor might focus on education, health care, and tax reform. These value tracks should support the organization definition statements and be fully defined in the strategic plan.

The challenge in developing a balanced portfolio stems from balancing resources against the potential benefits. A single project might benefit the tax reform value track, but it might absorb so many resources that the health care and education value tracks suffer. Balancing resources across the value tracks becomes the challenge. We can approach this problem from two perspectives: using a creative approach and using a strategic approach.

The **creative approach** involves generating project ideas from the staff. The organization considers a suite of projects that aim to provide value along the defined value tracks. You can accomplish this through classical facilitated group techniques, including brainstorming, the nominal group technique, the Delphi technique, and so on. The organization establishes early estimates for resource requirements for each project and then uses a weighted scorecard technique to select a project portfolio that offers the most benefits along the value tracks. Success depends on the accuracy of the estimates and the organization's self-discipline.

The **strategic approach** uses the organization's objectives as the primary driver. This approach is analogous to (if not identical to) developing a strategic plan for a for-profit organization. The organization defines short-, medium-, and long-term objectives, and then defines projects to meet those objectives. The challenge here is that the project mix could absorb more resources than are available. Unlike a for-profit organization, the not-for-profit is more restricted in its capability to raise funds to close the resource gap. The organization must choose to readjust its objectives or find more revenue. Weighted score-cards, balanced scorecards, and other previously mentioned techniques directly apply to this approach.

I generally recommend a **mixed approach**, in which the strategic planning committee defines the core strategic projects and allows the staff to design the rest of the value track projects. As you experiment with this approach, you might find that the staff gladly offers great ideas for all strategic projects.

Balancing an Internal IT Portfolio

What are good tools worth? The quality and quantity of tools in a tool set might differ between a master cabinet maker and a general carpenter, but the answer remains unchanged. All professionals' ability to perform their duties depends on appropriate tools. However, the cost justification might be difficult. The master cabinetmaker can easily justify expensive woodworking tools, but these would be wasted on the general carpenter.

Justifying IT projects has proven to be particularly challenging partly for this reason. For-profit organizations view IT as overhead or a cost center and try to reduce or eliminate that cost, starving the IT department of resources. Many organizations view IT almost as a low-level service organization, which has the effect of abusing precious organizational resources, frequently without appropriate business justification.

In this section, I take an investment perspective of IT projects and view IT as a tool supplier, creating both a stable IT department and an organizational working environment. Our tools include activity-based costing (ABC), life cycle costing, and our strategic plan.

IT Value Tracks

We can define two value tracks for internal IT departments. The first is to build and support a technology infrastructure upon which specific applications can reside. The infrastructure also offers common application services, such as e-mail, Web access, computer-based conferencing, and word processing. Let's call these infrastructure projects.

The second value track is to offer services to the rest of the organization regarding specific applications, including help with hardware and software selection, adaptation, installation, and support services. Let's call these client application projects.

Infrastructure Projects

The technology infrastructure is a tool of the strategic plan and executive management. Through the strategic plan, executive management should provide IT guidance regarding size and coverage for the infrastructure. Specifically, if the IT department knows that the organization plans to grow 20 percent within the next 12 months, it can create project plans to provide support for the growth. If IT is unaware of the growth, it will always be playing catch-up and will have ever-changing project requirements, yielding poor service, response, and support.

Additionally, as executive management establishes the culture of the entire organization, they must also establish the culture of the technology infrastructure. Such culture includes guidance for IT regarding security, up-time performance, and general support for organization applications. Continuing our earlier analogy, senior management should restrict general carpenters from wasting money on expensive cabinet-maker tools. Conversely, senior management should encourage the master cabinet makers to acquire the tools needed to do their job. This applies to application areas (finance, engineering, marketing, and so on) as well as IT.

If senior management ignores either of these responsibilities, one of two results follows: 1) IT takes on the responsibility independently, or 2) a level of anarchy occurs at the expense of the IT department as the organizations' departments fight over IT resources.

I don't intend to present a formal discourse on the merits and issues associated with the varying forms of IT management. I do claim that, as in all other projects, IT projects must roll up and support the organization's strategy and goals.

The technology infrastructure is not overhead, but rather an investment, as with any other organizational asset.

A sound, right-sized, properly supported infrastructure enhances the entire organization's capability to perform its work. Additionally, it enhances each department's capability to identify, install, and run appropriate tools for their jobs.

If this argument is insufficient, consider the converse situation, in which IT has misaligned the infrastructure compared to the strategic plan. Here, oversizing actually is more beneficial than undersizing. The latter results in downtime (resulting in huge production losses), security risks, lost archive data, expensive infrastructure patchwork, and poorly installed software tools that are difficult or impossible to support. Oversizing only wastes money, a lesser issue.

As the executive committee rolls out the strategic plan, the IT group must be aware of the plan and include its own projects to provide support for the plan. Funding for such projects clearly is the responsibility of executive management through the IT budget. I encourage all IT departments to promote life-cycle costing, otherwise the IT department will always borrow from the future.

Client Application Projects

In contrast, specific applications that different departments require are the responsibility of those departments. Acquisition, installation, and support for departmental applications is also an investment. The client, not the performing organization (in this case, IT), is responsible for justifying the cost of the project. In addition, the cost of the project itself must be included in the analysis and allocated to the client's organization.

This means that if the engineering department wants a new computer-aided design (CAD) system, the cost of analysis, purchase, installation, training, and support for that CAD system should be allocated to the engineering department, not the IT department. You can accomplish this through ABC or similar techniques. The lack of a charge-back system places IT in the difficult (and incorrect) position of having to capitulate to unreasonable requests—or play the role of the bad guy by saying no.

A sufficient charge-back system still can place engineering at odds with IT. As IT charges its services back to other departments, the cost of those services comes into question. If IT is poorly managed, it will have to overcharge for its services. Executive management must also decide if IT should be a profit center or zero-based. If it's a profit center, how much profit should it make? Only executive management can answer this question.

Even if executive management answers this question, a mismanaged or improperly run IT department will be both a financial and technological burden to the organization. You can resolve this through checks and balances (such as balanced scorecard or OGBS metrics) and by allowing the departments to outsource IT services. This philosophy requires the IT department to remain competitive with other solutions.

Many organizations have outsourced many of their IT services for this reason. An alternative to outsourcing the entire IT department is to allow departments to outsource specific projects as long as their projects comply with infrastructure requirements.

IT Portfolio Conclusion

Dividing IT projects (and services) into two values tracks enables us to properly align IT projects with the right client and properly allocate IT costs. With this philosophy, the organization's strategic plan should drive and align IT infrastructure projects, and executive management must define the desired technology culture.

In contrast, each department should define specific applications. Project costs should be allocated through an ABC or similar charge-back system. Individual departments must justify the application cost and IT support as an investment; this is not IT's responsibility.

Maintaining a Balanced Portfolio

The portfolio manager, the PMO, or another tactical authority can manage a well-balanced portfolio using tactical means. If the portfolio was well designed, the designer can pipeline the projects based on resource availability and strategic need. The PMO or portfolio manager can initiate projects at designated times with little or no strategic review or intervention. However, even in the most efficient and predictable environments, senior-level management must review the project status periodically, if just as a check and balance. Consider these typical reviews:

- **Regular portfolio reviews**—As with all on-going activities, senior management should review project portfolios on a regularly scheduled basis. Reviews should be presented by the PMO, portfolio manager, or project and program managers, or by an appropriate combination of these.

- **Phase gate reviews**—The PMO, steering committee, portfolio manager, or specially designated gate review teams should review projects at phase gates to determine progress and authorize subsequent phases.

- **Exception meetings**—Exception meetings can be conducted as needed to handle special situations. Unexpected exception meetings should be rare once project management matures in your organization.

The next section covers changes at the strategic level.

Handing Opportunities

Every organization must confront unexpected opportunities. Although these could seem auspicious initially, they can severely impact a project portfolio and result in more damage than value. Pulling resources from on-going projects could inadvertently damage those projects and the staff members moved. Frequently shifting resources leaves many work packages incomplete and demoralizes the staff. Fortunately for us, however, we can exploit the work package nature of project cost management. This becomes our strategy for handling opportunities:

1. Determine the true value for the opportunity using the same select/reject methods used to develop the portfolio.

2. Allow the portfolio designer to schedule the opportunistic project using standard means.

3. If resources become overloaded, the portfolio manager works with project managers to determine which work packages can be successfully outsourced to rebalance the workload.

Properly developed portfolios do not need to terminate or postpone ongoing projects to make room for unexpected opportunities.

Ideally, no projects should be cancelled or delayed past their true need date. Existing projects typically demonstrate an ROI greater than the cost of capital or a positive NPV, thereby justifying any needed borrowing to fund the projects. The serendipitous nature of work packages enables project managers to outsource work packages quickly, with little impact on project quality, schedule, or cost.

The only exception is if cash flow prevents real money from being expended on outside resources. However, if the strategic planning committee can justify resources, including the cost of internal resources, acquiring money to fund the project should not be an issue.

If some projects must be cancelled to make way for opportunistic projects, cancel them cleanly and swiftly, and don't look back. Keep such practices to a minimum, to keep from demoralizing project staff.

Handling Failing Projects

When project management is running properly, portfolio managers will know well in advance when projects are in trouble. Change management, combined with appropriate escalation procedures in the projects' communication plans, will inform executive management of project difficulties long before they are catastrophic.

Cancel projects only when their values can no longer be achieved or their value/cost relationship becomes adverse.

In other words, reevaluate the project based on the current select/reject criteria. If necessary, you can successfully terminate projects at phase gates or funding milestones. If a project must be cut, cut it. Many projects linger because of momentum or "sunk costs." Sunk costs are the costs already spent on the project. I agree with most experts:

Do not consider sunk costs when deciding whether to terminate a project.

That money is gone. Throwing more money at a bad project just increases your sunk costs—it doesn't get you a return. Okay, you made a mistake; cut your losses and move on.

Handling Changes in Organizational Environment

Well-balanced portfolios are a product of the organization's environment. As long as the environment remains relatively predictable, the well-balanced portfolio will remain stable. Under this premise, we can consider two levels of environmental change: microscopic and macroscopic.

- **Microscopic change**—Affects a portion of the portfolio, but not the project selection criteria
- **Macroscopic change**—Affects the selection criteria and, therefore, might affect the entire portfolio

We can define **microscopic change** as a relatively minor change affecting a small number of projects. For example, a competitor might announce a new product with many more features than your marketing group predicted. Another example might be an unexpected regulation that arises from a sudden geopolitical situation.

Such events require the portfolio designers, project managers, and key stakeholders to reevaluate their projects, to determine viability within the new environment. In essence, project designers and portfolio designers must re-approve their projects using the established select/reject criteria the organization already embraces. Portfolio and project designers can cancel or redefine projects to accommodate the new environment as appropriate.

Of course, I don't intend to oversimplify the issue. This disruptive situation requires extensive effort on the part of the portfolio designers, project designers, managers, key stakeholders, and executive management. The key functions and actions, however, are already in place; no new approaches are required. The portfolio managers and designers review the project mix to make sure that strategic objectives are still intact and that resources are appropriately distributed. They issue change requests to the appropriate project managers to address the issues. Project change management helps resolve the issues at the project level.

Macroscopic changes can affect the entire portfolio. These include such major events as organizational acquisitions, change in organizational direction (mission statements, value statements, and so on), changes in upper-level management, a global economic cataclysm, or even the change of a bond rating that significantly affects the cost of capital. Such changes require the strategic planning committee to reevaluate the very basis for the evaluation criteria and potentially determine new project selection criteria. Each situation is different, so the (potentially new) strategic planning committee should consider each one. From a project and portfolio perspective, however, when changes occur, they should be well planned to avoid as much disruption as possible. Fortunately, projects that show the greatest returns will probably survive, as long as their values align with the new organizational direction.

Summary

I save you some reading here by combining this chapter's summary with a brief discussion regarding the balanced portfolio doctrine. As with all activities you delegate to those outside executive management, I urge you to present clear guidelines to those delegates, to ensure that their work meets your needs and expectations. As you delegate the strategic projects to portfolio designers and project designers, you provide them clear success criteria through the balanced portfolio doctrine. Table 13.1 offers suggestions regarding the content of the doctrine through the summary organizational evaluation matrix.

Table 13.1 Balanced Portfolio Doctrine Organization Evaluation Matrix

Performance Item	My Organization's Performance High ← → Low				
My organization's balanced portfolio doctrine has clear project selection/rejection criteria for inclusion in the portfolio.					
My organization's balanced portfolio doctrine guides portfolio and project designs to ensure that all strategic value tracks are supported.					
My organization's balanced portfolio doctrine has guidelines for embracing high-risk, high-reward projects that don't endanger the strategic portfolio.					
My organization's balanced portfolio doctrine has guidelines to manage, limit, and focus pure research based on the organization's objectives.					
My organization's balanced portfolio doctrine clearly supports infrastructure projects needed to support the strategic goals.					
My organization's balanced portfolio doctrine demands organizational justification for internal projects.					
My organization's balanced portfolio doctrine provides clear guidelines for terminating failed projects.					
My organization's balanced portfolio doctrine provides for oversight and checks and balances for the portfolio.					
My organization's balanced portfolio doctrine provides for communication between executive management and the portfolio managers regarding the portfolio's progress and problems.					
My organization's balanced portfolio doctrine provides guidelines to handle opportunistic and consequential projects.					
My organization's balanced portfolio doctrine encourages participation through creative projects.					

14

Globalization and Strategic Outsourcing

S trategic outsourcing adds many benefits to an organization. When we combine these strategies with project management concepts developed in earlier chapters, we can reexamine outsourcing from a new perspective. By developing the proper outsourcing strategy, you can create a pool of resources sufficient to capture new opportunities without affecting your ongoing strategic projects. In essence, you create an **infinite resource pool.** For our purposes, I cite the goal of strategic outsourcing using this perspective:

> **Strategic outsourcing creates an infinite resource pool: providing the organization with sufficient resources to capture all opportunistic and creative projects without sacrificing ongoing projects.**

We cannot fully discuss outsourcing without also addressing globalization. Globalization has opened up new markets and ideas, and offers new and less expensive vendors. However, the rush to capitalize on globalization has cost many organizations money, clients, and respect. Many organizations that outsourced their IT or customer service activities overseas are now pulling them back. Other companies that outsourced their manufacturing overseas are reeling from quality issues and lawsuits. As with any other discipline, globalization and strategic outsourcing must mature.

In this chapter, I use previously developed concepts to structure an outsourcing doctrine that takes advantage of overseas opportunities as well as domestic outsourcing. I limit my discussion to outsourcing project opportunities. This excludes outsourcing entire departments, such as IT, customer service, or manufacturing. I also exclude selling overseas.

Outsourcing at the project level requires agility. The portfolio/project designers and managers must balance resources week by week and month by month. Capturing opportunities or handling emergencies frequently requires you to outsource work that was originally assigned to in-house staff, frequently on short notice. Let's refer to this as **portfolio agility**.

As an executive, you cannot make every outsourcing decision. You must delegate the day-to-day decisions to appropriate managers—in this case, the portfolio/project designers and managers. To accomplish this, you create a framework, a structure, and rules to guide those individuals to make decisions aligned with the organization by creating an outsourcing doctrine. Ultimately, your doctrine will help you take advantage of many outsourcing benefits:

- Gain strategic advantage by capitalizing on less expensive vendors.
  - Take advantage of foreign country pricing.
  - Capture pricing and quality benefits by using more experienced vendors.
- Improve resource efficiency.
  - Maximize the productivity of your in-house staff by allowing them to focus on their expertise.
  - Stabilize and balance staff.
- Reduce time-to-market and project delivery times.
  - Augment staff where needed to improve time-to-market or reduce project delivery times for strategic advantage.
- Improve strategic advantage and portfolio agility.
  - You will create a resource pool that you can tap quickly to adjust to an ever-changing marketplace.
  - You will capture and take advantage of less expensive solutions without sacrificing quality.
  - You will capture new technologies to improve your ability to address your marketplace.

Outsourcing Considerations

Outsourcing offers many advantages, but it also incurs risk. In this section, I present both positive and negative considerations that affect your approach to strategic outsourcing in a project environment:

- Giving away your strategic advantage
- Product quality considerations
- Project and organizational risk
- Resource considerations
- Globalization factors
- Management and oversight
- Environmental factors

Giving Away Your Strategic Advantage

Each organization retains certain technology, methods, or strategies that both separate it from its competitors and offer it advantages. When outsourcing, either you must avoid giving away your secrets to a vendor that could capitalize on them or you must enforce secrecy through nondisclosure and noncompete clauses in the agreements.

Nondisclosure and noncompete clauses work well within a country, but they become more difficult to enforce in other countries, especially distant countries that have different cultures and laws. You must know the laws of that country, know how well that country enforces those laws, and have sufficient legal presence in that country in case you need to enforce those clauses. Many companies have lost significant money because they couldn't enforce a contract overseas. Until you've established a strong relationship with your vendors, it's wise to assume that the technologies you outsource will be in the public domain.

> **When developing your outsourcing doctrine, avoid outsourcing technologies and procedures that give you strategic advantage.**

Of course, outsourcing not only saves money, but it can also help reduce your time to market. By getting your product to market more quickly, you get a jump on the competition even if they do get a hold of your technical advantage—this can make you the market leader and help you hold on to your advantage longer.

Product Quality Considerations

Losing your strategic advantage is not the only outsourcing risk. Product quality might be difficult to control among different vendors and countries.

Consider a classic IT project that builds a computer system. The system consists of a number of software and hardware components. Using the concepts presented earlier in this book, the project team develops a work breakdown structure with work packages. Each work package creates one of the components. The team decides to outsource some of the software work packages to a company in India, to save money and reduce the overall project time.

For simplicity, let's consider two possible vendor outcomes: 1) The components created by the vendor integrate seamlessly into the rest of the system, or 2) they do not.

Again, for simplicity, let's consider two possible ways the project team can manage the vendor: 1) The project team carefully inspects the completed products against clear, measurable performance characteristics, or 2) the team does not. This simplified perspective yields a 2×2 matrix, shown in Table 14.1.

Table 14.1 Possible Outcomes of an Outsourced Work Package

	Vendor's Components Work Seamlessly	Vendor's Components Are Flawed
The project team carefully inspects the components against clear, measurable performance requirements.	Testing goes quickly, the components are accepted, and the vendor is paid.	Testing goes quickly, defects are identified, and the product is returned to the vendor for repair.
The project team does not inspect the components.	The vendor is paid and the components are put on the shelf until system integration. System integration goes well (at least, regarding the vendor's components).	The vendor is paid and the components are put on the self until system integration. Integration goes badly; the project team expends an enormous amount of time fixing software components they didn't write and don't understand.

Now consider how we achieve any of the three acceptable results. To create components that integrate seamlessly, the vendor needs complete, clear, measurable performance requirements. The vendor also must engage in rigorous quality control to produce components that meet those requirements. Similarly, the project team needs clear, measurable performance requirements to test against before it can inspect the component.

Successful outsourcing begins with clear, measurable performance requirements.

This is true whether you are outsourcing components or services. In the case of services, you might have more trouble measuring the results. Also, you can outsource studies, investigations, or research. Here, you must place requirements on the researchers' performance, as well as any products or deliverables. For example, imagine that you hire a research company to investigate proteins that can dissolve calcified blood clots. The project includes requirements that stipulate acceptable research methods, the desired performance characteristics of the proteins (for example, that it be injectable and nontoxic, that it not impair normal blood clotting, and so on), investigation techniques (for example, all investigators must maintain lab notebooks in specific formats), and limits on the time and resources applied to the investigation.

The goal in specifying performance requirements for research is not to restrict the research, but to ensure that the research is done professionally and produces true, accurate results.

Globalization adds one final consideration in this area. Anecdotal feedback that I get from seminar participants indicates that even with clear measurable requirements, international language and cultural differences cause misinterpretations. The "thumbs-up" hand signal here in the United States means that everything's okay; in Australia, it means something totally different (look it up if you're interested).

As a seminar leader, I travel across the United States and can attest that you don't have to leave the United States to find cultural differences. I use a different presentation style when teaching in San Francisco than I do in Chicago, and I use a third style in New York City. I have a fourth style for the Southeast.

> **Prototypes, pilots, demonstrations, and other real, tangible, visible intermediate deliverables help ensure that both parties agree on the work and its results.**

Either the project team or the vendor can take these interim steps. For our scenario, their objective is to ensure that both the project team and the vendor have a common understanding of the requirements.

Project and Organizational Risk

Outsourcing regarding risk involves two perspectives. On one hand, outsourcing can reduce project risk by finding skilled, inexpensive vendors. On the other hand, improperly planned outsourcing increases risk, by entrusting unskilled vendors with part of your project. Let's first consider how you might use outsourcing to reduce organizational risk in a project.

Let's say you are planning a 20 percent growth in a particular market segment. Instead of hiring, plan to outsource the initial increase in workload. If your expansion is successful, you'll have the money and can continue to outsource until you can hire. If you're unsuccessful, you won't have the burden of paying staff that you can't afford or can't use.

> **Preplanned outsourcing enables you to anticipate and reduce organization risk.**

You can use this same approach to accept risky projects. Preplan your outsourcing strategy so that if the project takes off, you can cover the additional workload. If the project fails, you won't have unneeded staff.

On the other hand, as we've already seen, outsourcing itself is risky. You're entrusting some aspect of your project to someone in a different organization that has a different agenda. Additionally, despite your best interviewing, vetting, and prequalification techniques, some incompetent vendors sneak through and, occasionally, even the best vendors run into trouble.

Start slowly. Anticipate risks. Determine what works well for you before you open the floodgates for your strategic outsourcing approach.

Resource Considerations

One of the most overlooked reasons to outsource is simply to balance resource loads for the organization. In this section, I present concepts to balance a classical cross-functional matrix structure.

Earlier in this book, I presented the concept that organizations historically are structured for process-oriented functions. Next year's budgets are based on last year's budgets, financial managers base resource needs on their regular financial cycles, and even engineering managers who are familiar with project management look at last year's numbers to determine whether they should hire for this year. None of these methods considers project fluctuations.

Let's look at resource loading for a department. Remember one of the key roles of a functional manager:

**A functional or department manager must supply resources
for both regular process work and project work.**

If we plot the resource demands for the regular functional/routine work over time, we would expect to find a relatively flat graph. Some seasonal bumps might show up, or we may be expanding or contracting; but generally, our graph is flat.

Now let's add project work to the graph. Project work is not regular—it's not flat. It contains periods of high workload followed by periods of low workload. Adding project work to the regular process work yields Figure 14.1.

Functional managers must provide staff based on the upper curve. For this example, I assume that the portfolio designers/managers and project designers/managers have resource-leveled as much as they can and that the functional or routine work is increasing slightly.

This graph includes a very important assumption. The assumption is that we can determine the shape of the graph.

**Accurate resource demands can be determined only when
project managers plan their resource needs in advance.**

In other words, without accurate project plans, you can't determine the shape of the graph. Without mature project management, any resource planning is speculative at best. Even with this planning, as you can see, resource demands tend to be volatile. You can satisfy these highly volatile resource demands in several ways:

- Delay projects
- Hire and fire
- Outsource work
- Hire temporary help/consultants

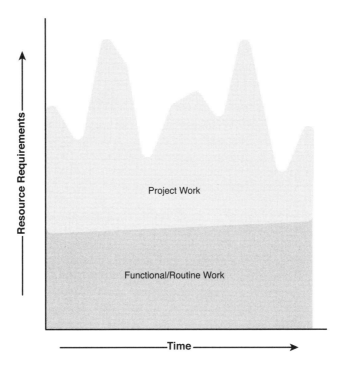

Figure 14.1   Resource requirements for project and process work

To determine your best outsourcing approach, consider the following:

Consideration	Discussion
Maintain your strengths	Use your own staff where you are strong.
Build new strengths	You might want to build new strengths to improve your strategic advantage. You can do this through training. You can also hire consultants who specialize in the new technology and learn from them.
Outsource what's easy	Some work lends itself to outsourcing, while other work does not.

With these considerations in mind, let's examine each alternative.

Delay Projects

This option is available for projects that have minimal benefits or projects for which you can delay the benefits without affecting the organization's strategic objectives. This option requires a solid, well-communicated strategic plan. When the strategic plan is vague or not communicated, the portfolio designers are left to guess and they assume that they can't delay any project. Certainly, delaying the wrong project will hurt the company.

Also recall from Chapter 4, "Strategic Alignment," that this approach can be disruptive and inefficient. Although it can succeed in some circumstances, you should avoid it as a general approach.

Hire and Fire

The logistics and resulting negative reputation you'll generate by frequently going through hiring and firing cycles ultimately will make it difficult for you to hire good talent. Large organizations with long-term projects (five to ten years in duration) might find this technique useful.

Outsource Work

This is a favorable solution for well-defined work that doesn't give up strategic advantage. It is also excellent for well-defined work that includes technologies in which your own organization is weak. Using the techniques already presented in this book, you should be able to fix-price the work to reduce both your financial and schedule risk. You won't have to worry about assimilating consultants into your team, finding work space, or dealing with personality issues.

Hire Temporary Help/Consultants

If you can't outsource the work packages because they lack definition, because they give away strategic advantage, or for other reasons, you might consider bringing in temporary help. You can hire in two areas: the functional/routine work and the project work. Generally, hiring temporary help to handle the functional/routine work is preferred. Refer to Figure 14.2.

This approach offers several advantages. First, day-labor or consultants who perform these routine functions tend to be less expensive and easier to find than those in specialized fields. Second, it's easy to evaluate their work because this work is routine. Third, and perhaps most important, you can hire the same people the next time you're overloaded. You won't have to retrain them, you won't have to deal with new personality conflicts or team issues, and they'll become productive more quickly.

You then can use your in-house staff for the project work. This will give them a break from their (perhaps) boring routine work, giving them a change of pace. You can also see how they'll perform in a project environment. Sometimes hiring consultants to do project work is more advantageous (see Figure 14.3).

Use this option when you need expertise that's not available in-house, or simply to reduce project risk.

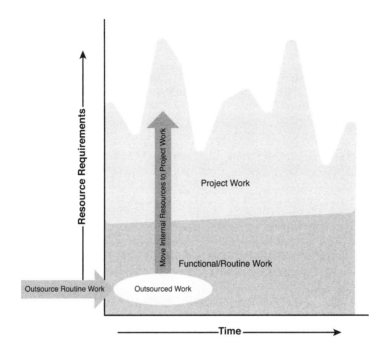

Figure 14.2   Hiring temporary help in functional/routine work

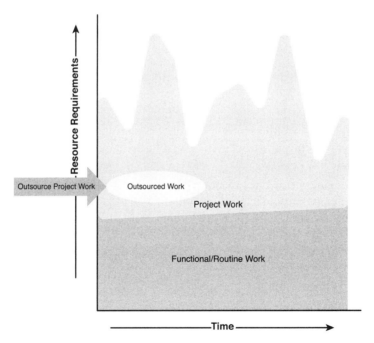

Figure 14.3   Hiring consultants for project work

Globalization Factors

I have addressed many globalization factors previously. I simply highlight them here for convenience:

- Even the best-written requirements can be mistranslated when dealing with different countries.

- Distance and culture can restrict your ability to enforce an agreement.

- Unless you've developed strong relationships, you run the risk of losing any technology you outsource.

Based on these concerns, outsourcing to other countries becomes a strategy instead of a tactic:

**The organization should commit to a country
or region where it plans to outsource.**

This statement might seem obvious, but most organizations overlook the effort to make that commitment. This means that you should put sufficient structure in place to support outsourcing to that country or region:

- Train appropriate staff on the culture, customs, and language for the region.

- Plan trips to the region regularly to establish face-to-face relationships.

- Start slowly, make small mistakes, and resolve them before making major commitments.

- Consider outsourcing in the same countries where you're planning to sell.

These techniques will allow your project teams to work more closely with your foreign partners and will produce the results you want.

Management and Oversight

Your ability to manage and track outsourced work plays a significant role in what you should and should not outsource. If you're running a flat organization (one in which many employees report to a single manager), you might have difficulty managing day-labor or on-board consultants. Also, if project management in your organization is still immature, you might have difficulty defining and tracking fixed-price contracts of outsourced work packages.

Environmental Factors

One final consideration that affects outsourcing is your current environmental factors. These include such items as cash and cash flow, tax situations, exchange rates, short-term geopolitical issues, workforce issues, and other environmental issues. Many environmental factors tend to be shorter-term issues, and you want your outsourcing doctrine to be more stable. Consider establishing a structure in which the doctrine is stable but can be adjusted over time to account for these shorter-term issues.

The Infinite Resource Pool and Portfolio Agility

The considerations I presented previously might seem daunting initially. However, with a little forethought and planning, you can establish an outsourcing strategy that allows your organization to move in virtually any direction on a moment's notice. Essentially, you can establish an infinite resource pool, with sufficient outsourcing capabilities to capture and take advantage of opportunistic projects, creative projects, new market directions, and advancing technologies. The infinite resource pool works hand-in-hand with portfolio agility (not to be confused with agile project management).

> **The infinite resource pool and portfolio agility allow the organization to move instantly to capture opportunities or avoid disasters.**

A mature project management discipline offers both the infinite resource pool and portfolio agility. Let's recap the needed techniques.

Serendipitous Work Packages

When mature project managers handle work packages, they can be outsourced easily. Whether you're outsourcing or not, work packages should have clear, measurable quality requirements. This is not an extra step; it's simply the sign of mature project management.

The cost of the work package also should include internal resources. This means that the cost of doing the work in-house is comparable to the cost of outsourcing (assuming comparable rates and talent). Again, this is not an extra step; it's simply a sign of mature project management. These two conditions enable you to outsource work packages using a fixed-price contract quickly if needed.

Pre-qualify Work Packages to Outsource

When your project management is mature enough and your work packages can be outsourced easily, you can pre-qualify those work packages that contain outsourcable technologies. Avoid work packages that contain proprietary technologies or processes, or technologies that offer you a strategic advantage.

Work packages that contain common technologies (such as standard engineering, construction, software development, and so on) are excellent candidates. You shouldn't have trouble finding vendors for such technologies, and you won't have to give up your advantages.

Place two flags on each work package. One flag indicates that the work package is an excellent candidate for outsourcing. So when the need arises, portfolio and project managers know they can outsource this work package quickly. The other flag indicates that the work package should not be outsourced for proprietary or other reasons. This allows portfolio and project managers to determine what they can and should not outsource quickly.

Prequalified Vendors

The final ingredient to agility is prequalified vendors. For this discussion, we consider both outsourcing strategies: outsourcing work packages and hiring day-labor or consultants.

For **outsourcing work packages**, consider the typical kinds of projects you do and determine the technologies involved in the greatest number of work packages. For these technologies, identify and establish relationships with firms that can perform the work needed. Establish a partnership relationship with such companies so that you can move quickly when needed.

For **day-labor or consultants**, look at the functional/routine work that you do, especially in departments that are frequently overloaded. Develop relationships with companies that can supply staff labor in those areas so that you can move your own staff into project work when needed. Maintain a partnership relationship with those firms so that you can get the same people on board each time you need them. This reduces conflicts, training, and start-up costs.

Management and Oversight

The final step to ensure a successful outsourcing strategy is providing sufficient oversight. Consider these tools for management and oversight for outsourced work.

Your Work Package Is the Vendor's Project

A well-defined work package is a project in all aspects, just on a smaller scale. Therefore, the vendor should manage it as a project. Your project team can then monitor its progress as it would manage any in-house project:

- The vendor should develop project phases with clear deliverables. These deliverables should have clear specifications that can be measured to ensure quality and compliance.

- The vendor should establish clear progress milestones.

- The vendor should demonstrate commitment through standard project management planning tools, including resource histograms, precedence diagrams with critical path, and so on.

- Your project team can monitor the vendor's progress just as in any other project. This includes regular status reports, formal change management procedures, exception reporting, and so on.

- You might require that your vendors be certified at a particular maturity level or use PMP-certified project managers.

Write the Right Contract

For simplicity, consider these three major contract types:

- **Fixed price**—A vendor agrees to perform the services or build the products defined in the contract for a firm, fixed price. If the vendor spends more money than expected, it must absorb the loss; if the vendor spends less, it keeps the savings as additional profit.

- **Cost plus**—The seller agrees to reimburse the vendor for all expenses incurred in the contract plus pay a prearranged profit. These are useful contracts for research and investigations and in situations when the results are unpredictable.

- **Time-and-materials** (**T&M**)—The seller agrees to pay the vendor a fixed rate per unit of time. This is the usual contract for day-labor—you pay the laborer or consultant an hourly rate.

You should outsource well-defined work packages with a fixed-price contract. If your vendor won't fix-price a well-defined work package, find another vendor. Occasionally, you'll want to outsource a work package that's less well defined. For example, imagine that you want to develop a computer system to control a section of an automobile production line. The production line might be well defined, but you want to experiment with a new user interface to make it easier for the line workers to control the line, to avoid mistakes.

One technique for handling these situations is to define two stages for the contract. The first allows the vendor to investigate and research the ill-defined or innovative areas. This might include a series of prototypes or pilots to evaluate different interface techniques. A cost-plus contract would be appropriate because you might discover an excellent technique early or it might take several tries. You can write a bonus clause in the contract to award the vendor for defining an acceptable interface early. These contracts are called **cost plus incentive fee** contracts.

After you've defined the interface, you can fix-price the rest of the system's development. You can write a bonus clause here as well, rewarding the vendor for finishing early. When you're augmenting your staff with day-labor or consultants, time-and-materials (T&M) contracts usually offer the best solution.

Verifying Productivity and Progress

Project management has a saying about progress:

You get six months behind in a project one day at a time.

Verifying productivity and progress for outsourced work is the same as verifying it for internal work. For outsourced work packages, your project team will demand that the vendors provide regular status reports, performance milestones with measurable results, inspections for work in progress, and other standard project management techniques. For day-labor and consultants, the management team can track progress just as it would for any employee to project team member. Successfully tracking productivity and progress involves three key elements:

- Ensure that the project team has sufficient maturity to manage the vendors

- Ensure that the contract has key elements to allow progress monitoring and remedies for nonperformance

- Ensure that you, as an executive, provide your project managers sufficient support

Payment Considerations

Vendors should demonstrate true progress before receiving payment.

Fixed-price contracts offer the cleanest payment options. Here, the vendor might receive progress payments after completing well-defined components or performance milestones that you verify. If you're outsourcing a computer system, you might make payments for a completed and approved design document, approved prototype, completed unit testing, completed integration testing, and final acceptance. You can verify each of these stages using well-defined techniques.

Cost-plus and T&M contracts are frequently paid monthly. This means that you can end up paying your vendors even if they make little progress. For such contacts, consider paying the profit portion of the payment only upon completion of specific milestones. Using our earlier example of automating the automobile production line, you might pay the profit portion of the agreement with each completed pilot or prototype. For another example, construction contracts allow the buyer to withhold a portion of each payment (called **retainage**) until work can be inspected or approved. When all the work has been done and all inspections are complete, the buyer releases the retainage as final payment.

T&M contracts are easier to monitor because the contractor is usually on-site and you can see their progress on a daily or weekly basis. Even if the contractors are off-site, you usually include them in weekly status meetings where you can determine progress.

Organizational Outsourcing Doctrine

The original purpose of this chapter was to develop an organizational outsourcing doctrine. As you can see, this doctrine can be more complex than other doctrines I've presented in this book. The additional work needed to develop a strong, long-lasting doctrine will pay off in the end with improved delivery cycles, more portfolio agility, and reduced costs. This is a template outline for an outsourcing doctrine.

1. **Goals for outsourcing**—In this section, state your primary goals for outsourcing work. Include each goal in a subsection of the document and include guidelines that project and portfolio designers/managers should use when considering outsourcing. Some examples follow:

   a. **Resource balancing**—Indicate the types of projects or areas in which you are willing to outsource to balance resources. For example, you might want to outsource in IT but not marketing, or you might take a technology approach and outsource in engineering but not IT. Finally, you can take a project approach by balancing resources to ensure that all strategic projects are completed on schedule. This section should concentrate on the goals for resource balancing. Your outsourcing doctrine will include more detail regarding this topic later.

   b. **Reduce time to market (or development cycle time)**—You might want to specify certain markets or products for which outsourcing is encouraged to ensure project success or reduce time to market.

   c. **Expanding technologies**—Include this section to identify technologies that you want to develop in-house or avoid in-house. With this information, portfolio and project designers can specifically outsource older technologies so you're not burdened with them, or hire consultants in new technologies so you can learn from them.

   d. **Increased agility**—If you're a research-driven organization or you like to capture opportunities or creative projects, identify the areas you want to capture. This directs the portfolio designers to outsource other project work, freeing up internal resources to capture these opportunities.

2. **Resource balancing strategy**—In this section, state your organization's strategies regarding resource balancing. This should present strategies regarding how to achieve the goals stated in the previous section. Include project management requirements (for example, project managers must plan detailed resource needs at least three to six months in advance) so that functional managers can plan.

   Also specify the requirements for functional managers (for example, functional managers retain at least prequalified vendors for work within their department) so they can support periods when project loads are high. You also might want to include stipulations for the portfolio designers (for example, portfolio designers must maintain at least three prequalified vendors in certain areas) to promote strategic outsourcing.

3. **Vendor selection**—In this section, identify your organization's strategies regarding prequalified vendors and vendor selection.

   a. **Technologies for prequalified vendors**—Include target technologies for which you want prequalified vendors.

   b. **Partnership philosophies**—State your organization's approach to developing strategic partnerships with vendors to establish long-term relationships.

   c. **Prequalified vendor maintenance**—State doctrine and philosophies for creating and maintaining the qualified vendor lists. This should include minimum qualification criteria for inclusion in the lists, as well as what criteria are important to the organization. For example, you might demand that vendors accepting fixed-price contracts greater than $100,000 run the contract with a PMP-certified project manager.

4. **Regions and countries**—State your organization's target regions and countries where outsourcing is promoted. Also identify regions and countries where outsourcing is discouraged or forbidden.

Summary

Globalization and strategic outsourcing can add a significant advantage to most organizations. However, you must carefully consider and plan your strategy to ensure success. With maturity, you'll develop a virtually infinite resource pool and portfolio agility, enabling you to capture new opportunities or prevent disasters without impacting your strategic plans and organizational direction. Table 14.2 offers your organizational evaluation matrix.

Table 14.2 Globalization and Strategic Outsourcing Evaluation Matrix

Performance Item	My Organization's Performance				
	High ←				→ Low
My organization has an established outsourcing doctrine to guide project and portfolio designers and managers.					
My organization plans to develop (or has developed) its outsourcing strategy slowly over time to discover and fix problems quickly and inexpensively.					

Performance Item	My Organization's Performance High ⬅————————➡ Low				
My outsourcing doctrine contains a clear purpose for outsourcing, including portfolio agility, expanding technologies, balancing resources, reducing time-to-market, and so on.					
My organization's project teams define work packages that can be outsourced as a normal part of their project planning.					
My organization knows which departments are resource bottlenecks, to foster outsourcing.					
My project managers determine resource needs well in advance.					
My organization has identified specific countries or regions where outsourcing is encouraged or allowed.					
My organization has identified specific countries or regions where outsourcing is discouraged or forbidden.					
My organization has identified specific technologies that can be outsourced.					
My organization has identified specific technologies that should not be outsourced.					
My organization aligns the contract type with the type of work outsourced.					
My project teams are skilled in monitoring and conducting oversight of outsourced work.					

*NOTE:

Chapter 15, "Optimizing Resources in a Multiproject Environment," (pages 247–264) is available for free online at www.ftpress.com/title/9780137136902.

Endnotes

Chapter 1

1. The *Guide to the Project Management Body of Knowledge,* 4th ed. (Newtown Square, PA: The Project Management Institute, 2008).

2. PMI and *PMBOK* are registered trademarks of the Project Management Institute.

Chapter 2

1. Initial concepts were developed by Stephen Gershenson, Gershenson and Associates, Boca Raton, FL.

Chapter 3

1. Stephen Gershenson, Gershenson & Associates; Michael B. Bender, Ally Business Developers; and Stuart Syme, Niedpath Solutions Group.

Chapter 5

1. Robert S. Kaplan and David P. Norton, *The Balanced Scorecard* (Boston, MA: Harvard Business School Press, 1996). The balanced scorecard provides a structure for developing measurable results along all organizational lines.

2. Literally: For Your Information. The message is informational only; no action is required.

3. Literally: Cover Your Ass. The message is sent for political protection only.

4. Thomas J. Peters and Robert H. Waterman, *In Search of Excellence* (New York: Harper and Row, 1982).

Chapter 6

1. The terms *responsibility* and *accountability* confuse most class attendees that I address. It's no wonder because the two terms do share a definition: "being answerable for." The confusion is so pervasive that many dictionaries cross-reference the two words, using *responsibility* to define *accountability* and using *accountability* to define *responsibility*—creating a circular reference. For our purposes, using the same definition for the two terms is not only confusing, it's redundant. Most dictionaries include the word *trustworthy* in some form for responsibility. In a business or work environment, someone who is trustworthy for accepting an assignment would be committed to doing that assignment properly, creating our definition.

2. *The American Heritage Dictionary of the English Language,* (Boston, MA: Houghton Mifflin Company, 1980).

Chapter 7

1. Derived from the *PMBOK Guide,* 2nd ed.

Chapter 8

1. The U.S. Congress enacted the Sarbanes-Oxley act following the failure of several major corporations. It contains requirements for accurate financial tracking of all organizational activities, including projects.

2. Activity-based costing is an accounting system in which the cost of all activities performed in an organization is allocated to the department that requests the work. For example, the HR department would charge back the cost of screening job applicants for an engineering position to the engineering department.

3. Value engineering is a concept that was developed during World War II. The project manager (or engineer) determines the purpose of an item—a work package, in this case—and tries to find other items that perform the same function for less cost.

4. Example derived from seminar materials developed by Ally Business Developers and used with permission

Chapter 10

1. Management by wandering around, or management by walking around (MBWA), is a prominent management technique in which the executive simply walks through areas, observing and engaging in light, casual conversation to encourage communication, receiving first-hand feedback and getting a feel for what's happening. Reference: Thomas J. Peters and Robert H. Waterman, Jr., *In Search of Excellence* (New York: Harper and Row, 1982).

Chapter 15

1. Eliyahu Goldratt, Jeff Cox, and David Whitford, *The Goal*, 3rd edition (Great Barrington, MA: North River Press, 2004).

2. Eliyahu Goldratt, *Critical Chain* (Great Barrington, MA: North River Press, 1997).

Index

MIRR (modified internal rate of return), 195, 207

mission statements, 77

momentum, 83-84

Monte Carlo analysis, 44

multiproject environments
    cross-training, 253-254
    deliverables-oriented
        assignments, 259-260
    multitasking, 251-253
    organizational agility, 247-248
    project synchronization, 258
    resource management doctrine,
        260-262
    resource utilization, 248-250
    single-tasking, 251-253
    theory of constraints, 255-257
    throttlers, 258

multitasking, 6, 251-253

N-O

nonprofit organization portfolio
    management, 221-222

NPV (net present value), 193-195,
    206-207

objectives. *See also* goals
    balanced objectives, 55-56
    comprehensive objectives, 55-56
    definition of, 21
    durable objectives, 56-57
    measurable objectives, 58-60
    specific objectives, 56-57
    strategic objectives, 9

OGBS (organizational goals
    breakdown structure)
    constructing, 69-74
        *business unit decomposition,
            72-73*
        cultural decomposition, 73
        *horizontal decomposition,
            71-72*
        time decomposition, 73-74
        vertical decomposition, 72
    example, 74
    overview, 67-68
    rules, 68-69
    value track, 68

opportunistic projects
    aligning, 83
    budgeting, 203-204
    definition of, 81

optimizing resource usage, 9

organization definition statements
    case study: Branch-Smith
        Printing, 78-79
    mission statement, 77
    overview, 75-76
    quality statement, 77
    value statement, 78
    vision statement, 77

organizational agility, 247-248

organizational alignment
    choosing organizational
        structure, 93
    definition of, 54
    executive management, 98
    functional management, 90,
        96-97
    goals of, 92
    organizational alignment
        checklist, 107

ownership, 93-95

PMO (project management office)

  overview, 101

  responsibilities of, 102-104

  structure and makeup, 102-103

portfolio designers and managers, 97

project designers and managers, 97-98

project management in process-oriented organizations, 89-91

projectized organizations, 91-92

steering committees

  CPOs (chief project officers), 105-106

  overview, 99-100

  phase gate review teams, 104-105

  as portfolio designer and manager, 101

  project management department, 104

  responsibilities of, 100

  structure and makeup, 100-101

organizational and resource charts, 45-46

organizational assumptions, 60-61

organizational development checklist, 87

organizational environments, 247-248

organizational goals breakdown structure. *See* OGBS

organizational infrastructure systems, 136

organizational outsourcing doctrine, 243-244

Organizational Performance Rating Sheet, 51

  project framework, 26

  strategic alignment, 66

organizational process assets, 127

outputs

  for Build process, 123

  for Close process, 127

  for continuous process improvement activity, 129

  for Define process, 118

  for Manage process, 125-126

  for Plan process, 121

outsourcing

  benefits of, 230

  cost management, 136

  environmental factors, 238

  globalization and strategic outsourcing evaluation matrix, 245

  globalization factors, 238

  goals of, 229-230

  infinite resource pool and portfolio agility, 239-240

  management and oversight, 238-240

    contracts, 241

    payment considerations, 242

    verifying productivity and progress, 242

    work packages, 240-241

  organizational outsourcing doctrine, 243-244

  product quality considerations, 231-233

S

salary banding, 141

schedule activities (WBS), 38

scheduling, 63

scope
  change management and, 171
  definition of, 20-21
  scope creep, 28
  scope definition
    overview, 32
    requirements definition, 32-34
    work definition, 35-38

scorecards, balanced scorecards (BSC), 209

SEI (Software Engineering Institute), 11

selecting projects, 63

senior management, 23

sensitivity analysis, 44-45

single-tasking, 251-253

size of tasks, 40

SMEs (subject matter experts), 22, 120

Software Engineering Institute (SEI), 11

specific objectives, 56-57

sponsors, 23

stakeholders
  agreement with objectives, 60
  relationship with project managers, 22-23
  stakeholder analysis, 113
  stakeholder management, 34

steering committees
  overview, 99-100
  as portfolio designer and manager, 101
  responsibilities of, 100
  structure and makeup, 100-101

stoplight graph, 176-177

strategic alignment
  balanced portfolios
    abandonment, 64
    balanced portfolio organization evaluation matrix, 215
    BSC (balanced scorecards), 209
    budgeting for, 202-205
    definition of, 201
    effects of unbalanced portfolios, 201-202
    implementing, 65
    manufacturing outsourcing project example, 213-214
    phase gates, 212-213
    postponement, 64
    prioritization, 62-63
    project selection methods, 206-208
    rejection, 63-64
    research projects, 210-212
    scheduling, 63
    selection, 63
    value tracks, translating to financial benefit, 205-206
    weighted scorecards, 209
  communication, 84-85

throttlers, 258

time-and-materials (T&M) contracts, 241

time decomposition, 73-74

TOC (theory of constraints), 255-257

tornado diagrams, 45

tracking costs
    earned value (EV), 146-147
    reporting and exception detection, 147-148
    schedules, 146

triggers, 113
    for Build process, 122
    for Close process, 126
    for continuous process improvement activity, 128
    for Define process, 116
    for Manage process, 124
    for Plan process, 120

U

unbalanced portfolios, effects of, 201-202

unexpected opportunities, handling, 225-226

unique projects, 19

V

value
    adding through project management, xi
    aligning projects with value tracks, 186-188

EV (earned value), 113, 131
    multiple project EV roll-up, 175-176
    tracking costs with, 146-147
    variance analysis, 148
EVM (earned value management)
    benefits, 131-132
    example, 137-138
    work packages, 138
IT value tracks, 222
NPV (net present value), 193-195
value statements, 78
value tracks, 68, 205-206

variance analysis (EV), 148

verifying productivity and progress for outsourced work, 242

vertical decomposition, 72

vision statements, 77

W-X-Y-Z

warm-body syndrome, 5

wasted resources
    multitasking, 6
    project du jour syndrome, 5
    view of projects as distractions, 5
    warm-body syndrome, 5

WBS (work breakdown structure), 18
    deliverables, 35
    phases, 35-36
    precedence diagrams, 38
    sample WBS, 36
    schedule activities, 38
    work packages, 35-37

FT Press
FINANCIAL TIMES

In an increasingly competitive world, it is quality
of thinking that gives an edge—an idea that opens new
doors, a technique that solves a problem, or an insight
that simply helps make sense of it all.

We work with leading authors in the various arenas
of business and finance to bring cutting-edge thinking
and best-learning practices to a global market.

It is our goal to create world-class print publications
and electronic products that give readers
knowledge and understanding that can then be
applied, whether studying or at work.

To find out more about our business
products, you can visit us at www.ftpress.com.